Flying Into the Sun

by Paul Ogier

Amistad Publishing

Flying Into the Sun

ISBN-13: 978-0692854211
Amistad Publishing

Second Edition Printing July 2019

First Edition Printing November 2018

Everything in this book occurred, but the names and identifying details of many characters have been changed to protect their privacy.

Editing and formatting by BZHercules
Spanish editing by Gabriela Rodriguez of Oaxaca, Mexico
Book Cover by Brandi Doane McCann

To recreate the story, I used notebooks and diaries written forty years earlier, as well as photographs, pilot logs, memory and interviews. Several entire passages and conversations were taken from the notebooks, including the one in which Mexican Federale Rafael Solas tells Steve that American women are cold in bed.

www.flyingintothesun.com
(pictures and information)

Praise for Flying Into the Sun

"Tourists in Mexico are warned not to drive at night. Cows, burros, dead animals or broken-down cars might be just around the bend—even bandidos. Tonight, the danger is crazed, drug-running gringos flying down the mountain, blowing past anything threatening their rhythm."

~Flying Into the Sun

"This is fantastic!! It's going to be BIG! I see a movie!"

~Chris Cantara, pilot & owner of Seaside Aviation, LLC

"So many great parts in the book. Magical Mystery Tour down the mountain was excellent. The book reveals a Mexico that tourists never see."

~Eric Knight, semi-pro surfer

"F*** awesome!!!!!!!!!!!"***

~Dave Bicknell, guitarist and software engineer

"Yup, I love books. And I'm always happy to find out about a surf/travel book that takes me back to places I've been to, or back to a time I've missed. Flying into the Sun is a mix of both...a time before smartphone navigation in rental cars or even planes, and what more a surfboard can be used for than just riding waves... Worth a read."

~thefreesurfer.com

Map of Mexico

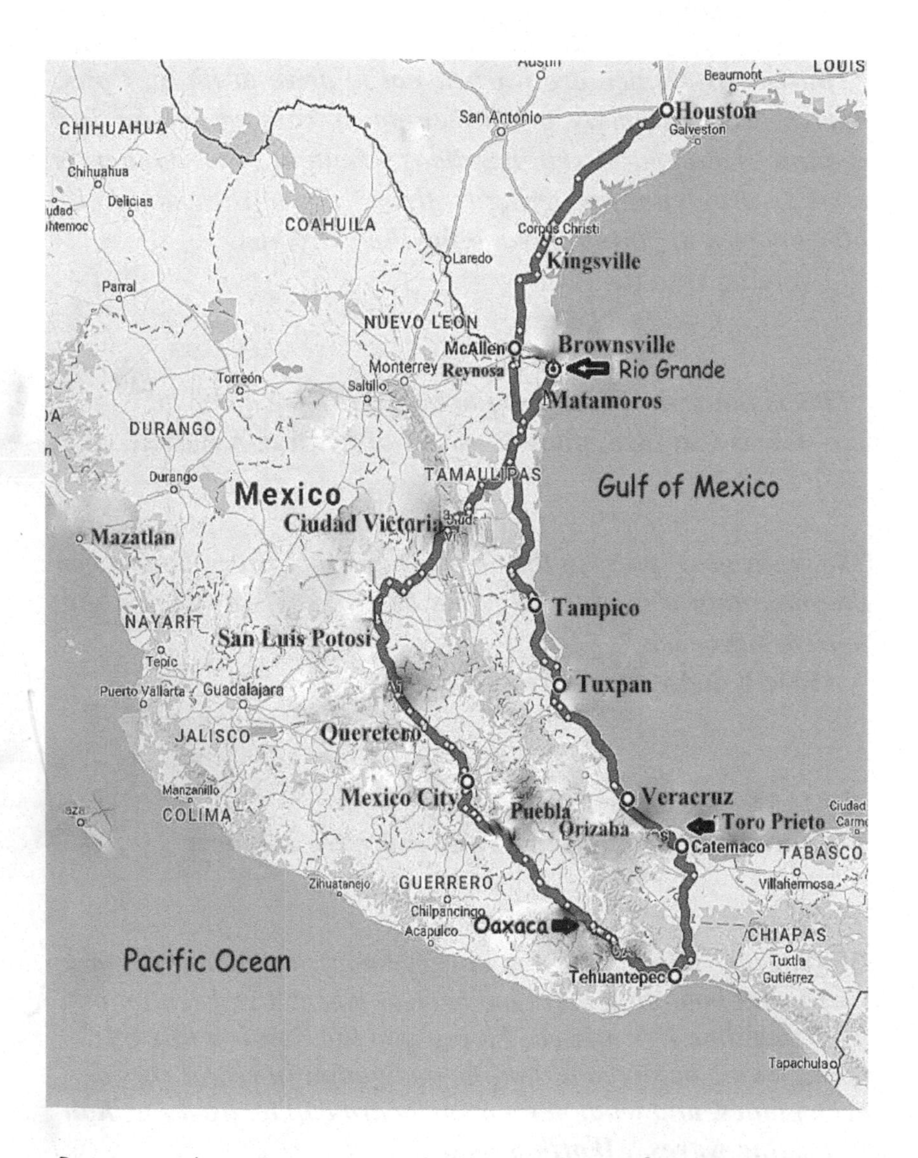

Route south to Oaxaca is in the center. Route from Oaxaca with the weed starts south, then up along the Gulf of Mexico.

Flying Into the Sun

SURFBOARDS, AIRPLANES and WEED

ACROSS the MEXICAN BORDER

a true story

by Paul Ogier

Chapters

FOR THE GOOD PEOPLE
OF MEXICO

PROLOGUE

Chicken
1979

"Buenas tardes, Capitán."

"Buenas tardes," I replied.

I sat down at the desk along the right wall of Veracruz's flight office and began filling out a flight plan.

"A dónde vas?" the agent asked from behind the counter.

The collar of his blue shirt was unbuttoned and his tie was loose. He had been helpful in my education of flight procedures in Mexico.

"I am flying to Los Leones north of Tampico to go fishing," I answered. We spoke in Spanish.

"Ah. Very good. And your friend? He is not accompanying you?"

"No. He must return to the United States for work."

The printer behind the counter ran for half a minute.

"Tampico has clear skies," the agent informed me.

I handed him my flight plan from Veracruz to Los Leones. He laid it on the counter and marked it with a pen while I read the printout of Tampico's weather.

"Muy bueno," he said and smiled, proud of me.

"Gracias."

He signed the top copy and detached it, then handed me the two carbons.

"Buen viaje," he bid. *Have a nice trip.*

I taxied the Piper Arrow to the gas pumps where the young fuelers topped off the wing tanks and filled the four plastic gas cans in the baggage compartment. We joked as they polished the windscreen, and I added a nice tip when I paid.

Although the wind blew from the east, planes were taking off toward the west to avoid making noise over Veracruz. The tailwind would increase my take-off distance, but Veracruz's main runway was a mile and a half long, so the slight increase in the take-off run wouldn't be a factor for my small single-engine Piper. I radioed ground control and taxied to the end of the runway.

After lifting off, I raised the landing gear and continued straight out farther than normal so the control tower wouldn't notice my turn to the south. I flew the highlighted course on the chart in my lap and watched for the landmarks circled in ink: a road, a power line, a river and another road. Eighteen minutes after takeoff, a narrow rectangle of gray appeared ahead in the green jungle. Even with 260 flight hours under my belt, I still got a feeling of accomplishment when an airport or even a landmark showed up exactly where it should.

I lined up with the runway and landed east, into the wind. On the rollout, I spotted our rental VW Rabbit parked behind some bushes two-thirds down the runway on the left. I spun around and set the parking brake adjacent to where Todd was dragging our two suitcases through the weeds. With the engine still running, he climbed onto the right wing and hoisted the suitcases behind him one at a time. I reached over and pushed the door open against the wind from the spinning propeller. Todd kept his back to the door as he shoved the luggage onto the rear seats. He started to say something but stopped in mid-sentence as he stared through the windshield.

"Fuck," I read on his lips.

I looked ahead. A truck painted in army green was hauling ass down the runway toward us.

"See you in Houston," I said.

Todd jumped off the back of the wing, and I latched the door. If there had been enough runway behind me, I would have spun around and taken off in the proper direction—into the wind and away from the truck. But there wasn't enough runway behind me. I'd go off the end before I could get airborne. My only option was to take off where I had enough runway—toward the truck. I shoved the throttle to the firewall and held constant, adrenaline-driven pressure against it.

Getting into the air before our paths met was not something I could hope for. When it comes to aeronautics, physics beats hope every time. It was down to an old-fashioned game of chicken. I stayed on the centerline of the runway and watched the airspeed needle slowly rise as the truck got bigger. If we hit, then we hit. Stopping and giving up was not an alternative. One stint in a Mexican penitentiary was enough for one lifetime.

Latin America 101

CHAPTER ONE

Mexico, Fall 1974

(five years earlier)

I turned to see who tapped my shoulder, and a skinny guy with a ponytail began speaking Spanish too fast for me to understand. Dan and I had just spent an hour at the outdoor market in Veracruz. This wasn't the first time we'd been harassed by an ambitious vendor or someone asking for a handout. We kept walking. Dan stopped and grabbed my arm.

"That smelled like pot. Maybe he was trying to sell us some," he said.

We walked back and found the guy with a filter cigarette between his fingers, but it wasn't tobacco he was smoking. He offered us a hit, then removed a small newsprint packet from the front pocket of his jeans. Inside were several marijuana flower tops so long he had to unfold them to show us. Dark red threads ran through each bud.

"Pele rojo. Sinsemilla," said our new friend. (Pe-lay ro-ho. Sin-se-mee-ya.)

Pele rojo meant a redheaded person, but the term apparently extended to red-haired marijuana flower tops. *Sinsemilla* was Spanish for *without seeds,* and their buds came from female plants that had not been pollinated, allowing them to grow larger and more potent. We bought the bouquet for three dollars.

"Tienes papeles?" I asked.

He delicately removed four cigarette papers from the pocket of his faded Black Sabbath tee-shirt.

"Un regalo," he said. *A gift.*

We said adios to our new weed connection, and Dan drove us south along Veracruz's seawall as I stashed the flower tops up under the dash.

*

Dan and I had departed Houston three days earlier with our surfboards strapped to the top of my green '66 VW Bug. While studying the map back in Houston, we noticed Punta Roca Partida jutting into the Gulf of Mexico from an east-west coastline a hundred miles south of Veracruz. The beach would catch a direct swell from cold fronts, and there might be nice waves peeling from the point. The closest town to Roca Partida was Toro Prieto, and it would be our winter home in the sun.

We crossed into Mexico and made camp on pure white sand under pine trees near Tuxpan. In the morning, an orange sun rose from the Gulf and brought shoulder-high emerald waves. It had been months since I'd surfed without a wetsuit, and I felt like Superman, flying light and free across the faces of the waves.

Outside the surf, pelicans descended in a line and glided inches above unbroken swells. Inland, beyond the pines, dark hills rose into the morning's pale blue sky, and pockets of fog still hung in low areas.

*

After sixteen years of non-stop education, rules and regulations, this trip was overdue. No more academic pressure. No more getting up early to drive the freeways at rush hour for a class at the University of Houston. No more wasting life. While sitting on my board surrounded by everything that mattered, it was clear I should have quit college the previous year, especially since there was no longer a college deferment for the Vietnam draft.

The remark of a classmate in writing class had nailed the college coffin shut. Both he and I were of the opinion that in order to write, one must first experience something to write about. Sitting in a classroom and listening to a teacher was a waste of time.

"If we had any balls, we wouldn't be here," had been my school chum's final say on the matter. I wondered if he took his own advice.

*

While Dan and I sat on our boards waiting for the next set, he squinted at something past the waves.

"Fins," he said.

Fins could be sharks, or maybe not. As I turned to look, he said, "Dolphins."

We watched five or six fins go in and out of the water beyond the surf. When they disappeared, we searched all around and tried to predict where they might emerge. A minute later they surfaced closer to us. Dan rubbed the layer of wax on top of his board with his palm. It sounded like the dolphin-speak in documentaries so I did the same. Whether the sound attracted them or not, two dolphins surfed toward us, completely immersed within an unbroken swell. When the pair got near, they turned right and stared at us through the water with their right eyeballs.

"That was weird," Dan said.

"They were checking us out."

A set came through and I caught the first wave. When I stood up, I found myself surfing in close formation with a dolphin on each side of my board. The two cruised parallel for a while, then shot forward, crossed, and returned alongside me. They repeated the maneuver twice while I tried not to hit them. As I paddled back out, I wondered if my avoidance tactics had disturbed their formation surfing. Maybe so, because they all resurfaced a hundred yards down the beach. Dan and I surfed in and drove to Veracruz where we spent the night and purchased supplies (and fresh sinsemilla flower tops).

As we drove south from Veracruz's market, we passed a hacienda-style hotel called the Mocambo and were out of the hustle and bustle of the city. I put in a Neil Young cassette, and

“Cinnamon Girl” started us off.

A straight road went through flat, green fields dotted with shrubs and small trees. When we drove through towns, metal-dome speed bumps stretched across the asphalt and forced us to come to complete stops sometimes. The bumps were called “topes” (tóe-pez), and road signs usually warned of their arrival.

As we slowed through the towns and their topes, locals gazed at the surfboards on top of the Bug, but some were more interested in who or what was inside. They looked through the windshield and stared into our eyes. There was considerable pondering going on, and I wondered about their conclusions.

Between towns, men plodded along the road in the shade of their sombreros. A few rode burros, while others walked and led their steeds by ropes. Several burros had bundles of sticks on their backs, and a few men carried sticks piled on their own backs.

An hour out of Veracruz, the Gulf reappeared to our left, and we cruised on a ridge of high, grassy dunes. We drove by the town of Alvarado with its tall Spanish church, then crossed a long bridge and became surrounded by hills and jungle. In thirty minutes, the land flattened.

“The turnoff shouldn’t be far,” I said. The map lay across my lap. Dan nodded.

Even though the only law enforcement we had encountered in Mexico had been at the routine checkpoint twenty kilometers south of the border, we decided not to smoke our newfound weed until we got off the main road. Our long hair didn't seem to be an issue with anyone in Mexico, maybe because we were strange enough just being gringos.

*

Too bad the same attitude didn’t prevail in Texas. The previous year during a nocturnal drive to South Padre Island to surf, a Kingsville deputy sheriff stopped me and a few friends south of Corpus Christi. The officer didn’t say why he stopped us, but it most likely had to do with the surfboards on top of our car—a textbook indication of hippies and illicit drugs.

"We don't go for long-haired hippies in this county," the deputy told us.

County patriotism was new to me. Regarding hippies, it was true I didn't cut my hair often and I liked to get high, but I heard hippies didn't bathe. Not me. I preferred to shower at least once a day. And hippies gave up everything and lived on communes and believed in free love. I had nothing against hippies. I admired them.

The deputy studied us, then added, "You are by far the scroungiest looking bunch I ever seen."

There was no pleasing this guy. Maybe a couple of the others were scroungy, but I certainly wasn't.

He informed us that if he found anything illegal in the car, anything, he repeated, we would get a free ride to the station for haircuts. It had been five years since Peter Fonda and Dennis Hopper were blown away by rednecks in *Easy Rider*, yet long hair and alleged scrounginess were still on the books as criminal offenses in King Ranch territory.

The lawman didn't find anything, and we departed with our scalps.

Not so fortunate were four surfer acquaintances arrested by the same deputy sheriff two weeks later. They had diligently stashed their pot but forgot about the open bottle of wine. The cops confiscated their car, and our friends were driven to jail where the deputy proved to be a man of his word by shaving their heads. Their experience was heightened by the LSD three of them had dropped an hour before their arrest.

Psychedelics in jail sounded like a bad trip to me, but they seemed to have made the best of it. Our friend said he was still tripping in the morning when one of the deputies came to work with bloody pieces of toilet paper stuck all over his cheeks because of razor cuts. It gave our friend the psychedelic uglies, big time. He laughed as he recited his tale and didn't seem to mind his own scabs on his shaved head. They were all released the next day—the deputy sheriff having done his part for the Get a Haircut/Keep America Beautiful campaign.

*

"This could be the turnoff up here," Dan said and took his foot off the pedal.

A sign displayed an arrow pointing to the left, but the top was bent down. We could only read the bottom half. It wouldn't have been Toro Prieto, but it could have been Punta Roca Partida without the Punta.

I looked at the map. "It's gotta be."

Dan turned left onto the dirt road, and I put in Jethro Tull's *Thick as a Brick*. A few minutes later, as Ian Anderson sang about society teaching the young man to play Monopoly and sing in the rain, the VW jerked to the right. The front right tire was flat. With all the potholes we had encountered, I was surprised this was our first. We had the spare on in twenty minutes.

"We can go back to that Vulcanizadora on the main road to get the tire patched," Dan suggested.

Mexico was inundated with shops that had huge tires hanging from trees with "Vulcanizadora" or "Taller" printed in white across them. We backtracked and got the flat fixed for eight pesos (64 cents).

Continuing on the road to Toro Prieto, we crossed a bridge with clear water rushing underneath. Changing the tire and waiting for the repair had made us grubby and sweaty. We put on our baggies and waded to some boulders in the middle of the river. The temperature felt twenty degrees cooler under the trees, and we sat and listened to the water rushing around the rocks.

"This might be a good time to sample one of those buds," Dan said.

He went to the car and rolled a joint. The pot was good. Its smoke expanded fast in my lungs, and I coughed. It sure wasn't dirt weed. It was straight from the fields. After a few hits, Dan dabbed the end of the joint in the river. Waste not, want not.

A breeze swept under the branches, and birds alerted the neighborhood to the two gringos smoking reefer in their river. We sat on our boulders and listened. We were in Mexico, almost at our destination. It was time to slow down and smell the sinsemilla flower tops.

We eventually unfastened ourselves from nature and got back on the road. Dan flipped the tape over, and *Aqualung* played.

Pastures rolled by with cows and horses and bulls with horns and low-hanging balls. Lime-green, dome-shaped hills appeared on our right. Beyond them, dark green mountains faded in the distance and humidity. We drove past cornfields and groves of avocados and oranges, and fields of what looked like corn but without ears of corn.

Peasants and burros with sticks walked along the road, and a shepherd herded his goats to the side so we could pass. Forty minutes later, a green Gulf of Mexico filled the windshield.

The road curved right and paralleled the Gulf until it narrowed abruptly and offered us a fork. We took the left branch toward the Gulf, and several houses bumped by before we ended up in front of a tin roof supported by varnished tree posts. Wooden tables sat on the dirt under the front part of the roof, and a store or restaurant made up the back half. A man stood in the shadows behind a counter, watching. Dan and I got out and made our way through the chickens pecking at the dirt. The man raised a hinged section of the counter and came through.

He was short and thin with thick, coal-black hair and a brown face. With his abrupt mustache and upright posture, he resembled a 50- or 60-year-old Mexican Charlie Chaplin. He held his right hand out rigid and we shook.

"Soy El Mio. Siéntese," he said and pointed to one of the tables. We sat down.

El Mio? That meant "mine." Was his name Mine? Maybe I misunderstood.

"Soy Steve. Esto es Dan," I told him.

"Mucho gusto," he said.

"Su nombre es El Mio?"

"Si." He nodded.

"Quieren refrescos?" asked El Mio.

"Si, una Coca, por favor."

"Dos," said Dan.

El Mio brought our refrescos and returned behind the counter. I looked around. Where we sat had been just a spot on the map a week earlier—an idea. Now we were part of this parallel reality. From under the roof, I could see only four small houses, but there was no shortage of roosters and chickens and pigs: baby pigs, medium pigs, big pigs and huge pigs. Some might have been hogs. My knowledge of swine extended only to Arnold on the TV show *Green Acres*.

Dan and I were anxious to scope out the surf, so El Mio guided us along a path and through a slot between tall sand bluffs. We looked out on a tranquil green Gulf that stretched 800 miles to Texas. In front of us, transparent waves too small to surf peeled evenly into a little sand cove. We weren't disappointed. Our plan was to wait for cold fronts to bring swells. Down the beach, far to the right, Punta Roca Partida rose out of the water like the Rock of Gibraltar.

"Es esa Punta Roca Partida?" I asked El Mio just to make sure.

"Si, es La Roca," he answered.

Dan and I looked at each other. The point was at least a mile away. Maybe there was a village closer to it, or maybe we could drive over and camp out.

Between us and Punta, I noticed a low, flat island a thousand yards from the beach. Birds swarmed like gnats above it.

"What is that?" I asked El Mio in Spanish.

"An island," he answered.

"Does it have a name?"

"It is the home of the pelicans."

In the distance, the birds didn't look that big.

"All of them?"

"Si." He smiled.

We took a different path back to the store and came upon a clear, fast-moving river. El Mio told us it was Toro Prieto's source of drinking water and where villagers bathed and washed clothes. El Mio talked non-stop as he guided us around, and although he spoke fast, we got the gist of what he said.

As we approached El Mio's store, a woman emerged from an area of thick bushes a hundred feet to our left. El Mio saw us looking and said those bushes served as their bathroom. Three pigs ran squealing and grunting into the brush. El Mio pointed to corn cobs lying nearby. With words and gestures, he explained that the cobs were for wiping el culo. He grinned as he told us the pigs kept them clean for the next user. Dan and I had brought our own supply of toilet paper.

That evening, El Mio cooked fish and rice on a kerosene stove and told us almost everyone else in the village used wood stoves, which explained all the stick-toting. A cute girl wearing a sleeveless black-and-white dress brought a pitcher of cold, pale-green liquid. She was slender and tan with sun-tinted brown hair that fell past her shoulders.

As Dan and I drank the limeade mixed with some sort of alcohol, I noticed a line of minuscule ants running from the bottom of the pitcher to its rim. When I pointed out the ants swimming in our limeade, El Mio smiled.

"No toman mucho." *They don't drink much.*

I asked El Mio how he could serve cold drinks without electricity, and he said a truck brought ice every day. He pointed down the dirt road we had driven.

The girl brought a second pitcher, and El Mio introduced us.

"Está es mi hija, Isidra." *This is my daughter, Eeseedra.*

"Hola, Isidra," I said. "Soy Steve." I started to shake her hand, but she held hers still.

"Hola, Esteef."

Dan introduced himself, and she walked back behind the counter.

By the time we finished the second pitcher of limeade, it was dark. When El Mio lit an oil lamp, I went to the Bug and retrieved our Coleman lantern. After placing it on a table, I pumped it and lit the filament with a match. El Mio watched and nodded.

Men from the village meandered in. They wore neat clothes and looked like they had spruced up. Dan and I were an attraction. The lantern intrigued them, and several came to our table and asked about it. After a beer or two, they became more talkative and wanted to know where we were from, and what we intended to do with the tableros on top of our car.

I knew "olas" meant waves, but the only "ride" I knew was manejar, which related to driving a car. I basically answered, "We like to drive our boards on the waves."

Most of the men in the village were campesinos, they told us, and worked in the fields, planting and harvesting corn, fruit and sugar cane.

After three pitchers of whatever was in the limeade besides ants, Dan and I didn't feel like setting up our tents. We laid our sleeping bags on the hard dirt between the tables. In the morning, over huevos rancheros and refried beans, we decided to stick to our plan and wait for a cold front. We would remain in Toro, and if the waves weren't good enough, we could hike or drive to Punta Roca.

El Mio led us to a wooden shack with no roof and said we could stay in it if we wanted. Villagers helped us cut palm fronds and construct a thatched roof. I had learned enough in boomtown Houston to be able to build tract homes, but this was my first thatched roof. That night, Dan and I discovered the Bug's AM radio could pick up KILT in Houston. We began monitoring the nightly news for impending cold fronts.

After settling in, we asked where we could put our trash but had difficulty getting our point across. Apparently, the residents of Toro utilized everything, and what they didn't use, the pigs ate. We had learned firsthand the pigs indulged in a non-discriminatory diet. Some pigs were so big, they were the size of calves and shook us awake in the middle of the night when they scratched their backs against the corners of our hut. We ended up piling our trash a short distance from the shack where we planned to burn it.

A few days later we were walking along Toro's dirt main

street, and through a window we saw one of our discarded Pringles' potato chip tubes at the center of a dining room table. Forks, knives and flowers protruded from the top of the red cardboard tube.

Because of Dan's magazines, we became the source of social unrest in Toro. While loading the car in Houston, I had noticed the stack of *Playboy*s in one of Dan's boxes but didn't give them much thought. I was more interested in the three-book set of *The Teachings of Don Juan* in the same box. I had read Carlos Castaneda's first book and was anxious to read the next two about Don Juan, a Yaqui Indian medicine man in Mexico who guides Carlos Castaneda in his spiritual quest to become a Man of Knowledge.

According to Don Juan, when most people begin a quest to learn, their purpose is faulty and their intent is vague. They hope for rewards that will never materialize because they aren't prepared for the hardships involved. In the first book, psychedelic peyote buttons help Castaneda master the first stage of learning.

Dan's *Playboy*s quickly proved useful at the twenty-kilometer checkpoint south of the border. As Dan gathered our documents for the soldier in charge, I was told to pop the VW's hood. Two soldiers rummaged through our things while another walked around the Bug and looked inside.

When the two in front discovered Dan's magazines, the other two soldiers joined them, and they began leafing through what they called "*Los Libros de Mujeres* (*The Books of Women*)" and joking with each other. We got out and Dan handed our visas and car documents to the chief, who only glanced at them before giving them back. The soldiers continued to paw the magazines, and we became impatient.

"Tell them they can have one," Dan said to me.

"Pueden tener uno si quieren," I told the soldiers.

They looked up from the naked women to verify their good fortune. As we drove away, I saw the soldiers in the rearview mirror, still in a huddle over their *Libro de Mujeres*.

From then on, we put the *Libros de Mujeres* on top of our stuff in the trunk to persuade soldiers to wrap up their search, and we kept our passports, visas and car papers together in the glove box so we could hand them over quickly.

The scandal in Toro Prieto began when the men who had helped with our thatched roof saw Dan's box of *Playboys*, and we let them look at a few. Our abode soon became the place to be for the men in the village. They would stop by to say hello, then sit down in front of our shack and talk with us for a few minutes before one would utter the magic words "*Libros de Mujeres*" with a guilty smile.

When the women in the village learned what their husbands were up to in their off-time, they ostracized me and Dan, not even reciprocating a measly "Buenas" when we walked by. While the men lounged on the grass and perused *Los Libros*, their wives stood on the hillside with infants in arms, looking down at the decadence brought by the gringos. To top it off, these episodes unfailingly occurred immediately after Dan and I had partaken of the sinsemilla.

I thought about *Star Trek*'s prime directive not to interfere with the culture of alien civilizations. Although I didn't remember pornography mentioned in the TV series, we had absolutely interfered with the culture of Toro. Something needed to be done. Dan and I consulted.

While several of the men lay on the grass enjoying the naked mujeres, I went into our shack and returned with half the *Playboys*. I handed them to the largest aficionado.

"We don't want them. They are yours. Un regalo," I told him. *A gift.*

He stared at me.

"No, no puedo," he said and shook his head, most likely having considered the consequences with his real-life mujer.

I held out the stack to the hombre next to him, but when he reached for them, the first guy had a change of heart and intercepted. Word quickly spread we were no longer pornography dealers, and the women became friendly again.

Since Toro now possessed porn, Dan and I had still violated the prime directive, but at least we were no longer a part of it.

*

We survived on the supplies we had bought in Veracruz: tuna and sardines, cans of Chef Boyardee, peanut butter sandwiches, pop tarts, and we supplemented our diet with items El Mio stocked in his little store. In the evenings, Dan and I often ended up at the tienda for dinner and cervezas. Isidra and I talked.

"Cuantos años tiene, Esteef?" she asked me. *How old are you?*

"Tengo veinte años. Y usted?" *I am twenty years old. And you?*

"Tengo veinte años, tambien." *I am twenty, also.*

"Donde aprendiste Espanol?" she asked. *Where did you learn to speak Spanish?*

"En escuela."

I had taken one semester of Spanish in college and the usual classes in high school.

At night, Isidra and I sat in the VW and listened to cassettes. She rested her hands on the steering wheel and focused through the windshield as if she were driving. I put in Pink Floyd's latest album, *Dark Side of the Moon*, and the introduction to "Time" played with its cacophony of alarm clocks.

"Es esa música?" she asked. *Is that music*?

"Por Pink Floyd, si."

She asked if a lot of music in los Estados Unidos sounded like that, and I told her no. Her natural beauty and expressions shone in the amber and blue lights of the dash as she concentrated on the song.

Could a girl from a remote Mexican village understand lyrics about ten years passing you by before you realized you missed the starting gun?

"Dónde vive en los Estados Unidos?" she asked. *Where do you live in the United States?*

I removed the map of Texas from the glove box and spread

it across our laps, then reached up and flipped on the overhead light.

"Yo vivo aqui," I said and pointed to where Texas and Mexico were separated by the thin blue line of the Rio Grande. "Estamos vecinos." *We are neighbors.*

"Si." She smiled and stared at the map. "Está muy lejos. Cuanto tiempo a manejar aqui?" *It is very far. How long did it take to drive here?*

"Un dia," I answered.

I couldn't read her expression, but, like me, she may have been wondering how such a different world could be just a day and a blue line away.

"Tiene una novia?" she asked. *Do you have a girlfriend?*

"No. Tiene un novio?" I answered. *Do you have a boyfriend?*

"No."

*

One evening, El Mio and I sat at a table and talked. He glanced at Isidra, who was working behind the counter.

"Ella es muy presentable, no?" he asked. *She is very presentable, no?*

I looked over at her. It took a few seconds to realize that El Mio had just asked me if Isidra would be an acceptable wife to take back to the United States. Isidra and I had known each other three weeks. We had only talked and walked along the river and beach—no kissing, no nothing. If she had given me signs, maybe I would have made a move, but I didn't know anything about Mexican customs. American customs were hard enough to figure out.

"Si, ella es muy presentable," I answered.

When I returned to our shack, Dan was lying on top of his sleeping bag reading Carlos Castaneda's third book, *Journey to Ixtlan*. I picked up the second one, *A Separate Reality,* and thought about what El Mio had said.

The surf remained small, but Dan and I often paddled out in the afternoon for rejuvenation in the warm salt water, and to watch the lines of pelicans glide by after a hard day's fishing.

We also explored, and would fill our canteens with river water and hike all around. One Saturday afternoon, we stumbled upon a group of locals hanging out in a barn, listening to a guitar player sitting on a wooden table at the front. We hadn't met any of them, but they knew about us—everybody knew about us—and we were invited in. Some looked almost our age, but most were younger.

After performing a few folk-sounding Mexican songs, the singer asked if either of us played. I took the guitar and began finger-picking Neil Young's "Tell Me Why," but the guitar was so out of tune, I stopped to tune it. I used the low E string for reference, and when I got to the last string, it snapped—just like that. I hadn't even raised the pitch of the first string. The smiles in the group went blank, and mild shock appeared on the guitar owner's face.

"Tiene una otra streeng?" I asked. *Do you have another string?*

"No." He shook his head.

No problema. I'll buy a new one.

"Hay una tienda?" I asked. *Is there a store?*

"Aqui no," he answered.

Of course there wasn't a store nearby that sold guitar strings. The closest one was probably three hours away by car—as if anyone had a car. I felt bad. I was only trying to tune the guitar for them, and now they didn't even have an out-of-tune guitar to play. Strike two on the prime directive front.

"Disculpame," I said. *I'm sorry.*

Dan and I walked out of the barn. Like everyone else, Dan stayed silent. He was most likely disappointed in me too.

KILT finally announced that a cold front had passed through Houston. If the front moved as fast as its winds—about twenty miles per hour—the swell would arrive in a day and a half.

At dawn, our thatched roof blew away, and everything inside was strewn and drenched—including us. Apparently, cold fronts picked up speed as well as strength when they crossed the Gulf of Mexico.

Strong winds made the big waves unrideable for two days. It was not what we expected, though in hindsight, it should have been. Wind that comes from behind the waves makes them choppy. Wind that races 800 miles across the Gulf of Mexico blows them to shit. On the third day, the wind subsided. The waves still sucked, but we were afraid the size would drop overnight, so Dan and I paddled into the brown chop and attempted to surf the unpredictable peaks.

Villagers gathered on top of the sand bluff in their sweaters and serapes. They had waited weeks to see the beings from another planet do what they had come to do. We did not impress them. The few waves we caught allowed us to drop in and ride along the face for only three or four seconds before they closed out, breaking all at once. We spent most of the time paddling to keep from being swept down the beach by the wind and current. All of our observers except one disappeared after twenty minutes, and I was pretty sure it was Isidra who remained. I tried hard to get at least one decent ride and failed.

That evening at El Mio's, no one mentioned our surfing. Maybe they thought what they had watched was normal, or maybe they didn't want to embarrass us by mentioning it. Dan and I were bummed out. The attraction of staying in Toro the entire winter, living the laid-back tropical life and surfing warm waves, had lost an essential ingredient.

*

El Mio told us Isidra and her cousin were preparing a meal for Dan and me. I understood it would not be just a regular meal but a special family meal. He said Isidra was a good cook, muy buena, and grinned.

During dinner, El Mio sat at the end of the table while Isidra sat opposite me, and Dan faced her cousin, Taña. Dan had made it clear early on that he wasn't interested. Taña was no Isidra in the looks department. We ate sliced beef, rice with an orange-colored hot sauce, and a vegetable called ayote, which tasted like squash. Dan and I complimented the chefs.

Two hours later, as I lay in my pup tent inside our roofless shack, I felt queasy. Dan said he didn't feel so good either. Within minutes, we were both outside throwing up. Diarrhea ensued. Throughout the night, we crashed through our tent openings to make it out in time. To try to reach the community bushes would have resulted in disaster. When our illness continued for three days, Dan diagnosed us with amoebic dysentery.

"It's an omen," he said. "No waves, dysentery and no pot."

The sinsemilla had helped us through the worst of our infirmity but was now depleted. Smoking always put us in a good mood. Dan wanted to leave and find another place to surf. I considered it. The only attraction in Toro for me now was Isidra, and who knew how or if that would work out? I couldn't argue about the bad surf, and we might get sick again from the food or the river water we were drinking.

"Any ideas where to go?" I asked Dan.

We tallied up. I had $290, and Dan was rich with $600—enough to travel far and long. We unfolded the map and saw the Pacific was just a jaunt across the Isthmus of Tehuantepec. From there, we had the option of going north up the Mexican coast or south to Guatemala. El Salvador was on the other side of Guatemala, and a friend and I had surfed big waves there the summer after graduating high school.

Dan read through our Sanborn's car insurance documents and found that we were covered in all of Central America. Even though passports weren't required in Mexico, we had brought ours, which was a good thing because most of the Central American countries required them. El Salvador it was.

When I told El Mio of our plans, he nodded, no smile, and stared at me. I looked around for Isidra, although I didn't know what I was going to say. Would she think our time together meant nothing to me? Would she care?

Dan and I stopped by the tienda in the evening for final cervezas, but Isidra didn't show up. After packing our things in the morning, we parked in front of the store and settled our account with El Mio. There was no sign of Isidra. I couldn't leave without saying goodbye. When I asked El Mio where she was, he told me she had walked to the river. I grabbed my camera from the car. I had taken a good picture of El Mio and his wife with all their children, but Isidra had been absent.

Isidra was sitting on a rock, facing the river. As I approached, she stood and turned toward me. When I got closer, she backed away. I stopped.

"Me voy," I said. *I'm going.*

"Ok."

"A El Salvador."

"Adios," she said.

"Yo regresaré después El Salvador." *I will return after El Salvador.*

She looked at the ground in front of my feet.

"Una foto," I said and held up the camera.

"Por qué?" she asked. *Why?*

To remember you, I almost answered before I realized that wouldn't sound right.

"No lo sé. Para tener," I said. *I don't know. To have.*

When I raised the camera, she shook her head and started to turn away. I snapped a photo. Afterward, she allowed me to get close enough to shake her hand goodbye.

El Mio stood behind the counter when I got back, and I bought two Cokes for the road. Over his shoulder, I saw the miniature driftwood surfboard I had been carving before our roof blew away. It lay on the table where Isidra did the store's paperwork. I had intended to give it to her when I finished it.

We said goodbye to El Mio, and Dan bounced us along the dirt road that had brought us to Toro four weeks earlier. He requested Crosby, Stills and Nash, but both CSN albums were on opposite sides of a tangled cassette, so I put in Jackson Browne's *For Everyman*.

The same countryside rolled by, but the movie through the windshield now had more depth. I knew about the shacks we passed and the campesinos who lived in them, where they got their water, why they toted sticks, and that the fields with the stalks resembling corn were sugar cane fields. Caña dulce. I had sipped its juice and chewed the canes.

CHAPTER TWO

El Salvador

Bandidos

We slowed for the topes at Santiago Tuxtla and San Andrés Tuxtla, then turned south around Lake Catemaco. At the Isthmus of Tehuantepec, we made a right and drove its hundred miles with a gusty tailwind rocking the Bug the entire way. At the Pacific, Dan turned south and we drove a half hour before coming to a stop behind traffic. I stuck my head out the window and saw soldiers in green uniforms at the front. We were still 200 miles from the Guatemala border.

The cars inched forward while several trunks were opened and searched. A soldier carrying a rifle walked to my window. He bent down and looked across to Dan. I took off my sunglasses. He was younger than us and said nothing as he turned to me then back to Dan. His face was pocked, and his oval eyes were as black and shiny as obsidian. I couldn't read them, but I got the impression we were his first long-haired surfers. Another soldier walked to the back of the Bug and looked through the rear windshield at our boxes, tents, Coleman lantern and everything else.

"Papeles," the soldier finally said.

Our documents were in my lap, ready to go. If Dan and I aspired to become Men of Knowledge per *The Teachings of Don Juan*, being Men of Papers was a step in the right direction.

The soldiers could search all they wanted. The only thing that would interest them would be the *Libros de Mujeres*. He returned our papers and motioned us on with no search. At the Guatemala border, we were told we couldn't enter the country without yellow fever vaccinations. We backtracked to a clinic near Tapachula for inoculations and still crossed the border before sunset.

Ten minutes into Guatemala, a loud bang came from the engine compartment, followed by a consistent pop, pop, popping of what sounded like an air rifle firing. We got out and opened the engine hatch. A spark plug was lying on the sheet metal to the right of the engine. The Bug had blown a plug, and the threads of its hole in the engine were stripped.

We had just passed a huge tire leaning against a tree with the words "Taller Mecánico" emblazoned in white, so we limped back to the shop. During my senior year in high school, I had rebuilt the engine of a 1959 Karmann Ghia by reading *How to Keep Your Volkswagen Alive* by John Muir. Later, I worked at Kevorkian's VW repair shop. I was curious as to how this problem would be resolved.

The mechanic picked up a huge bolt from his work table and drilled a hole in it. Then he screwed the spark plug into the bolt so that the firing part stuck out the bottom. After drilling a bigger hole in the cylinder where the spark plug normally went, he screwed the bolt with the spark plug into the new hole. We paid him fifteen pesos and hit the road.

With a name like the Pan American Highway, we figured it would be the route to take, so we turned north from the coast and climbed a muddy road into rain and mist and night. The so-called highway dragged us through every city, and after depositing us in their centers, offered no clue how to exit.

"All paths are the same, but only one has a heart," Dan recited as we circled Quetzaltenango's town square at midnight trying to figure out which street would get us back to the highway.

He was quoting *The Teachings of Don Juan*. The correct path was one with a heart, and would make for a happy journey as long as you stayed on it. It would give you strength, while other paths would weaken you. With Don Juan's guidance, Dan and I followed the path with heart out of Quetzaltenango and all the other towns we encountered during the night.

As soon as we came to a decent road back to the coast, we jumped on it. Our map showed the coastal highway as paved, but long sections were dirt and rock. When there was pavement, we often drove even slower to avoid the fathomless potholes.

Sometimes the road gradually rose six or seven feet as it approached rivers, only to end abruptly in mid-air, then resume in mid-air on the other side of the river. Spray-painted arrows on plywood signs and trees directed us off the road before we became Evel Knievels, but the real feat was not to miss those signs in the dark. Bridges might some day connect the two sides.

By sunrise, Dan and I were beat. We set up camp on a volcanic sand beach and slept. In the afternoon, we learned how fast you can run with your surfboard on sunbaked black sand and still get the soles of your feet scorched. The waves were small, but they had Pacific Ocean power and hinted of what lay in store for us. Before crossing into El Salvador the next day, we parked in a river and washed the car and ourselves. Afterward, we put on clean clothes—our border-crossing clothes.

When my high school friend Jack and I had gone to El Salvador three years earlier, no information had been available regarding surf spots—only that there was surf. A taxi drove us down the coast in search of waves and dropped us off at a fishing village called Majagual. We spent two sleepless nights in a thatched room above a raucous bar while trying to surf big, closed-out waves during the day.

The second afternoon, a fisherman on the beach urgently tried to tell me something. I finally understood that the water had many big fish that ate people, and that *tiburon* meant shark. I paddled out and relayed the message to Jack.

Back then, Jack and I continued south to Sunzal Point and ended up as housemates of a Peace Corps worker who lived across the road from the point. We shared the house and the rock point break with two Floridians who surfed with their ankles tethered to their boards by bungee cords. When they wiped out, they didn't have to swim all the way in or over rocks to retrieve their boards. Jack and I took a bus to the coastal city of La Libertad and bought bungees and leather, and the Floridians showed us how to make leashes. It changed everything. We had freedom to try things we wouldn't have before.

Dan and I now rolled into La Libertad and discovered that El Salvador had been discovered. The town was jammed with surfers in baggies and huaraches. After a month of not seeing another gringo, we were culture-shocked. The waves would surely be crowded. We drove to the point to check out the surf and parked under palm trees in front of a new restaurant. Where waves normally peeled across the mile-wide bay, there was only smooth blue water.

We sat on a porch overlooking the ocean, and someone sitting nearby told us a surfer from Texas had married a local girl and built the restaurant two years earlier. My pride about being in El Salvador before it was discovered diminished. Not only had another surfer come to Salvador soon after me, he had married a Salvadoran girl and built a restaurant. He was a person who went for what he wanted.

The guy we were talking to said he knew someone who was looking for roommates to share a big house in town. Dan and I drove to the house and talked to a curly-haired surfer from New York City named Lenny. His hometown surf breaks were Long Island and Coney Island, which I thought was just an amusement park. We liked the house and unpacked the Bug. Lenny told us there were more surf spots north and south of La Libertad, but a vehicle was needed to get to them. He said most of the surfers in town had arrived in El Salvador by bus or plane and didn't have cars. The outlook for uncrowded surf improved.

We set up our hammocks on the porch and waited for surf. A week passed with no waves, and a bummed-out attitude descended upon the surf community. When there were waves, surfers fought for them. They paddled past others to get closer to where the wave would begin breaking so it became *their* wave. But when it was flat, we were all brothers (and a few sisters) in mourning.

Dan and I became bored.

"We should go for it," he said.

He was talking about returning to Mexico and bringing back weed to La Libertad.

"To smoke or sell?" I asked.

"If we're going to do it, may as well make it worth our while. This place needs something."

I agreed. I laid Castaneda's *Journey to Ixtlan* on my stomach and looked over at Dan in his hammock.

"We've got to get our passports renewed in a few days anyway," I said.

When we had entered El Salvador, the customs official only wrote fourteen days in our passports. To get an extension, the normal routine was to drive up to the capital. Leaving the country and re-entering would also get us an extension but wasn't worth the hassle—unless an incentive was added. I looked up at the tin roof and visualized a map of El Salvador, Guatemala and Mexico. I saw the army roadblock 200 miles into Mexico.

"Let's look at the map," I said and went into the house to get it.

I laid the map on the tile between our hammocks and pointed to where we had run into the roadblock.

"If we go to Veracruz, or anywhere far into Mexico, we'll have to go through that roadblock," I said.

Our eyes settled at the same spot on the map. Dan reached down and put his finger on it.

"This road here, before the roadblock. It goes up to this city, Tuxtla Guttierez. It looks big. Maybe we can score there."

We rose from our hammocks and walked to the Bug to see where we could hide some pot. A strip of metal trim ran along the bottom of the back of the rear seat's backrest. We removed the trim and particle-board cover. Inside the backrest were four large black springs and mucho available space.

We kept our mission to ourselves and told our new acquaintances we were exiting the country to get more time stamped in our passports. Lenny said he knew an agent at the border who would give us ninety days if we asked. He wrote the person's name on a scrap of paper and said a few dollars would facilitate the request.

As we journeyed north, Dan and I studied the roads and the border crossings at Guatemala and Mexico. Four hours after crossing into Mexico, we turned right and climbed the mountains to Tuxtla Gutierrez. There were no army or police stops along the way, and we settled into a hotel near the town center. All we needed now was a connection. After dinner, Dan and I split up to improve our chances of scoring. I walked to the zocalo (the town's main square) and sat on a bench, then strolled about and had a cerveza or two.

*

I woke up when Dan came into the hotel room and sat on his bed. He hadn't had any luck finding weed, but he thought he had scored with a cute American girl until she left for a few minutes and returned with her sister who was single, unlike herself, and not attractive. She had led him on, Dan complained.

"I made a connection," I told him.

He straightened up.

"Some guys were smoking pot, sitting at the town square away from the crowd. I sat down a few benches from them and they waved me over. One said he knew where to get kilos of some good mota. That's what he called it."

"Mota," Dan repeated.

"We're going to meet on the road south of town at noon. Five kilos for a hundred and fifty bucks."

Dan nodded.

"Are we buying the same stuff you smoked with them? Was it good?" he asked.

I removed a half-joint and a book of matches from the top drawer of the dresser and handed them to him.

"It's not like what we bought in Veracruz. The guy said the weed is compressed into bricks. But it's strong and tastes good. And the bricks will be easier to stash."

Dan took a few hits and was back in a good mood.

The next day, we met my connection at a closed restaurant on the highway and followed him a short distance up a dirt road. After consummating the deal, we hid the five bricks inside the backrest and raised it upright. A sleeping bag and cardboard box in the luggage area went up against it.

Although we only had two borders to cross, we would be stopped on both sides of each, so there was a potential for four inspections. That didn't include any pop-up roadblocks the army or police might spin across our path.

Leaving Mexico and entering Guatemala went smoothly. The agents stamped our passports, issued car papers, and we were on our way. They didn't even ask us to open the hood. In Guatemala we stayed on the coastal road, and the border with El Salvador came earlier than expected. It was night, and Dan was kneeling on the rear seat, reaching over the backrest to re-stash some pot when two soldiers appeared in the headlights. I hit the brakes and told Dan to get back up to the front, pronto.

"I'm almost done," he said.

"Hurry, we're at the station."

One of the soldiers motioned me forward, and I continued slowly. I had to go fast enough not to raise suspicion, but I didn't want them to see Dan climbing back up to the front. Dan fell into his seat a hundred feet before we got to them. Good thing it was dark.

A soldier walked to my side, and another went to Dan's. My guy held a clipboard and asked for our papeles. Dan handed me our documents, and I gave them to the soldier. He walked around the front of the car and disappeared into a small building on our right. No one told us to do anything, so we stayed put.

The soldier on Dan's side walked directly to the back of the Bug and shined his flashlight through the back window. Had he seen Dan climbing over the seat?

"Venga," he called. *Come.*

Did he see some weed or skewed trim Dan hadn't finished reinstalling in his haste? Shit. What were we thinking—smuggling marijuana across international borders?

Dan and I looked at each other and got out of the car. I walked in slow motion around the back to where Dan stood. The soldier pointed a finger through the rear window where his flashlight aimed. Our own flashlight lay on the floor behind the back seat. It was on and illuminating the entire left half of the luggage area as well as the backrest and trim. I saw that all the screws were in place and no contraband was in sight. Exhale.

As the soldier and I looked at each other, I tried to read his thoughts on the matter. I finally shrugged, and so did he. Dan opened the passenger door and reached over the back seat for the flashlight. As we followed the soldier into the office, I gave Dan a very dissatisfied look. The first guy handed us our passports and car papers, and we drove away.

Two hundred feet down the road came El Salvador's entry. I parked in front of the immigration office and we walked inside. Where did I put that piece of paper with the customs official's name? It was probably buried inside my duffel bag. A real Man of Papers would have kept it secure with all the other documents.

"I'll put money in the passports," I said to Dan. "We could luck out and it'll be the right guy."

I slid both passports to the official behind the counter, one with a U.S. ten-dollar bill inside. American dollars were valued in El Salvador. He looked at the passports and money, then up at me.

"We would like ninety days, por favor," I said. It seemed like he was waiting for an explanation.

The officer nodded and removed the bill. I watched as he stamped our passports and wrote ninety days in both. Alright.

He began to close them but hesitated and stared at my open passport. He looked up.

"You have already been in the country. I am sorry. I cannot give you ninety days," he said in Spanish.

What? What kind of law is that? He stared at me with droopy, sorry eyes. Did he want more money?

I took another ten-dollar bill from my wallet and placed it on the counter.

"No puedo," he said. *I can't.*

He shook his head and drew a line through the ninety days and wrote fourteen days underneath.

"You can go to the capital for an extension," he told us and closed our passports.

Dan was standing to my right, watching. He reached in front of me to grab the second ten-dollar bill, but I placed my hand on his arm to stop him. The official turned to Dan with an expression that appeared hostile in any language. Then he gave me a stare that I took to mean "your friend just fucked up."

But I could have been wrong. Maybe I was the one who fucked up. What was apparent, though, was that we had breached some rule of bribe etiquette. The agent slid our passports to us—without the cash.

The next day, we began spreading joy across the land, selling ounces for thirty dollars and transforming the heretofore sullen attitude of the surf community into something positive. Everyone became upbeat and optimistic, taking stock of things that had become mundane: the banana and coconut and papaya trees that grew in our yards, the hummingbirds that siphoned nectar from red and yellow and blue flowers, and the gigantic afternoon thunderstorms that mushroomed over the Pacific, drifted into town and dumped rain to cool our world and make it pleasant for an evening stroll through La Libertad. Best of all, a swell arrived.

As expected, the point at La Libertad was crowded, so Dan and I drove north and checked out other spots. Sunzal, where Jack and I had surfed with the Floridians three years earlier, also had too many surfers. We continued north to the town of El Zonte and surfed a right point break at a small half-moon cove by ourselves.

A few nights later, I had it in my mind that I needed to get out of the hammock to do something—that Dan and I were waiting, but I couldn't remember for what. How long had we been lying in our hammocks listening to Genesis' *Lamb Lies Down on Broadway*? It was a double album, and one side of an LP ran about twenty minutes, and two sides of an LP fit on one side of a cassette. I had flipped the tape over, so we must have been lying in our hammocks for at least forty minutes. Did I flip it over twice? That wouldn't make sense. I tried to figure out which side was playing but couldn't. One thing certain was that I was thirsty. My mouth felt like cotton.

Dan hadn't said anything in a while. Or had he? His eyes were open and aimed at the underside of the porch's tin roof. I looked up and saw a line of ants moving across a wood beam that supported the rafters. Is that what Dan was looking at? As I stared at them, another line of ants appeared to the side. I turned to look at those, and a third line of ants appeared in my periphery. When I turned to those, they quit moving as if they saw me looking and stopped, all of them at the same time. What kind of awareness was that? And why would they care if I watched?

While I observed, the ants melted into the wood—into a dark brown line. After some focusing, I realized there were no ants. I had been looking at a split in the wood beam. I turned back to the previous lines of ants. They, too, no longer existed.

I remembered what Dan and I were waiting for. We had traded a few ounces of weed for a dozen hits of blotter acid and were waiting to come on to the hits we had taken. The waiting was over. I extricated myself from the hammock and went to the refrigerator for a cerveza.

After our beers, Dan and I walked down to the water. We sat on big rocks and watched phosphorescent waves peel across the bay under the full moon. Instead of sand, the beach was made up of different-size round stones. We listened as they rolled around on top of each other in the surf. I felt their vibrations through the boulder I sat on—Earth's vibrations.

Sometime later, we walked along the shore to the town cemetery. The moon shone so bright that our shadows were as distinct as if the sun had been out. We wandered among the tombstones and read their names and dates without a flashlight. Back at our house, we smoked a doobie and put Fleetwood Mac's *Future Games* in the tape deck. We settled into our hammocks and listened to the long mellow songs and the faint surf and rolling rocks. I closed my eyes, but my brain didn't sleep for a while.

I awoke around noon with the post-psychedelic blues—the emptiness caused by loss of the acid-enhanced perception. Late afternoon, Dan and I paddled out at Libertad Point and surfed with the crowd. Although we both caught waves, neither of us liked to fight for them. I preferred my communion with Mother Nature more peaceful.

Dan and I decided La Libertad was not for us. Hanging out in Surf City was not the reason we had traveled south from Texas. In addition, our house did not have soul—a concept we learned from Carlos Castaneda. We had gotten off track. The next day, Dan and I drove to El Zonte and found a house to rent—a ranchita (*small ranch*), the owner called it. We moved in the next day and watched the sun set behind our own point break. Back on track, just like that.

The swell stayed decent, and we surfed the point alone until a surfer we had met in town got off the bus with his board. Dan and I were a little bummed, but, really, three surfers at a point break wasn't the worst thing in the world. Scott was from North Carolina and had grown up surfing on Cape Hatteras. As we paddled out, Dan and I mentioned we had each taken a hit of acid.

I caught a few head-high waves and got acclimated to the acid, then a real set came through and I was dropping, almost free-falling, down the face of a big wave. It was peeling right, so my back was to it. When I hit the bottom, I sank my fin and looked above my right shoulder at a twelve-foot wall of sun-sparkling colors and geometric patterns. I accelerated out of the bottom turn and shot ahead to the top, just below where a million tiny white bubbles popped and sizzled.

The wave began to tube, so I slowed and let it fold over me while the shoreline disappeared behind my personal waterfall. Before the wave closed out, I shot through the aperture, went down a little, then up and over the top and into the air. I came down weightless and landed hard on my board while the ocean glittered all around. I was still living the ride when the top of the wave blew back, and cool, fat droplets showered me.

I paddled back out and took a place between Dan and Scott, who sat too far out. He was playing it safe—away from the rocks. I was about to tell him to paddle closer to us when a big fin rolled over at the surface five feet behind him. Fuck.

"Shark behind you," I yelled.

Dan turned to me.

"Fucking shark," I yelled. Dan didn't hesitate. He paddled.

Catching a wave would have been the quickest way out of there, but a glance to sea showed none on the horizon. I paddled fast and hard behind Dan and hoped Scott did the same. He was the one most likely to be attacked. But if he got ahead of me, I would be the chosen one. When I'd made some distance, I turned to Scott and saw he had kept up with me. At that moment, the shark's fin came out of the water the exact distance from him as before. Behind the shark, a wave broke.

"It's right behind you. Catch the wave in," I yelled.

I clenched the rails of my board, and was rocked to the beach by an avalanche of white water. Scott caught the same wave. Dan stood on the beach, watching. My high had disappeared for the moment. Funny how adrenaline tops acid.

*

The time for our passport renewal arrived, and we drove up the mountain to San Salvador. The line at the counter moved slowly. When we handed the official our passports, he studied them and said, "Un momento" and disappeared through a door in the back. Un momento later, he returned and ushered us around the counter and through the same doorway. Inside the office, a chubby Salvadoran in a brown uniform sat behind a big desk.

"Siéntese," he said.

We sat down in front of his desk.

He stared at Dan and me for several seconds, then held up two ten-dollar bills and a piece of paper, all stapled together.

"Did you give this to an official at the border?" he asked in Spanish.

I focused on the money for a few seconds before I answered.

"Yes," I said. We couldn't lie about it.

"Why did you give money to a government official?"

The tricky part would be predicting the consequences of any potential answer. The only way to play it was the ignorant, naïve route. We were just twenty-year-old, stupid, gringo, college kids. What would they do?

"Because we wanted to stay longer in your country," I answered, which wasn't an explanation, but it was the truth.

The colonel or major or whatever kept his eyes on us and shook his head. We had upset him.

"You have committed una ofensa grave," he said sternly.

If those words had similar meanings to the English they resembled, it wasn't good.

"You have forty-eight hours to leave the country," he told us in Spanish.

He wrote in our passports and made it official by striking them with a hand-carved wooden stamp. When he gave them back, "48 horas a salir del pais" was etched into a new page. *48 hours to leave the country*. Fuck.

*

Dan and I watched the waves from the back porch of our ranchita and wondered what we were going to do. We had just settled into a house with soul and its own point break, not to mention our steady income. What would we do with the pot if we returned to Mexico? But we didn’t want to go back to Mexico.

That evening, we told our surfing acquaintances in La Libertad about our misfortune. They came up with something we hadn't thought about.

“Costa Rica,” they said. “Head south.”

“Good surf.”

“No crowds.”

“Go for it.”

CHAPTER THREE

Costa Rica

The Brotherhood

Honduras came first, followed by Nicaragua, then Costa Rica. Before each crossing, we washed the Bug and ourselves in a river and put on our border clothes. The coastal route was a mix of asphalt, broken asphalt, potholes and rocks, and the Bug was not happy about it. Thin aluminum tubes protected the pushrods at the bottom of the engine, but nothing protected the aluminum tubes. The rocks we drove over kept bumping and bending them, and oil began to seep at their ends. The solution was simple—keep adding oil. We stopped for oil more often than for gas. One night, we were forced to make a pit stop at a small factory for whatever oil they were using in their machines. The Bug didn't mind. That oil would be gone in four hours, and a flashing yellow light would alert us to its thirst.

In Nicaragua, we sidetracked to a black sand beach that sparkled silver in the sunlight and dropped steeply into waves that broke right onshore. A grove of coconut trees extended from the beach to nearby hills, and Dan and I sat in their shade as parrots flew under the fronds, squawking en masse. We dropped some acid and went swimming. It was the first time since Toro I had gone in the ocean without a board, and I floated serenely on my back while surging in and out with the swells.

Afterward, Dan and I sat at the top of the steep beach and timed it so our somersaults coincided with waves crashing onto the sand below. We were back on top, drying and baking, and I was staring at white foam receding on shiny black sand when I felt a tapping on my leg. I turned to Dan. His face was twisted as he pointed over his shoulder.

A campesino stood six feet away, wearing a ragged straw hat and a baggy shirt tucked behind a rope belt. I saw why Dan was making a face. Four dead iguanas hung from the guy's right shoulder and down his chest. Below that shoulder was no arm. Under the brim of the hat, his right eye appeared as a white marble, and a vertical scar cut into the cheek below. The sight of him and his iguanas may not have affected someone level-headed, but Dan and I were not level-headed at the moment. I laughed. Then Dan laughed. Then Iguana Man laughed. The iguanas did not laugh, but one opened its eyes. They were alive.

"Fresca," the man said and grinned. *Fresh*. His missing teeth were balanced by an equal number of silver ones. Did he wink at me?

Dan and I managed a conversation with the guy and found out his wounds were sustained in a machete battle during a border war between El Salvador and Honduras. We declined to purchase any iguanas, and he continued down the beach.

Upon entering Costa Rica, we had yet to decide on a precise destination. The Nicoya Peninsula was near the border, but friends had surfed there, and I remembered the pictures they took of too many sharks patrolling the water close to shore. Dan and I continued to the capital to scope the lay of the land.

After a few nights at a hostel in San Jose, we headed to Quepos on the Pacific. For a couple of days, we paddled across a wide river adjacent the town and surfed decent-sized waves on a long beach. We caught a few good rides, but most of the waves closed out.

Further exploration revealed a white sand beach alongside a tranquil ocean thirty minutes south. The bartender at a restaurant told us we were at one of three coves just designated a national park named Manuel Antonio. We could get to the other ones by crossing a tidal river up the beach. There were actually five coves, and all had been owned by a private citizen until Costa Rica declared eminent domain and took possession of the first three.

We drove over the sand to the tidal river and looked across to where the road disappeared into the jungle. The river was too deep for the Bug to cross, so we parked it on the beach and waded to the other side. We hiked under a solid canopy of branches and breathed thick, flowery air as parrots and red macaws fluttered overhead. In ten minutes, the path opened to white sand and blue water with two peninsulas extending out at each side. People swam and waded in the water, and tents were set up under a row of trees at the top of the beach.

Dan and I drove back to our hotel and checked out. When we returned to the beach, the river was down because the tide was lower, so I circled back over the sand to pick up speed, and we splashed across.

We spent the next several days snorkeling for puka shells, stalking schools of yellow and blue fish and hiking the rocky ocean ledges to the fifth cove and beyond. It would have been paradise except for the monkeys that dropped from the trees and stole from campsites and cars, and the psychedelic-colored land crabs that tried to creep into our sleeping bags at night. One left a claw on Dan's finger when he tried to evict it from the rear floorboard of the Bug. During the day, hundreds of crabs moved as one, amassing over entire sections of the beach like something out of a science fiction movie.

The peninsula on the right side of the cove was nearly an island since it was connected to the shore by only a narrow strip of sand. The monkeys supposedly lived there, so one afternoon Dan and I set out to explore Monkey Island and maybe find their lair and everyone's stolen stuff.

We climbed up through a jungle so dense, the atmosphere had been sucked dry, and our lungs worked hard to breathe within the vacuum. At the top, we shimmied out a branch that extended horizontally from a rock cliff and sat with our legs dangling over the cobalt Pacific hundreds of feet below. A yellow trimaran motored from around the point and passed directly below us. I yelled down, but neither of the two sailors in the cockpit looked up.

After descending back into a shady forest, we sat against a fallen tree and smoked a joint.

"I don't think this is where the monkeys live," Dan said.

"They could be out stealing."

Leaves dropped onto the forest floor nearby. But leaves shouldn't make that much noise. Dan and I looked up. Nothing, and no more falling leaves or branches. When we stood up to continue our search, the dropping resumed. We looked up again and hell broke loose—monkeys from hell. Dozens of them bombarded us, and they were no longer hiding. They jumped up and down on high branches and threw things at us, and something brown and soft hit Dan in the shoulder. It was shit. Monkey shit. We ran, and they chased us from above and threw more branches and shit. The only quick way out was to jump into the water and swim across the cove to our beach.

*

Tents were for short-term residence, so we rented a shack on the road between Quepos and the coves for five dollars a month. It came furnished with its own outhouse and water well. There were very few houses along the road, and the only one we could see from our new home was a bamboo mansion that two rumored ex-gold smugglers had built. The Bug was happy to have a home too. It quit leaking so much oil, probably because the engine wasn't getting as hot with the shorter drives.

After moving into our shack, Dan and I were driving back from Quepos when, up ahead, a girl in jean cutoffs and a scarf around her head was thumbing. Dark red hair fell from under the scarf onto her shoulders. I stopped.

"Hola," said Dan from the passenger seat.

"Hola," she replied.

"A dónde vas?" I asked, across Dan.

"La playa." *The beach.*

"Vamos." *Let's go.*

Dan got out, and she climbed into the back. I would have preferred her in front, but Dan had seniority.

Sylvia told us she was from Panama and had been vacationing in Costa Rica for two months. She said her nickname was Panama Red, which is a type of weed from Panama—a very good type. As we drove, Bob Dylan sang "Like a Rolling Stone" on the cassette deck, and she started singing along in English.

"Habla inglés?" I asked, looking at her in the rearview mirror.

"No." She returned my gaze, then looked out the side window and resumed singing.

"No entiende las palabras?" I asked. *You don't understand the words?*

"No," she said and added, "Un poco." *A little.*

I dropped Dan off at our house and drove Sylvia to the beach.

"Necesita regresar a su casa?" she asked. *Do you need to return to your house?*

"No."

We sat at the bar in the beach restaurant and drank a beer or two. She told me she had seen me before. I was surprised I hadn't noticed her.

The next afternoon, Sylvia and I rendezvoused at the restaurant and walked across the tidal river to the strip of beach that connected Monkey Island to the cove. She took off her halter top and leaned back in the sand. I had heard topless sunbathing was popular in Europe and other places, but hearing was different than experiencing. Afterward, we swam in the cove, then lay down on a towel and kissed. That night, Sylvia stayed with me in my room (the back porch of our shack) and soon spent every night there.

Later, when Sylvia needed to retrieve clothes from where she had been staying, I drove her. She walked across the front porch to the side of the house, raised a window and crawled through. The front door opened and I went in. When I asked why she had to go through the window, she mentioned something about not having a key. Sylvia grabbed her stuff and we left.

Her temperament was something new for me. She would get mad for unknown reasons, and I figured it had something to do with the hot-blooded Latin thing. She once slapped me in the face, flew out the front door and disappeared down the road to the beach. I thought that was the end of her, but in the evening she strolled up to the shack wearing a thin, blue halter top she had somehow fashioned from a handkerchief of mine.

One night, the landlord's wife came to our house, worried and almost in tears.

"Mi hijo, mi hijo. Yo no sé dónde está." *My child, my child. I don't know where he is.* Her son should have returned from the beach hours ago, she said.

"Vamos a ver," I said. *Let's go see.*

I drove her to the restaurant on the beach where her son sat on a bar stool, drinking beer with his buddies. He was 18 or 19 years old and told his mother he would get a ride home in a little while.

*

"Something's going on," Dan said as he looked out our window.

Sylvia had hitched into town, so it was just us at the shack. I looked up the road and saw two black-and-white police cars parked in front of our smuggler neighbors' bamboo palace.

"We need to hide our stash," I said.

Dirt and rocks surrounded the shack. I went to the back and placed the baggie in a hole in the dirt, then put a rock on top of it.

When the policia arrived, Dan and I were sitting nonchalantly at our dining room table. Dan laid down his paperback as I welcomed them. The chief asked for our passports and told us they needed to search the shack. He directed one man to look inside the house and the other to search outside. No one went to the Bug, where five pounds of mota were still hidden in the back seat. Dan and I and the police jefe sat at the table and waited. The policeman who had gone to the back returned too soon. He held up the plastic bag containing our pot and cigarette papers.

How did he find it, and so fast? Had he seen me hide it? I know I had kept out of view.

He handed the baggie to the chief, who examined it. There was only enough weed for three or four joints. The chief said nothing, and we waited until the other officer finished his search inside the house.

"Come to the oficina de policia tomorrow morning at ten," we were told.

El Jefe put our passports in his shirt pocket, and the three police walked across the road to our landlord's house. Fifteen minutes later, the police cars continued in the direction of Manuel Antonio.

"What do you think they'll do?" Dan asked.

"I don't know."

"How can they prove it's ours, anyway?" he said. "They found it in the back yard, not in the house or on us. It could've been there before we got here."

He had a point, but the Quepos cops wouldn't buy it.

"We didn't deny it," I said. "And they didn't arrest us. If it was serious, they would have taken us in, don't you think?"

Dan stared at his fingers tapping the table-top.

*

At ten a.m., we sat across a desk from the police chief and awaited our fate. He opened a drawer and pulled out our bag of pot, then looked at us for a few seconds before laying it on the desk. He stared at us some more, then looked down at the weed.

We get it. It's our weed. We're muy malo.

"Marijuana is illegal in Costa Rica," he said in Spanish.

I nodded in acknowledgment of our sins as did Dan. We were just college kids on a break, trying to catch a few waves. It wasn't like we were criminals. The officer looked at Dan and me a bit longer, then slid our passports across the desktop to us.

"Gracias," we told him.

I stood up and looked down at the plastic baggie on his desk. We had plenty of pot, but those cigarette papers were hard to come by. We'd have to go back to inhaling the 50-year-old wallpaper from the walls of our shack. *Cigarette papers aren't illegal, are they, señor?*

As we walked out of the police station, I figured it had to have been our landlord telling the cops what great hombres we were that got us off.

A few days later, our gold-smuggling neighbors told Dan they learned the reason for the search. Someone had informed the police that gringos living on the road to Manuel Antonio were selling marijuana. The snitch was Sylvia's ex-boyfriend. The window she had gone through had been at his house.

He belonged to an association called The Brotherhood of Eternal Love, based in California. Six months earlier, Costa Rica cops had busted him for possession of hash oil that his Brotherhood had been moving through the country. The government confiscated his passport and told him they would return it after he spent all the money in his Costa Rica bank account. That was his punishment. When he discovered Sylvia had ditched him for me, he had somehow found out about our selling weed and told the cops. *Brotherhood, indeed.*

Even before Sylvia came into the picture, Dan and I had been spending less time together. He now hung out with friends in Quepos. Dan had been a good traveling and business partner, and I must not have been too bad, either, since he had asked for a divorce only once. We took the pot out of the back seat and divided it so we could each sell what we wanted whenever we wanted. I buried mine out back (far from the house, this time).

*

Two weeks later, I ran into one of our ex-gold-smuggling neighbors in Quepos. We talked a little, and he asked, "How do you feel?"

"What do you mean?"

"Physically," he said.

"Fine. Why?"

"Your eyes are yellow."

My eyes are brown. I didn't understand.

"The whites of your eyes are yellow," he said. "You feel good?"

I thought for a second. "Actually, I have been kind of tired."

"I think you've got jaundice."

Jaundice?

"Is your piss dark yellow or brown?" he asked.

"Come to think of it, it has been dark. I wondered about it."

He gave me directions to a doctor who confirmed the diagnosis. But jaundice was just a symptom of many diseases, the doctor told me. I could have malaria, typhoid, typhus, dengue fever or hepatitis. There was no way to tell, he said. My eyes were yellow because my liver couldn't remove impurities from my body. Mosquitoes were the source of some of the diseases, but unsanitary living conditions could also have been the culprit.

There had been no shortage of mosquitoes on our expedition. And regarding unsanitary conditions, there was the river water we drank and bathed in at Toro, the dinner that gave us dysentery, the bad fish I ate in La Libertad, the yellow fever vaccination at the Guatemalan border, and who knows what else.

The doctor prescribed hard candies. It would help the liver, he said. I ate hard candies for several days and became more tired. I also developed a fever. When I told Dan about my jaundice, he was certain I caught it from Sylvia.

For the first time in all our travels, the heat and humidity became uncomfortable, and I felt I wasn't going to get better in Costa Rica. I told Dan I planned to fly back to the U.S. and he bought my remaining weed.

When I left a day early, Dan was at the beach so I wrote him a note. In San Jose I checked into the same hostel where we stayed when we first got to Costa Rica. That evening I walked to an old theater to watch *Papillon*, a movie with Steve McQueen and Dustin Hoffman about two French criminals who were imprisoned on Devil's Island off the South American coast.

I was sitting up in the almost-vacant balcony when Dan walked in holding a bag of popcorn. I waved him over. He told me he had come to San Jose to find me but hadn't expected to see me in the theater. He just wanted to watch *Papillon*. Dan said he had put his original share of the pot back into the seat of the Bug. I had been driving around with it for two weeks without knowing it.

The next morning, Dan removed the weed, stuffed it in his backpack, and hopped a bus to Quepos. The only luck I had finding long-term parking was a police storage yard, which would have been funny if Dan's pot had still been in the back seat. I flew to New Orleans, then took a bus to the Spring Branch district of west Houston where my parents lived.

The bathroom scale read 128 pounds; my normal was 145. Not too bad. A Houston doctor confirmed I might have any of several tropical diseases, but that I would eventually get better with no treatment. His only advice was not to drink alcohol for a year so that my liver would heal. I wasn't a big drinker anyway.

At the library and bookstores, I learned that massive doses of vitamin C hastened the recovery of most of my potential tropical diseases. I took massive doses of vitamin C, and in four weeks I was well enough to join the carpenters' union. If I played my cards right, I might someday aspire to journeyman and earn a good, honest living and contribute to the gross domestic product. It wasn't college, but my father seemed happy about it. Two months later, I had enough money to quit and fly back to Costa Rica.

*

Before I could drive the Bug from the police storage yard in San Jose, I spent two days replacing stolen parts. When I made it back to Quepos, the ex-gold smugglers informed me Dan had flown to Colombia. He was probably sitting in a dormant volcano drinking yagé with the Indians and learning the meaning of life. That was what we had both planned to do.

Instead, I sold the VW for $600 and bussed up through the

same six countries Dan and I had driven with the weed. I even surfed in El Salvador, where immigration officials never noticed the prior forty-eight-hour eviction stamped somewhere in my passport.

Mexico Business

CHAPTER FOUR

Oaxaca & The Zapotecs

When I returned to Houston, I learned Dan's mother had committed him to a mental institution after he told her about our acid trips in Central America. Why he mentioned them to her was beyond me. My father had become a lawyer after retiring from the Navy and worked from his own neighborhood law office. Dan telephoned him and was out before I got back. My father told me Dan hadn't been in a big rush to be released because he had a new girlfriend inside the facility. Afterward, Dan chose to reside with a friend of ours rather than with his mother.

Dan and I had our differences in Mexico and Central America, but we had also shared experiences none of our friends related to or cared about. To us, though, they weren't just experiences. They were life. Three friends who had quit college the same time we did were back majoring in finance, law and computer science. Dan and I made plans to continue our own education. We would return to Mexico and bring weed back to Texas.

First, we needed a source; a destination, a spot on the map. Tuxtla Gutierrez, where we bought the kilos we took to Costa Rica, was too far—not to mention the nearby roadblock. The city of Oaxaca (Wa-háw-kuh) caught our attention because it shared its name with excellent weed we sometimes got hold of in Houston. Oaxaca lay in a valley where two mountain ranges come together one thousand miles south of the U.S. border. The medium-size city looked big enough to find a connection and allow us anonymity.

We loaded up my newly acquired '66 Plymouth Valiant and tied our boards on top to maintain a gringo surfer image. The boards would also come in handy for crossing the weed. We passed through the twenty-kilometer checkpoint, and I put in The Eagles' cassette, *On the Border*. "Already Gone" played—my adios to the Machine.

On Mexico's mile-high central plateau, a straight modern highway took us south across an infinite brown plain dabbed with cactus, rocky peaks and spires of black lava. At two checkpoints, we were on our way pronto, but near Querétaro, older officers moved between the soldiers and were not distracted by our magazines of naked women. The search was more thorough than at previous checkpoints. We could not return this way with the mota.

Twelve hours after crossing the border, we descended into the bowl of smog and traffic that was Mexico City. Our fast pace fizzled on a congested road with stop signs, brake lights and car horns. An hour later, we climbed out of the city on the south side. The air cleared, and snow-capped Popocatepetl Volcano and neighboring Iztaccihuatl rose into the twilight. Eight more hours to Oaxaca.

I reached under the dash for the baggie of joints, and we celebrated our transit through the Federal District with Mexico playing across the windshield and Carlos Santana playing through the speakers. By the time Popo and Izta disappeared behind us, Dan was asleep facing the passenger window. Including the leg from Houston, we had been on the road for twenty hours.

Just before morning, we came to a vista spot on the right. Dan and I got out and looked down. Beyond a low ridge, twinkling city lights competed with the dawn. Oaxaca was no longer just a spot on the map. Dan settled into the back seat, and I stretched out in front.

At noon, we checked into a hotel and walked around town, scoping everything out and making our gringo selves visible to potential connections. The next day, we played tourist and visited Monte Alban, a city of pyramids and temples built by Zapotec Indians 1,000 years before Christ. We learned the Zapotecs considered themselves the very first people, and believed all life sprang from the Tree of Life in nearby Mitla.

*

Dan and I were sitting on a bench at the zocalo like we had done the previous two nights when someone sat down to my left.

"You are American," he said.

He appeared to be a few years older than us, clean-cut, and with a fairly respectable haircut. He wore striped green slacks and a black-and-white checkered shirt. Maybe it was Mexican fashion.

"Yes," I answered.

"You need something? Smoke?"

I nodded. "Si."

"Un poco? O mucho?" *A little. Or a lot?*

"Un poco mucho," I answered.

He smiled and nodded.

"I can help. Venga." *Come.*

We followed him a couple of blocks to a small park and sat on a bench together. His name was Guillermo, but he told us his friends called him William because he spoke English. William is English for Guillermo. He knew where to get some "materiál."

"What is the price?" I asked. "Per kilo."

"How much do you need?"

"Possibly fifteen kilos."

Smalltime. But fifteen kilos equaled thirty-three pounds, which Dan and I could sell for $350 a pound. We would make $11,000 on a $500 investment. Our expenses amounted to gasoline and hotels. By keeping our load small and easily manageable, there would be less potential for problems—and failure.

"Thirty dollars a kilo, más o menos," answered William. "It depends on what they have and the quality of mota you want."

"We want it good," Dan said.

"Claro." William nodded. *Of course.*

"Who are we buying it from?" I asked.

"The people in the mountains. Los Indios. You will meet them."

"When can we do it?"

"Tomorrow night."

William told us we would not need to bring money. If the Indians had what we wanted, we would return later to complete the business.

The next night, I drove south from Oaxaca with William in the passenger seat and Dan in the back. Fifteen minutes out of town, William pointed to a truck inspection ramp on the left side of the road.

"Normalmente, it is used for truck weighing and inspections. But during the day, police sometimes put roadblocks and look in cars for mota and armas," he said. "Do not drive past here with the materiál."

As we drove by, I looked across the road and saw the station was closed.

"I will show you where you are able to go around," William said.

A few minutes later he pointed to a dirt road on our left.

"You turn there," he said. "Is a store. Go left after the store. Drive ten minutes and you will be past the checkpoint. You will see a road. Turn left. Do not turn before."

I looked at Dan in the rearview mirror. We weren't going to drive north after buying the pot. We didn't know William. He might be planning to snitch us out to cops or his friends or whomever. Also, Oaxaca was a known pot-growing region, and the popular transport route was surely to the north. The cops had to know that. Dan and I would go in the opposite direction, south, then up across the Isthmus of Tehuantepec before heading north along the Gulf of Mexico.

"Los Indios do not know themselves as Indios," William said. "Some people call them Indios to say they are lesser. They are good people. You will see."

"What do they call themselves?" Dan asked from the back.

William turned to him and shrugged. "They are the people who live in the mountains."

A sign for the town of Tlacolula appeared in the headlights, and William pointed to a turnoff.

"There. Go right," he said.

I followed his directions, and a minute later we stopped at a small store with an illuminated Superior beer sign on its roof.

"We must bring a gift for the people in the mountains," William said.

Dan and I followed him into the building and to the back wall where bottles of liquor lined the shelves.

"Mezcal," William said. He picked up a bottle of amber liquid with a label that read Monte Alban. A fat worm or hairless caterpillar bounced along the bottom of the bottle.

"Do not worry. Is not alive. Is un gusano. A worm," William said.

"We were at Monte Alban yesterday," said Dan.

"Is the best mezcal," William said as he picked up another bottle. "This is good too, but Monte Alban is best."

The second bottle had a label with Gusano Rojo printed next to a cartoon of a drunken señorita worm wearing a dress. Inside, another dead worm rested at the bottom. William put the Gusano Rojo down and picked up another bottle of Monte Alban.

"This is for our friends in the mountains," William said as he held up a bottle. "And this is for us." He raised the other one.

I paid for the mezcal and we continued driving. In ten minutes, we exited the highway onto a dirt road that cut across flat land with few trees. When we passed through a sleeping town, six or seven dogs attacked our tires and doors viciously. They may have been normal perros during the day, but at night and in the pack, they were a frothing, collective evil. They chased the Valiant until we were out of the village and continued barking in case we had any ideas of returning.

Mountain silhouettes grew under the starlight and eventually flanked us. We continued through the valley, listening to the sound of chirping crickets and dirt crunching beneath our tires. The air became chilly, and I rolled up my window. After dipping across a dry riverbed, William had me turn left, and we drove another five minutes.

"Turn off the lights. There, next to the casa," he said and pointed to the right.

I switched off the headlights, made a right and parked with the shack on my left.

"We wait," said William.

He lifted one of the mezcal bottles from the floorboard, took a long swig and held the bottle out to me. I wanted to stay alert and ready for anything that might happen, then considered one sip might relieve any potential anxiety. I took a drink and passed the bottle to Dan. It burned my throat as if I had just drunk gasoline.

"Many people take a limón after, or beer," William said. "Los Indios like it alone. Me, también." He took another swig.

"If the Indios offer you anything, you must accept," William told us. "Many times, a cigarette is a gift from them. They are poor."

"We don't smoke," said Dan. He took a drink and handed the bottle to William.

"You put the cigarette behind your ear," William said. "It is a courtesy. But is the same in all Mexico. You should not refuse a gift. Los Indios will offer you something. It is their custom. Like the mezcal we bring."

William took another drink and looked back at Dan.

"Okay," said Dan.

"How long do we wait?" I asked.

"Maybe they bring samples. They know we are here. And why. But not for which mota and the quantity. You said you want colas. Some people ask for the materiál in bricks."

"Colas" was slang for flower buds, and would bring a better price than if pressed into bricks. Another five minutes passed, and a light appeared in the shack's window.

"We go now," said William.

He led us to the front door and tapped lightly. It opened, and a short, stout man with black hair trimmed straight across his forehead greeted us. He wore matching loose white pants and shirt that resembled a karate outfit.

Light flickered from an oil lamp on top of a wooden table in the back right corner. The table and its one chair were the only furniture in the room. There was a door at the center of the back wall where the man must have entered. He said something to William in a language other than Spanish, and William and our host sat down on the dirt floor. Dan and I joined them.

As William and the Indian spoke in the strange language, Spanish was tossed into the mix but not enough for me to understand. The Indian's short sentences had a rhythm and ended abruptly with a spitting sound. William handed him the unopened bottle of mezcal. He smiled, unscrewed the cap and took a drink, then passed the bottle to me and said something. I looked at William.

"He asks where are you from?"

"Los Estados Unidos. Tejas," I told him.

The Indian pointed to his chest and spoke again.

"He tells you his name is Francisco, and he is Zapotec," William said.

"Soy Steve," I said to Francisco and pointed to my chest. He turned and smiled at Dan.

"Dan," said Dan.

As the mezcal made another round, Francisco removed a green and brown bud from the pocket of his pants. He held it up. Red threads were entwined throughout, similar to the weed Dan and I had bought in Veracruz eight months earlier.

"Colitas puras," Francisco said and smiled. (Co-lée-tahs poo-rahs.) *Pure little flowers.*

He handed the flower top to William, who traded it to Dan for the mezcal. Dan put the bud to his nose and nodded, then passed it to me. It smelled strong and fresh, and when I squeezed it, resin stuck to my thumb and fingers. I gave the bud back to Francisco.

"Bueno," I told him.

"Fuma," Francisco said as he handed the flower top to William. *You smoke.*

William got up and went to the table and began rolling a joint. Francisco pulled a baggie containing cigarettes from the pocket of his shirt and handed it to me.

"Gracias," I said. "Para mas tarde." *For later.*

I removed a cigarette from the plastic bag and placed it behind my right ear, then passed the bag to Dan.

William lit the joint and took a couple of hits. He walked around the table and handed it to me. The weed tasted as good as it smelled, and I blew out the smoke before it expanded too much.

"Muy bueno," I said to Francisco.

He smiled.

"Good enough?" I asked Dan after he took a hit.

The weed was obviously good enough, but I thought Francisco might want to hear it from Dan.

"Bueno," Dan said, exhaling. "What's the price?"

"You want fifteen kilos?" William asked.

"Yes," Dan answered. I nodded.

William talked with Francisco, then told us the cost would be 450 pesos a kilo—about $540 for thirty-three pounds. And it was available now if we wanted.

"No. Tomorrow night," I said. "If that's okay."

William translated and Francisco nodded.

"How does it come?" I asked William. "Flower tops or bricks?"

William consulted with Francisco.

"Stems of colitas, with each kilo tied with string," William answered.

We said goodbye to Francisco and maneuvered through the silent night until we encountered then fled Satan's canine corp. We were asleep in our hotel room before two a.m. The next day could be a long one.

After breakfast, Dan and I bought plastic garbage bags, duct tape, drinking water, batteries and snacks. We filled the gas tank, checked the tire pressures and topped off the radiator.

"The farmacia might have something we can take to keep us awake," I suggested.

"Like No Doze," said Dan.

At the farmacia, I explained to a woman in a pale blue uniform that we would be driving late and needed something to stay alert. She went to the back of the store and returned with a box of Octodron.

"Este es el más fuerte," she said. *This is the strongest.*

After returning to the hotel, we translated the ingredients and learned Octodron was an amphetamine—speed, and would have required a prescription in the States. It would suffice.

At ten o'clock, we picked up William and stopped to buy two bottles of mezcal. When we got back on the road, he opened one and took a drink. Dan and I abstained. We needed our senses in good working order for the trip down the mountains.

I parked with the shack on my left and a burro tethered to a tree on the right. Francisco led us out the back door and along a narrow trail through tall brush. We came out at a small clearing with several wooden shacks. An oil lamp hung from the porch of one house and allowed us to make our way to a hut at the clearing's opposite edge.

Another Zapotec stood inside, wearing the same white outfit as Francisco. We shook hands, and he spoke with Francisco before leaving the room. Francisco motioned for us to sit on the dirt floor.

"He has gone for the materiál," William said.

William presented the mezcal to Francisco. He took a drink and handed the bottle back to William. They conversed in their blend of Zapotec and Spanish, and when the mezcal came around, Dan and I took a sip or two to be polite. Another Zapotec entered, and we shook hands. He sat down against the back wall and began to chant, pausing every once in a while to take a drink of mezcal. Francisco occasionally interrupted his conversation with William to chant along.

A mantel extended from the front wall above a fireplace. At the mantel's center stood a framed picture of the Virgin Mary with her head and body surrounded by a golden halo. A worn black-and-white photograph of someone leaned against her, and on each side was a stone figure resembling a cat. A thin plume of smoke rose from a bowl at the mantel's right end. The chanting continued.

"What's going on?" I whispered to William.

He talked to Francisco, who turned to me and said something in a mix of Zapotec and Spanish. I didn't understand.

William translated, "A person in the village has died, and they are helping him on his way to the next life."

"Is that the Virgin Mary?" I asked and pointed to the framed picture.

"Is the Virgin of Guadalupe. She is Indian and has appeared to the people in Mexico. She is important for all Mexico, not only to the people in the mountains."

William looked up at the mantel. "The panthers are important to the Zapotecs," he added.

I wondered how many sacred virgins there were.

When I turned to Francisco again, he smiled. I looked back at the altar. In their conquest of Mexico, Cortez and his priests had tried to extinguish the Zapotecs' heathen gods and replace them with their one true Christian god. But the Zapotecs had combined the two religions and even created their own Virgin Maria.

The Indian who had left earlier returned with a burlap bag. When he opened it, the scent of flowers filled the room. After delicately separating a bud from its hand-tied kilo, he handed it to William, then sat down against the back wall and began chanting with the other Zapotec. The flower top was red-hair sinsemilla, the same as the sample we had smoked the night before.

Dan and I knelt before the open bag and inspected the thirty-three pounds of puras colas. The most pot I had seen before were the five kilos we bought in Tuxtla Guttierez. But those had been bricked, and barely resembled what lay before us. This would go for $350 a pound, possibly more.

William rolled a joint and took a hit before passing it to Francisco. I didn't need to test it. It was obviously good, and I wanted to stay alert. When the joint came around, Dan and I took only a hit or two as a courtesy. I removed the Octodron from my shirt pocket and washed it down with a swig of mezcal. Dan did the same.

CHAPTER FIVE

The Rio Grande

Francisco and his friends watched as Dan and I removed the back seat from the Valiant's floorboard and stuffed the plastic garbage bag of weed up into its frame. They continued to smile as we shook hands and drove into the still night. No dogs attacked, and Dan declared it a good omen.

Before reaching the highway, William had us drop him off near a small cluster of houses among scrub trees and cactus. He said to call when we wanted to do more business. As we drove off, I watched him in the rearview mirror but couldn't tell if he walked to one of the houses or just wanted to separate from us. If he had set us up, he wouldn't want to be a part of the bust. But it also made good sense to put distance between him and the materiál. At the highway, I turned right and we began our run—south.

It was after midnight. We were pumped and would be more pumped when the Octodron fully kicked in. The road descended evenly, and I downshifted into the turns as we zigzagged our way down. Pine and oak trees disappeared, and only shrubs, scraggly trees and cactus appeared in the headlights. The curves were uniform, and the distance between them was consistent;

well-engineered. I was able to hold the wheel straight for several seconds before going into the next curve.

"Topes," Dan announced when we came to the first town.

Whoever spotted the sign or the actual topes first called it out. Some could be severe. The topes of San Pedro Totolapa were worn and a few were missing, but I slowed anyway. We wanted to skate through Mexico incognito.

I got into a groove. By downshifting and going in and out of neutral, I could maneuver the curves without the use of brakes or gas. Forty mph seemed to do the trick, though I eventually had to use brakes.

"How about some Tull?" I suggested.

Dan put in Jethro Tull's *Benefit*, and the flute intro of "With You There to Help Me" reverberated within our capsule. I sank back into the vinyl and merged with the road and Earth.

We wound down the mountain on our Magical Mystery Tour, slowing for towns and topes and listening to music. My eyes flashed up and down between the speedometer and the headlighted reality in front of us. Dan changed tapes and pointed out curves without reflectors and potential obstacles. A burro standing on the side of the road never flinched when we passed six inches from its head. It was either asleep or very lazy.

Tourists in Mexico are warned not to drive at night. Cows, burros, dead animals or broken-down cars might be just around the next bend—even bandidos. Tonight, the danger was crazed, drug-running gringos flying down the mountain, blowing past anything threatening their rhythm.

Around four a.m., the winding wound down and our descent shallowed. When we reached the town of Tehuantepec, we were only a few hundred feet above sea level, and warm, humid air entered through the open windows. We turned left onto 185, and Dan drove us north across the Isthmus of Tehuantepec.

Sometime later, he nudged me from my separate reality of red and yellow protozoa swimming across the black backdrop of my eyelids. The Octodron was keeping my body awake, but my brain had other ideas. Dan turned down the music.

"There's the road we talked about," he said.

I looked up. The road paralleled the one we planned to take fifteen miles further and appeared on the map to be newer and more direct. It would save time, but we were unfamiliar with its checkpoint status—and a better road was more likely to have them.

"Wanna go for it?" Dan asked.

We had been awake for twenty hours. Add that to the Octodron, pot and mezcal, and it probably wasn't the best time to be changing the plan.

"The sun'll be up soon, and if there are checkpoints, they may be manned sooner than we're used to," I said.

Twenty minutes down the road, with two hours remaining before our driving curfew, we finally turned toward Texas. We planned to drive only at night—after potential checkpoints had shut down and before they might open in the morning. North of Santiago Tuxtla, we stopped for gas at a Pemex station.

An hour later as I tried to sleep facing the passenger window, the sign for Punta Roca Partida flew past my half-opened eyes. An image of Toro and Isidra and El Mio appeared in my foggy head.

"You wanna visit Toro?" Dan said.

"Too far." I turned and saw he was joking.

Just past Alvarado, we stopped at a typical highway motel with a courtyard to hide the car from prying eyes. For less than three dollars, we got a room with two narrow, sagged-out beds and a curtain for the bathroom door. Dan and I had camped on the side of roads, in deserts and on beaches. The room was fine.

When I woke up, Dan was gone. I looked through the window to the parking lot and saw the Valiant, safe and sound. On the dresser, an aluminum pot was on our Coleman stove, and a jar of instant coffee stood beside it. I was a light sleeper, especially when trying to stay alert for sounds of car intrusion, but I had slept through Dan coming in and out of the room and making coffee.

I looked at my watch. Four p.m. It felt good to know I had

slept a solid eight hours.

Dan came in holding a paper bag.

"I had empanadas at a restaurant across the highway. I got you some," he said as he placed the bag and a can of Coke on the nightstand.

"Gracias," I said. "How long have you been up?" I bit into a chicken empanada.

"Hour and a half maybe."

"How does the road look? Much traffic?"

"So-so. Not bad."

"Okay. I guess we split when it gets dark."

Dan lay down on his bed and closed his eyes.

The bypass west of Veracruz was uncharted territory for us, but we weren't going to drive through a big city with the back seat full of weed when we had an alternative. The bypass worked out fine and probably saved us thirty minutes. As we passed Poza Rica, towering flames of a gas refinery lit up low, ragged clouds and transformed night into an eerie, brimstone twilight.

North of Tampico, rain cut our visibility, but we both saw the taillights of a car or truck ahead swerve into the left lane. Dan took his foot off the gas. I leaned forward and peered through the wipers and rain. The vehicle had tried to avoid something but didn't miss it completely. A big silhouette dropped to the ground, and the vehicle drove back into the right lane and kept going.

"That car hit something. It's on the ground," I said.

"I see it. It's a cow," said Dan.

As we got closer, our headlights spotlighted the cow lying on its side with its four legs extended horizontally. It was spinning on the wet road like Curley of *The Three Stooges*. Dan slowed more.

"Keep going," I said. "Go around. Go around."

Dan steered to the left lane. Through my window, I looked down at the revolving bovine.

"That was weird," said Dan.

"Let's get outta here. We might get blamed for it."

Every traveler in Mexico has heard stories of drivers taken to court and made to pay for livestock casualties. Now would not be the best time to get stopped and questioned for cowslaughter. Dan accelerated.

Traffic thinned, and after midnight only a few semis were on the road. Dan and I switched seats near San Fernando, and I drove the last hundred miles. As usual, the twenty-kilometer checkpoint was open for business but it was on the other side of the road for the inspection of southbound traffic going deeper into Mexico. As we passed, I saw the station was dark outside.

Before reaching Matamoros, we made a right onto a gravel and shell road. Our destination was a beach I knew from when a carload of us had crossed the border for a day surf trip in Mexico three years earlier. We had hoped to find nice waves peeling off a sand bar at the Rio Grande river mouth. The waves sucked, but the memory of looking across the river to the U.S. and thinking the Rio Grande wasn't grand at all stayed with me.

When Dan and I got to the beach, we still had eight miles of hard-packed sand to drive across in order to reach the river. I switched off the headlights, and we finished our journey by dawn's light. The only people we passed were two fishermen waist-deep in the shore break. I parked near the dunes, and we laid our boards on the sand as if we planned to surf. I stretched and looked across the river, then out across the Gulf where the sun would soon rise. We did it.

The beach was deserted. We needed to bury the weed. Make hay before the sun shined. Dan and I jerked the back seat from the floorboard and removed the plastic bag of kilos.

"I'll stash it in the dunes for now. Then we can figure out where to bury it," said Dan. He disappeared with the bag over his shoulder.

I laid a towel in front of the car, unfolded a beach chair and sat in it. Dan returned and fell back onto the towel. To our left, seagulls cried and dove at the brown river water emptying into the Gulf. I closed my eyes. I was beat. We had accomplished the run all according to plan, but as much as we deserved a rest, we had work to do.

"We should bury it now before anyone comes," I said without opening my eyes.

"Let's do it," said Dan.

I took the army-surplus folding shovel from the trunk and followed Dan into the dunes. He carried the bag halfway to the river, and we buried the weed in a dip between two dunes. I placed a chunk of wood directly on top of the buried treasure and stuck a piece of driftwood upright in nearby sand.

We would cross the weed from the U.S. side after clearing customs at Brownsville. For the time being, we were law-abiding tourists in need of rest. We drove down the beach and took a nap. When we woke up, we removed everything from the car and searched for evidence of our cargo: seeds, leaves, anything. Afterward, the car looked too clean, so we threw clothes and Coke cans on the back seat and floorboard.

Since the Valiant was registered to me, I drove. Dan opened the glove box and got our papers ready for customs.

"Request?" he asked.

I thought for a second. "Eagles. *On the Border*."

Dan fished out *On The Border* from the shoebox and fast-forwarded to the title track. Glenn Frey sang that he was out on the border and didn't have time to listen to any law and order. He was busy trying to change his water to wine.

At Matamoros, Mexican customs took our Mexico visas and car permit and we continued across the bridge. Traffic was solid, but we moved steadily. On the U.S. side, two cars ahead of us stopped for less than a minute before driving on. Our turn came, and Immigration Man stuck his head out of his booth and gave the Valiant and our boards the once- or twice-over. He squinted at us and pointed to our right where cars were being inspected. We didn't take it personally. The parking bays were full of cars. He may not have singled us out because of our long hair and surfboards.

"Identification and car registration," the customs official said. "And please exit the vehicle."

Dan reached into the glove box and handed him our passports and car papers. We exited the vehicle.

"Where you boys been?"

As he looked at me, I became aware he was not going to believe any lie I came up with. And one lie will get you twenty when he starts with the follow-ups. Sometimes the truth is best.

"Surfing," I answered. "Near Tuxpan."

We could pass for surfers. And I was ready to answer a question or two about Tuxpan, and even tell him about surfing with porpoises. But I doubted he knew much about Tuxpan.

"Hmmmm," he said and glanced at Dan, standing quiet and respectful.

The agent flipped through our passport pages, then stared at me for a few seconds, most likely due to my lack of resemblance to the passport photo. The picture had been taken with my hair tied back in a ponytail, giving me a clean-cut appearance from the front. In real life, I may have seemed scroungy to him. He looked at Dan again, who always appeared more clean-cut than me with his borderline long hair and clean-shaven jaw. When did he shave?

The official held on to our passports and walked around the Valiant, pausing and knocking here and there. After rapping both surfboards with his knuckles and trying to pinch the rails, he opened the Valiant's left door and bent down.

When he came back into view, he studied me and Dan for a moment, then signaled ahead. Ten seconds later, another agent arrived with a slobbering German Shepherd at his side. I looked at Dan. He was looking at the dog. The new agent led the canine snitch to the left door, and it jumped onto the back seat and paced rapidly left and right while whining. I wasn't sure how a drug dog was supposed to act when it smelled pot, but I imagined this was how. I had no doubt we had cleaned the car thoroughly. I hoped. They couldn't throw us in jail for seeds or suspicion, could they?

It hit me that someone might be observing us on camera or through a window or somewhere. I turned from the car and looked toward America but kept the dog's movements in my periphery.

The dog's handler gave a short whistle, and the German Shepherd jumped out of the car. The first agent bent down behind the left door again. A minute later, the back seat rose into view. After a couple more minutes, the agent emerged and said something to the canine officer, who led the German Shepherd to the wheel wells and doors and muffler. Door panels, I understood. But the muffler? A telescopic rod with a mirror at the end materialized from somewhere, and the agent inspected the Valiant's underside. Dan and I watched without interest. We were tired surfers who patiently understood such inconveniences were necessary to keep America safe from drugs- and arms-smugglers. It was a small price to pay for liberty. The dog did not repeat its erratic behavior.

Before returning our passports, the agent gave us an "I know you two are up to something" look but didn't say anything. He just handed back our passports and pointed to America, and that was where we headed.

Our first stop was McDonald's, USA. We ordered hamburgers, fries and milkshakes, then drove to a Motel 6 and slept. I awoke before Dan and went to the car to determine what to throw out in case we were stopped on the beach or at the Border Patrol checkpoint driving back to Houston. The folding shovel could be explained as a camping necessity, but I didn't want to explain anything. It went into the discard pile. While waiting for midnight, Dan and I celebrated our successful run by watching *The Godfather II* at a movie theater and eating real Mexican food at El Patio.

We departed at midnight and would return to the motel after we crossed the weed. Traveling up Highway 77 at three a.m. with a load of pot under the back seat wouldn't be cool. This wasn't Mexico where checkpoints shut down at night in a civilized manner so people could go home to their families. This was Texas where the checkpoints were manned continuously in an uncivilized manner. A couple of scraggly surfers driving in the wee hours might look suspicious to the Border Patrol or the deputy barber of Kingsville.

We made a right at the beach and drove three miles to the river with the Gulf on our left shining under a quarter moon. Thick salt air blew in from the open windows and felt comfortable on my skin and through my hair. I had surfed similar nights at Galveston and the Surfside pier. Everyone had. At the river, I pulled in close to the dunes so the Valiant's silhouette blended into the landscape. We got out and looked across.

"What do you think?" I asked.

Dan looked upriver, then turned back to the beach.

"Looks good," he said. "Except for the moon."

"I know." We hadn't considered the moon. But it was only a quarter.

I looked beyond the river mouth to the lane of shimmering light that extended across the Gulf to the moon. Cloud ghosts stalked the horizon. Maybe they would chase away some of the moonlight. Dan stared upriver. I turned to where he was looking and saw a dim yellow light on the Mexican side, far away—probably a farmhouse.

"Let's go for it," I said.

We had brought both boards. If law enforcement happened along, Dan and I were dawn patrollers hoping to catch some morning glassy waves, although perhaps a tad early. But the sleeping bird doesn't catch the gusano. After changing into my surf baggies, I carried my surfboard to the river.

I tied the roll of duct tape to the end of the board's leash and placed it on the nose, then wrapped the flashlight strap around my wrist and pushed it up to near my shoulder. I put the board in the water and waded in alongside. The river was cool, soothing. Moonlight reflected off ripples in the current, and I heard waves breaking beyond the mouth of the river. I slid onto my board and paddled.

The current pushed me slightly downriver, so I aimed the nose upstream to hold a straight course and made it across in less than five minutes. I took the board to where the dunes began and hiked into them.

The landscape looked like another world in the moonlight. My upright marker was not where it should have been. I resorted to quick shots with the flashlight. No luck. Could someone have been watching and stolen our weed? The fishermen? I sat down in the sand and scanned from a lower perspective to try to see the deadwood marker against the night sky. Nothing.

I walked toward the Gulf to where the dunes ended and the hard, flat sand began. From there, I went south until I found the Valiant's tire indentions, then hiked straight into the dunes. I turned right and walked to where the deadwood marker stood upright in the sand, patiently waiting. After securing the plastic bag full of weed to the top of my board with duct tape, I dragged the conglomeration to the river.

As I swam ahead of the board, towing it by the leash, it tugged left and right. The board's fins were designed to be at the back but were now in front because that was where the leash attached to the board. I spun the board around and pushed it from behind using a quiet frog kick.

Dan was waiting at the riverbank. He dragged the board to the back of the car and cut the duct tape with a knife. While he placed the sandy garbage bag into the trunk, I strapped my board onto the racks.

"What happened? You took forever," he asked as he drove from the river and I dried off with a towel.

"I couldn't find the weed. Everything looked different. I ended up having to go back to where we parked the car so I'd have a starting point to search."

Dan turned and stared at me for a second. I didn't blame him. I was surprised too. Shocked. It was like being on the moon.

"Why were you pushing the board from behind? Was it easier that way?"

"I tried pulling it, but the fins in front made it tug to the side."

Dan drove quietly for a few moments.

“Next time, we should attach a rope to the front or take the fins off,” he said.

After departing the beach, Dan detoured onto a side road where we repacked the pot under the back seat. We returned to the motel and slept until mid-morning.

In my dozen or more surf trips to South Padre, I had always been waved through the Border Patrol checkpoint on Highway 77. This time was no exception, and there would be no more obstacles on our drive home as long as we minded our p's and q's while driving through the King Ranch.

CHAPTER SIX

Solo Run

I only knew Todd through other surfers and when our crowd happened to meet for lunch at the University of Houston cafeteria. When I was a beginner surfer in high school, he had been the part-time manager of our local surf shop, and that memory of him stuck with me. Todd didn't smoke pot, but I heard he wasn't averse to selling it. I gave him my sixteen pounds, and a week later he handed me $4,800. Business was his thing.

While I decided what to do and where to do it, I lived with my parents. My father and I had become cordial in our old age. During my senior year in high school, he and I disagreed about the length of my hair. I had also declined an appointment to his alma mater, Annapolis Naval Academy, which didn't help our relationship. He finally got over the long hair but still had a problem with my dropping out of college with only a year to go. He was making progress, though, and for my part, I occasionally picked up one the U of H course brochures he left lying around.

Dan stayed with our friend Richie and his mother a few blocks from my parents' home. We didn't socialize often, but three weeks after our run, we were both surfing in front of the blue octagon beach house at Surfside.

"You ready to do it again?" he asked.

"You don't think it's too soon?"

"What's too soon? I sold all mine. Didn't you?"

"Yes."

But I didn't need money at the moment. I was twenty-one and had either been in school or working my entire life. Doing nothing felt good, and I was seeing a girl I had met on the beach. I was content.

"Have you read *Tales of Power*?" he asked.

"No. Not yet."

My zeal for Don Juan's teachings had waned. Becoming a Man of Knowledge now seemed distant—almost like a tropics- or drug-induced delusion.

"I'm not ready to go down again," I told him.

Dan didn't appear bothered by my decision, though I often couldn't figure his thoughts. A set came through, and we surfed different directions.

Two weeks later, I became bored. Surf on the Gulf sucked during the summer unless a hurricane hit and a north wind swung around to give the waves shape. But no hurricanes spun on the horizon, and Mexico came to mind. I couldn't remember the exact feeling, but I knew I was always comfortable down there; free, warm, natural. I wondered if Dan still wanted to do a run. Was being content even a good thing? It was the same as being satisfied.

*

"Dan's gone," Richie's mother said. She peered up at me from behind the half-opened kitchen door.

"Where to?" I asked.

"He didn't say."

"Do you know when he's coming back?"

"He didn't say that either. Dan doesn't tell me anything, and he didn't tell Richie. He drove away the day before yesterday. You comin' in? You're lettin' the air out."

"No, I gotta go."

Maybe Dan had only gone to Padre Island or somewhere else

to surf. I found it hard to believe he would do a run by himself. He couldn't even speak much Spanish. Then again, I wasn't exactly fluent. And it was me who swam the river. But swimming the river's not difficult. Finding the weed in the dunes—that's the hard part. The more I considered it, the more I decided Dan could pull it off as long as he stuck to our routine. Still, I felt kind of betrayed, or maybe just disappointed. It had been our thing; we had learned to do it together. He did ask if I wanted to go, though.

A week later, I was painting the Valiant with a rental sprayer in my parents' carport when Dan pulled into the driveway.

"When'd you get back?" I asked.

"Yesterday." He grinned.

"Did you do a run?"

"Yep."

"Oaxaca?"

"Just like before. Except I stayed at a different motel coming back, and I took that other road to Veracruz. The newer one."

"Did you check it out on your way down?" I asked.

"No. I got to it really early during the run, so I figured any checkpoints wouldn't be manned yet. I just went for it. But there weren't any checkpoints. I didn't even see any truck inspection stations."

It sounded reckless, but he had succeeded.

"Did you use William?"

"Yep. Francisco asked about you."

"What'd you tell him?"

"That you'd be back, but I didn't know when." Dan turned to the Valiant. "Your car looks good. Green will blend in with the jungle."

I chose the color because I liked green, not for camouflage, but he did have a point.

"It's smart not to have it shine. Not as noticeable, less eye pollution. I don't know why everyone wants to drive shiny cars," he said.

I hadn't planned on the dull finish, but it was my first time painting a car. It looked okay but a bit amateurish, which might help with the incognito effect for Mexico.

"Did you paint it a different color 'cause you're goin' down?"

"I was thinking about it. The car needed paint anyway. You probably don't wanna go again."

"I've got to sell the keys I brought back. Why don't you go by yourself? They have some good shit right now. Better than before. Come by later and I'll show you."

"Richie's house?"

"Yep. Come on over."

*

Dan hadn't exaggerated about the weed being good. I could smell it as soon as he opened one of the pound-size Ziploc bags he kept hidden in Richie's garage. He told me he had put two fish on the back floorboard during his run to throw off the dogs at customs. But no dogs were summoned, and the agent let him pass after only a few questions. Dan's hair was shorter, and I wondered if he had cut it for his run.

I left four days later and crossed at McAllen to avoid becoming known at Brownsville and Matamoros. Incognito meant no surfboards or racks. Boards were a hassle anyway. When I got back to the U.S., I'd buy a Styrofoam boogie board to cross the load.

My *Libros de Mujeres* weren't vintage like Dan's magazines, but the young soldiers at Reynosa's twenty-kilometer checkpoint didn't complain. I punched play, and "Already Gone" by The Eagles came through the Valiant's two rear speakers.

Approaching Monterrey, jagged mountains rose from the red and brown plain into an azure sky. I had forgotten how good the visibility was in Mexico. The pure air gave colors color. I turned south before Monterrey, and the mountains passed off my right. Beyond Ciudad Victoria, the road wound up through the Sierra Madre and emerged onto the central plateau.

Only two roadblocks slowed my pace. Soldiers at the first one looked in the trunk, and I was on my way. It only cost me a

Libro de Mujeres. At the second stop near San Juan del Rio, a fat officer in a blue municipal police uniform checked my visa and car papers.

"Amigo," he said as I was about to drive away.

"Si."

"Your sunglasses," he said in Spanish.

"Si."

"They are blue. My uniform is blue." He pointed to my sunglasses, then to the overstuffed shirt of his municipal police uniform.

My shades were a mirror type with dark blue plastic frames and cost only five dollars. I had another pair, but I didn't want to give any away. They were a necessity in the bright sunlight of the high plateau, and I liked having a spare. The policeman cocked his head and gave me an imploring smile. He looked like a big spoiled kid, and I got the impression he might throw a tantrum or something worse if he didn't get what he wanted.

"Muchas gracias," he said as he put on his new shades. I drove off and made a note to stock up on sunglasses for the next trip. They might be a worthwhile supplement to *Los Libros de Mujeres*.

I arrived at the Oaxaca overlook before dawn and slept on the back seat until mid-morning. After checking into the hotel, I telephoned William, and we arranged to drive to the mountains later. If our friends had some good materiál, I might even be able to head out that night. I hiked around town and bought a few things, then returned to my room for a late nap. At ten, I checked out of the hotel and picked up William at the zocalo. We stopped for mezcal.

Francisco greeted us at the door, and we walked to the hut at the edge of their small subdivision. Two Indians stood inside. I recognized one from before but didn't remember his name.

"Santiago," he told me as we shook hands. "Mucho gusto a verte." *Good to see you.*

Santiago apparently spoke more Spanish than Francisco. Gurtrek was the name of the Zapotec I hadn't met before.

We all sat down on the dirt, and William talked with Francisco and Santiago. The Zapotecs conversed in low tones and politely waited for each other to finish talking before responding. Gurtrek sat to the side and glanced at me—smiling, of course. I wondered how big a novelty Dan and I were to these people. Surely, other gringos must visit. I nodded to Gurtrek, and he reciprocated. The mezcal made the rounds.

Santiago left the hut and returned five minutes later with two sinsemilla buds that looked the same as Dan's weed. William rolled a joint, although I didn't need to smoke it to know it was good. And if I was making the run afterward, it would be best to have all my wits available—especially since I'd be doing it alone. When the doobie came, I took a hit to be polite and told Francisco I wanted to purchase ten kilos. It was still smalltime, but without having to split it, I'd end up making more than before. Santiago left the room again, and the joint made its way back to me.

A few minutes later, Santiago returned with a burlap bag and laid it on the floor. Red-hair flower tops poked out the top, and the room took on a mixed scent of flowers and dry straw. Francisco hung a fish scale from a wood beam and reached for the burlap bag. From my jacket pocket, I removed the scale I had bought in Oaxaca and handed it to him. I had noticed last time that theirs was old and stretched out. Francisco smiled and attached the new scale to the beam. After weighing out ten kilos, he unhooked the scale and held it out to me. I pointed to him.

"Un regalo," I said.

Francisco moved the scale toward his chest. I said, "Si," and pointed to him again. He smiled wide. We toasted with one more swig of mezcal, and I downed an Octodron.

After fitting the pot into the back seat, I opened the trunk and removed the two fish I had bought at the market. I laid them on the back floorboard and unfolded the wrapping paper. Dan came up with a decent idea now and then. The Indians grinned. It was either a good joke or very smart. Francisco spat out some sentences, and I turned to William.

"Francisco says you are welcome anytime, and they hope to see you soon. They tell you that they are your friends," he said.

I shook hands with the three Zapotecs and dropped William off near the same cluster of houses as before. The midnight Magical Mystery Tour was less of a mystery this time, and I got into the road-groove sooner, snaking my way down and making a game of using as little braking as possible. One thing I missed about Dan was not having someone to change the cassettes. I put in *Close to the Edge* by Yes and sank into the seat while Mexico flew by, asleep.

Down the mountains, left and right, through villages, dogs and topes, and Tehuantepec arrived way ahead of schedule. I turned left onto the road that Dan pioneered and made it north of Veracruz before curfew. I checked into a motel and slept, then resumed the mission under cloak of darkness.

On the home stretch south of Matamoros, and with dawn approaching, the needle on the Valiant's temperature gauge began to creep up. I slowed and turned the heater on full-blast to dissipate the engine heat—a technique that worked during long mountain climbs. The needle stopped for a minute, then continued its journey up. I pulled to the side of the road and left the engine running to keep the coolant circulating.

When I raised the hood, water was shooting horizontally from several breaks in the radiator hose and the motor knocked painfully. I rushed to the trunk, retrieved a tee-shirt, and used it to remove the radiator cap. I grabbed a jug of drinking water from the back seat and poured it in. The knocking immediately subsided to a tapping, which was a big relief. Then a rumbling came from deep down, followed by an eruption of steam.

I had no more water, so I turned off the engine and hoped for no permanent damage. When the geyser ceased, I saw that the hose had come apart in so many places, it no longer resembled a hose. After removing it, I wrapped it over and over with duct tape until it became a duct tape-rebuilt radiator hose.

I leaned against the right front fender and looked east across the fields—to where the sun would soon rise. Maybe there was water for the radiator out there. I hiked through the tall yellow weeds and discovered a shallow pool of brown water. Three trips with the plastic jug filled the radiator. I sat in the driver's seat and gently turned the key one click to check the engine temperature. The gauge's needle moved from the left and stopped a quarter up. I held my breath, pressed the gas pedal and turned the key more. The engine started right up, and the needle slowly climbed and settled at its normal, middle position. I inspected the radiator hose and declared it leak-free, at least for the time being. After adding another jug of swamp water to the radiator, I drove away and made it to the river ten minutes after sunrise. The weed went into its resting place, and I drove down the beach to mine.

When I awoke from my nap, cars were parked on both sides of me, and colorful beach umbrellas had sprouted everywhere. Families were swimming in the Gulf, walking on the sand, throwing Frisbees and setting up barbecue grills. I must have been tired. Humanity stretched all the way to the river. What was going on? It was only Friday. I glanced at my watch—a little after ten and too early for this much activity. I sat on my towel in a daze and stared at the people when it hit me that it was the Fourth of July. Apparently, Mexicans liked to celebrate America's independence too—at least close to the border.

While shaving with a pot of salt water, I wondered about the situation on the U.S. side. I drove to the river and looked across. There were even more people and cars over there. And tents. Some tents were probably for shade and changing clothes, but some would be for overnight camping. This could be a problem.

At Brownsville customs, an officer shuffled through my passport pages, glanced at the car's registration and let me drive through. When I stopped for gas, I left the engine running and checked the radiator hose. A man filling his tank in front of me walked over and peered at the Valiant's motor.

"That's a slant six," he said.

I was anxious to get to a motel and not start new friendships. "Yep."

"They're great engines. I had a Dodge Dart for years. Listen to that thing purr."

Man, if you only knew. The motor did sound pretty good, though. As I drove to the Motel 6, my mind drifted to the masses on the beach, but I needed rest in order to think.

I slept for five hours, then lay in bed staring at the ceiling. How could I cross the weed with all those people around? I might have to wait until after the weekend. I drove to McDonald's for a burger and fries, then went back to staring at the ceiling. An idea came to me, but I'd have to play it by ear. I changed into my baggies and sandals. On the way to the beach, I stopped at a gas station and bought a big inner tube and a six-pack of beer. I filled the tube with air and stuffed it into the trunk.

After maneuvering the Valiant through three miles of sun-worshiping patriots on the beach, I parked near the river mouth. Fishermen were casting into the Rio Grande where I had crossed before, but today I would be going a different route. I carried the inner tube, a roll of duct tape and a can of Budweiser into the surf. When the water came to my waist, I sat inside the tube and paddled backward through the small waves. People frolicked all around as I drank my Bud and shared in their patriotic reverie. I must not have been paying attention to the current or something because my tube drifted slowly across the Rio Grande's discharge.

When I merged with the aquatic fun on the Mexican side, I let the surf push me to shore. No one appeared to notice me, so I carried the tube up to where the dunes began and sat on the sand, using the tube as a backrest. I lounged and surveyed the beach on both sides of the river. While everyone celebrated, I disappeared into the dunes with the inner tube.

I fashioned a duct-tape basket in the center of the tube and placed the garbage bag of kilos inside. After pulling the tube out of the dunes, I leaned against it like before and observed the beach activities for a minute. Then I dragged the tube into the water, jumped on top of twenty-two pounds of sinsemilla and drifted to America.

When the surf washed me onto the beach on the U.S. side, I thought it might look suspicious dragging a supposedly weightless inner tube across the sand, so I left it near the water and backed the car up. After lounging for a few minutes, I hoisted the tube and its cargo into the trunk and stabbed the tube with a knife. I shut the trunk and made my way back through the bikinis and Frisbees and arrived in Houston before midnight.

CHAPTER SEVEN

Oil Initiative

"What about bringing hash oil back instead of weed, like the Brotherhood was doing in Costa Rica?" Dan suggested.

We sat on Richie's back porch discussing our travails and safer ways to proceed with the business.

"Is that made from pot or hash?" I asked.

"The oil I've smoked came from pot," he said.

A couple liters of hash oil would sell for more dinero than twenty kilos of weed and could be concealed a lot easier.

I knew there wouldn't be exact information regarding hash oil production at the Houston Public Library, but I ran across books about moonshiners and their illegal whiskey stills during the Prohibition era of the 1930s. The bootleggers hid out in remote mountains while they manufactured their product, and Dan and I would have to do likewise. The moonshiners reminded me of the Zapotecs who lived in their mountain hamlets and avoided the outside world. As I sat and read about the arrests and shootings caused by a law that was eventually repealed, a similar situation came to mind.

At B. Dalton bookstore in the Northwest Mall, I thumbed through a magazine called *High Times*. Surprisingly, the new publication's focus was the smoking of marijuana. A picture in an advertisement caught my eye. It showed one metal sphere sitting on top of another identical sphere with curly copper tubes connecting the two. The contraption resembled the moonshiners' whiskey stills in the books at the library.

"Convert Herbs into Potent Oil," the ad promised. Neither marijuana nor cannabis was mentioned, but the intended application seemed obvious considering the magazine's theme. I put a check in the mail and had the apparatus shipped to my parents' house.

According to the instructions, all Dan and I needed to produce potent oil was rubbing alcohol, white unleaded fuel and potent weed. Alcohol, we could get in Mexico, but we purchased the cans of white fuel in the U.S. If we were asked about it at a checkpoint, our Coleman lantern and stove would explain its purpose. Dan and I planned to rent a remote shack in the countryside near Oaxaca, buy weed from the Indians, and return to the shack to make the oil.

We strapped our boards on top of the Valiant and stopped at South Padre Island for a surf break on the way. The friend who had gone to El Salvador with me the summer we graduated high school now lived on the island. I looked him up.

Jack was just under six feet tall and lean, like me. His sun-bleached brown hair was combed back and fell behind his ears to his shoulders. He built custom beach homes for a living and surfed whenever he wanted. He had escaped the Machine and graduated to the good life. I was envious.

Dan and I surfed with Jack for a few days, then crossed into Mexico. We spent one night in Oaxaca, then drove southeast down the valley in search of an oil-producing abode not too far from our mountain friends. Fifteen miles south of their village, on the opposite side of the valley, we spotted a lone building alongside a dirt road. Dan pushed open one of its double wooden doors and we looked into a barn with a dirt floor and a high, corrugated tin roof.

When we walked back to the car, a thin old man with a

bundle of sticks balanced on his shoulders was examining our surfboards. Gray hair hung beneath his stained, beat-up cowboy hat, and short, white whiskers poked out from his brown cheeks. He touched our boards and bungee cords with the tips of his fingers. Maybe he was comparing how our boards were tied to how his sticks were attached to his back. The bungee cords may have been his first.

"Buenos dias," I said.

"Buenas tardes," he replied.

In Mexico, if the time is one minute past noon, "Buenos dias" becomes "Buenas tardes." He stared at me and moved his head left and right until I realized he was looking at himself in my sunglasses. I took them off.

"Sabes quién es el dueño de esa casa?" I asked. *Do you know who is the owner of that house?*

He turned to the barn, then back to me. His eyes settled on my shoulders, maybe my hair. He looked over at Dan.

"Esa," I said and pointed to the barn, thinking the word "house" may have thrown him off. "El dueño?"

He nodded and pointed down the main road to the nearby village while his other hand rested on Dan's board. Perhaps he was attaining power from it. The old man did resemble my idea of what Castaneda's Don Juan looked like.

"Alli. La primera casa. La casa grande en la izquierda," he said. *There. The first house. The big house on the left.*

We thanked him, and he pulled the front of his hat down and continued up the dirt road with his sticks. I looked past him to the mountains and saw no houses.

The owner of the barn agreed to rent it for seven dollars a month although we planned to complete our hash oil production in less than a week.

Inside the barn, the night turned cold. As I lay in my sleeping bag reading Castaneda's *Tales of Power* by lantern, spiders and big black ants crept across the walls and ceiling, distracting me.

Dan extinguished the lantern, and I was almost asleep when something plopped onto my head. My fingers quickly ran through my hair, but I found nothing and chalked it up to a clump of oily locks shifting. A minute later, I definitely felt something move across my scalp. I cupped my fingers and pulled whatever it was from the roots of my hair and threw it to the floor. By the time I found the flashlight, the creature had fled. Dan woke up, and we set up our tents inside the barn. I didn't sleep well.

The morning was still frigid when Dan began putting on his jeans, and the biggest, ruby-red scorpion any gringo has ever seen dropped out of one of the pant legs. Dan picked up a shoe and smashed it until it became a ruby-red, bloody mess with its tail still twisting and stabbing. Before he resumed dressing, Dan turned his pants inside out for a thorough examination. I did the same.

The temperature climbed to at least 90 degrees before noon. We opened the doors, but no breeze came through—only the hotter air from outside. Sweat ran down our faces and onto our arms as we assembled the hash oil still. The second night was as cold as the first and left us tired and grumpy in the morning. Spending a week in a scorpion- and spider-infested barn while slaving over a hot still was not what we had in mind. We decided to shelve our oil production and ask the Zapotecs if they could make it for us. Dan and I checked out of the barn and found sanctuary in a cool, comfortable hotel in Oaxaca.

William said our friends in the mountains didn't make hash oil, but they sometimes got it from their compañeros. When we journeyed to their village in the evening, Francisco told us they didn't have any oil but could find some for us.

"Cuanto tiempo piensa?" I asked. *How much time, do you think?*

"Una semana," Santiago answered. *A week.*

They did, however, have some good sinsemilla, and Dan and I returned the next night for twenty kilos. We said goodbye to our Zapotec friends and told them we'd be back soon for the oil.

I started us down the mountain as Dan put in *Days of Future Passed* by The Moody Blues. The run was routine, and I volunteered for the river crossing.

CHAPTER EIGHT

Learning to Fly & Rainbow Weed

While I waited for Todd to dispense my materiál, I split my time between Sheryl's apartment and my parents' home. In two weeks, I drove down to South Padre Island to visit Jack and investigate life in the Rio Grande Valley. When I arrived, he had just moved into a rental house on the mainland with his girlfriend, Beth. The single-story home in Laguna Vista stood alone on a sandy marsh and had a clear view across the water to Padre Island. He offered me the extra bedroom if I wanted to share the rent. I did.

Jack wasn't building custom homes for a living anymore and hadn't for a year. That was just his front. His current business involved moving other people's weed across the Rio Grande, 700 to 800 pounds at a time. One of Jack's partners knew a family that lived on the Mexican side of the river. The weed was loaded onto an inflatable raft from their property, rowed across the river and transferred to a Jeep.

Every night for two weeks before a scheduled crossing, Jack and his associates stationed themselves along the river and used night vision goggles to observe the Border Patrol's routine. They communicated on portable citizens band radios and relayed their observations in code.

Occasionally Jack and his colleagues were contracted to get

a load past the Border Patrol checkpoint on Highway 77. They packed the kilos into the cabin of a 23-foot Boston Whaler, motored out the Port Isabel jetties and turned north along the coast. Thirty miles up, they cut back in through the Mansfield jetties and offloaded the weed on the mainland.

Until the previous month, Jack and I hadn't seen each other for almost two years, yet we somehow had ended up on parallel paths. It was nice to be able to talk to someone about my business and learn other aspects of it. Jack had more experience crossing the Rio Grande than me but was curious about the supply side in deep Mexico. His mother had been born in El Paso, and her family was from the state of Chihuahua. Her great, great, great grandfather had been its governor in the 1850s. Even though she spoke fluent Spanish, Jack had only picked up a little while growing up. He listened as I described my dealings with the Zapotecs and the late-night connections and magical midnight drives. He and I discussed bringing up a big load from Oaxaca but couldn't figure out a plan without too much risk. I wasn't in a rush to expand anyway.

As a man of leisure, I sat on the back porch of my new home and watched the egrets, herons and ducks, and the clouds that formed at the coast and swept west across the marsh, growing taller along the way. The wind blew from the Gulf, and the air was clean and salt-fresh. Below the clouds, a Piper Cherokee hummed east toward Padre Island. I had learned the names of general aviation airplanes in elementary school when my youthful goal in life had been to be a pilot. The Piper Cherokee disappeared, and I got up and drove to the Harlingen airport.

A flight instructor explained what it took to become a private pilot and sold me a vinyl flight case with "Piper Flite Center" stenciled in gold on the front. Everything I needed to learn to fly was inside the case, including an official logbook to record my flights. The school taught in low-wing, four-seat Piper Warriors similar to the plane I had just watched from the back porch. I scheduled my first flight lesson and drove home to study.

The lesson didn't go well. I wasn't sure if the instructor didn't take me seriously because of my long-hair surfer appearance, or if he was just a terrible instructor. We ran through the four basics of flight: climbs, descents, turns and straight-and-level. Then we climbed to 2,500 feet where he demonstrated "stalls" by pulling the control wheel back and bringing the nose up until I saw only blue sky and cloud tops. He held it in that position while the plane slowed to nothing and the wings rocked left and right. Then he shoved the wheel forward, and I levitated from my seat and stared down at the green and brown rectangles of Earth.

After four of these demonstrations, I told the instructor I felt nauseous. He pulled the throttle back and landed on a grass, agricultural runway, but not before I vomited through the small vent in the Plexiglas. We got out, and he handed me paper towels to clean the window and fuselage.

I didn't get sick during the second lesson, but the instructor still seemed like he had somewhere else he'd rather be. For my third lesson, I was assigned a different flight instructor, and things got better. He reviewed my logbook entries to see what maneuvers I had been taught and discussed beforehand what we would practice in the air. The next four days, I flew twice a day; once in the morning and again in the afternoon.

Driving home in the evening, a joint waited in the ashtray to relieve my nausea and help me contemplate what I had just experienced in the sky. Half the maneuvers I learned were called ground reference maneuvers. The goal was to fly above specific patterns on the ground like a road or a rectangular field without letting the wind blow you off course (the same concept as pointing a surfboard a little upstream when paddling across the Rio Grande).

We were down to landings. If I could just keep from flaring high and running out of airspeed, then falling three feet to the runway and bouncing hard, I might be allowed to solo. My instructor assured me I had reached a typical learning plateau, and sometimes it helped to take a break and think about it.

During my hiatus, I practiced the entire landing procedure while sitting in an armchair, while driving my car, and while waiting on my board between sets. Friends paddled over and asked about the flying lessons. I told them how alike aerodynamics and hydrodynamics were, and that side-slipping your board down a wave was the same as side-slipping a plane to lose altitude. They nodded in understanding.

When I returned to the airport five days later, the instructor had me do twelve takeoffs and landings. A few weren't bad. The next day, I did better. As we taxied back for the fourth one, the instructor told me to stop. He got out and yelled over the engine and prop noise.

"Do two touch-and-goes and make the third landing a full stop." He held up three fingers. "Don't forget to talk to the tower."

Solo. I taxied to the end of the runway with no one in the right seat to ensure I didn't screw up. Anticipation, not fear or anxiety, ran through my body; anticipation of exactly what, I didn't know. But it felt big.

When the tower cleared me for takeoff, I pushed the throttle to the firewall and maintained pressure against the stop so it wouldn't slip back—a technique drilled into me from day one. The Piper Warrior accelerated into the headwind along the centerline of the runway, and we lifted off. I climbed to a thousand feet while making my turns to the downwind leg.

As I flew parallel to the runway, I concentrated on my altitude and power setting. The landing routine I had practiced would commence in less than a minute when I got abeam the end of the runway. I had no time to contemplate what a wondrous thing it was to fly solo. I needed to stay ahead of the plane, ready to do what I needed to do when the time came.

My first landing was fine, not great. I didn't bounce. It was satisfactory. I pushed the throttle forward, raised the flaps and climbed back up. The second one was better. On downwind for the third landing, I looked around at the world below. I didn't feel like landing yet. I wanted to fly to the beach and see what surfing looked like from 1,000 feet and to cruise over to where the Rio Grande emptied into the Gulf. But I landed as instructed.

Inside the flight office, my instructor used scissors to cut a big square off the back of my shirt. He wrote my name and date on it with a black Marks-a-Lot and stapled it to a wall covered with dozens of other shirttails. I paid for the lesson, and that was that—no celebration, no cake, no champagne. It was like a post-psychedelic depression. I had been in the sky, floating above the world with my own three-dimensional perspective, and now my reality was a drab office, no cake, and a shirt with no back.

I got into the Valiant and drove away. Even though I had done a decent job in the air, I didn't feel like I was in complete control. It seemed as if I had been guiding the plane as someone would a horse. If the horse wanted to make trouble, what could I have done about it? I wondered if I should have even soloed.

*

I returned to Houston for a visit and found that Dan had just gotten back from another solo run. He was in Richie's garage, bitching.

"Fucking Greg stole two pounds. Does he think I don't know he did it?" he ranted.

"You're lucky he didn't steal more," I said.

Even though Dan could have been more discreet about stashing his weed, I was surprised a friend would steal another person's pot. Apparently, criminals could pop up in your own back yard. Greg had attended a neighboring high school with Dan. I barely knew him.

"I know where he lives," Dan continued.

"What about the oil?" I asked.

"No oil. That's why I brought back weed. Francisco said they'd get it in a week, but you know what that means."

"No problems on the run?"

"No. I thought about taking the road that goes from Oaxaca straight across to Veracruz but didn't."

I had considered that road too. It would shave off a lot of time, but it was uncharted territory. And it would require going north toward Oaxaca after making the connection.

*

A cold front swept away Houston's pollution and left behind an indigo sky that beckoned me west to Lakeside Airport. At the flight school there, an instructor reviewed my logbook and scheduled a lesson for the next day. He sold me a Houston air chart and a manual for a Cessna 150. I drove to Sheryl's apartment and memorized airspeeds and weights, read about the plane's systems, and studied the map and its symbols.

Unlike the low-wing Piper Warrior I flew in Harlingen, the Cessna 150's wing was on top of the fuselage. The plane was also smaller and lighter with only two seats instead of four. The instructor explained that Lakeside Airport was an uncontrolled airport and had no control tower. Pilots just announced their position and intentions over a specific radio frequency. We taxied to the runway and took off without obtaining permission from anyone—my kind of airport.

Because of its lighter weight, the Cessna's responses to my control inputs were more sensitive than the Piper Warrior's, and I over-controlled. But after forty minutes, I felt more in command of the little Cessna than I ever had in the Piper. It took me another two sessions to solo, but I didn't mind. As we cruised west of Highway 6, I gazed down at the fields and farmhouses. Subdivisions of tract homes were sprouting from the same fields I had canoed over during floods as a kid. I wondered how they solved the flooding problem.

The air was cold and smooth in December, and I spent days drifting solo on my magic carpet ride above a neat and orderly Houston. The chart lay open on the right seat, and I watched its symbols become reality on Earth.

Returning to Sheryl's apartment or my parents' house in Spring Branch, I always took Barker Cypress Road to avoid the rat race on I-10. I hit play on the tape deck and pushed in the cigarette lighter. Smoke entered my lungs, dissolved the nausea and continued down my arms and legs for a peaceful easy feeling. Barker Cypress curved gently through pine groves, rice fields, and yellow and brown checkers of unharvested corn. Farmhouses with wraparound porches and vegetable gardens stood in contrast to the progress that skipped over them to the west. I drove and watched and contemplated my flight while Jackson Browne sang about being caught between the longing for love and the struggle for the legal tender.

*

When I returned to Laguna Vista, Jack and I decided to venture south for the hash oil. I pressed play on the cassette deck as we departed the twenty-kilometer checkpoint south of the border, and "Already Gone" filled the cab of Jack's 1968 Ford pickup.

Although this was Jack's first run, he had driven through Mexico twice before on surf trips. He leaned back against the headrest with his arms stretched to the wheel and his prescription sunglasses aimed ahead. His lips moved with the lyrics. Compared to his night job, this was probably a vacation for him. I lit one of our pre-rolled joints, and we watched Mexico's landscape and people and burros play across the windshield.

Twelve hours later, we had topped the ridge before Mexico City and were descending into its smoggy heart when the engine quit. Jack steered to the shoulder, and I shut off the music. He tried the ignition. The motor turned over but only backfired. I raised the hood and listened while Jack turned the key again. Backfire. Out came the tools. We confirmed the basics; gas spurted inside the carburetor and the distributor points sparked. It could be something serious.

We troubleshot the engine all the way to the particleboard timing gear. Part of its rim had disintegrated, and many of the teeth were gone. The Ford was a clunker, so Jack had the foresight to pack a box of spare parts. Of course, there was no extra timing gear. Those only gave out every 100,000 miles or so. About now.

I stayed with the truck while Jack hitchhiked toward the city with the broken gear. Night fell, and he didn't return. I slept inside the camper and dined on pop tarts and Campbell's SpaghettiOs. The next afternoon, as I began to wonder what was going on, a car swung across the road and parked behind the pickup. Jack got out, accompanied by a man carrying a big toolbox.

"The gear is super rare," Jack told me. "I went to a lot of parts stores and shops. They had gears the same size, but they all had one tooth too many or one tooth too few. This guy's got a repair shop, and someone delivered the right one to him."

The mechanic held up the new gear and smiled. In an hour and a half, the truck purred like un gato. We paid the guy and drove away. Two wasted days.

Before reaching Mexico City proper, we turned right and drove around the inside of the valley bowl before climbing out on the south side. The air cleared as we descended from the rim, and the sight of snowcapped Popocatepetl and Iztaccihuatl in the pink dusk was comforting. As Jack drove, I lit a joint and put in a Stephen Stills tape.

*

"El aceite viene," Santiago told us as we sat inside the connection hut at the edge of their village. *The oil is coming.*

"Cinco dias, no más, tal vez antes," he added. *Five days, no more, perhaps before.*

Five days meant "who knows when."

The ever-elusive oil.

William said he had friends on the Pacific who could make hash oil, but they needed a week's notice. Francisco noticed our frustration and said something to us. I looked at William.

"He says they have very good mota," William said.

I looked at Francisco.

"Muy especial," he repeated with a serious look and no smile.

Jack and I hadn't come to Mexico for marijuana. We came for oil. But we could at least extend our friends the courtesy of looking at their very special mota. In a few minutes, Santiago entered the shack carrying a wooden egg crate with "Huevos Ramirez" stenciled in red and black on the side. He placed it on the dirt floor, and a pungent piney odor greeted my nostrils. The flower tops were twelve to fifteen inches long and sparkled with gold-dust pollen. Along with the usual red hairs, strands of orange and purple ran through the green and brown buds.

"Rainbow weed," said Jack.

It was muy especial, for sure, but we had come for oil, not pot. Where could we stash it? The truck didn't even have a back seat. Jack and I conferred.

We would figure something out.

"Thirty kilos, más o menos," I told William. "We can tell you exactly tomorrow night."

William translated to Francisco, who nodded.

The next morning, Jack and I got under the pickup and saw where we could tie the kilos under the bed. We visited the ferreteria and stocked up on bailing wire and plastic garbage bags. In the evening, we picked up William and the mezcal and drove to the mountains.

When it came time to stash the pot, we found it simpler just to secure the crates themselves under the truck's bed. After tying them to the frame with the bailing wire, we said goodbye to our friends and dropped William off at his usual spot before the main road.

Jack drove. I didn't mind sharing the fun. He leaned forward and stared through his glasses and the windshield, studying the curves and becoming one with the road.

"Your choice," I said with the shoebox of tapes in my lap.

"*After the Gold Rush,*" he answered after some thought.

I remembered when Jack had interpreted the lyrics of the title song for an English class in college. He understood that Neil Young was singing about the apocalypse in the Bible. Jack was a good Catholic, and his interpretation was convincing, but my take was that mankind had moved away from nature and ruined the world. Maybe the two interpretations were related.

The peaceful acoustic songs on the album complemented the sleeping villages we barreled past but contrasted our own mad pace down the mountain. Jack took us all the way to the Isthmus and across it. After turning north, we stopped at a Pemex station for gas. Jack walked over to me as I kept an eye on the attendant filling the tank.

"Two of the crates are hanging down," he whispered. He looked around. "You can see 'em."

We departed the gas station and quickly turned onto a dirt road. The crates were still secure, but the wires had stretched. More bailing wire solved the problem, although we had to pull over a few times along the way to tighten the wires again. North of Veracruz, we stopped at a motel with a discreet courtyard for the truck, and slept until noon.

*

"What if we crossed the weed from Mexico? Tonight?" Jack suggested when we woke up.

"Someone could be on the other side," I said.

"If there's any moonlight, we can check it out with the binoculars. And when we paddle over, we can turn around if we see anyone."

Maybe I was in a rut. Jack did have more experience crossing loads than me.

"It might even be safer than parking the truck on the U.S. side," said Jack. "If things turn to shit, we can ditch everything and get away in Mexico."

I thought about it.

"One of us could paddle across without the weed to check it out," I suggested.

The twenty-kilometer checkpoint for southbound traffic on the opposite side of the road remained my only concern. I had never driven past that checkpoint with a load during the daytime. We still had nine hours to drive. If we waited a couple more hours, it would be dark when we drove by, and we'd still have time to cross and also retrieve the kilos before dawn.

We left the motel just before dark and sailed past the checkpoint with no problem. Jack parked at the river mouth, and we looked across with binoculars. He removed his board from the camper, eased it into the water, and paddled over in stealth mode. Ten minutes later, he returned. We put the egg crates into garbage bags and onto the front of our boards, then crossed in tandem, Jack leading. On the other side, I followed him into the dunes, carrying my two crates. We didn't need to bury them. We'd be back in a couple hours.

To maintain tradition, I put "On the Border" in the tape deck as we drove from the beach. U.S. Customs directed us to a search bay, but the agent only looked in the camper and asked the usual questions before letting us go. We drove to the river and retrieved our rainbow weed.

*

Before we began dividing the kilos into pounds at our house, Jack said he wanted to show me something. He laid a bed sheet on the carpet, and we spread all the flower tops across it. We weighed out pounds with his Ohaus scale and bagged them, setting aside the gnarly, mutant buds. This was the Especial—our personal stash. It would only confuse the masses if they saw it.

After all the pounds were weighed, the sheet was bare except for an amber tint that looked like fuzzy dirt. Using the edge of his driver's license, Jack scraped the sheet outward from the center until a little mound of fluffy powder appeared. He pushed the mound into a vial and poured a small amount into a stone pipe. After taking a slow hit, he handed it to me. The smoke went down smooth, and the expansion was quick. I coughed a thick white cloud, and it left a perfumed taste in my mouth. Jack told me we were smoking pollen from the flowers. We continued to scrape until we had half a cup of pollen.

*

As a carpenter in Houston, I had become friends with Ron, a surfer from Santa Cruz who told me pot sold for a lot more in California than in Texas. Before my father's assignment to Naval ROTC at Rice University in Houston, I spent ten years of my youth in California, living in four different places. I had returned twice to surf.

One summer, I rented a tiny trailer and surfed the Santa Ana river mouth every morning. A Texaco station across the river hired me to pump gas, but first I had to visit a beauty salon and be fitted for a short-hair wig to hide my long hair. I would have thought California to be more progressive in such matters. The Texaco manager said my hair didn't bother him, but some of his older customers might be put off by it.

Another summer, a friend and I drove my 1959 Karmann Ghia to California. Trestles on the Camp Pendleton marine base became our favorite surf spot. The three white-sand point breaks were named for the elevated train tracks nearby: Lower, Middle and Upper Trestles.

Just north of Trestles was Cotton's Point where James Arness, aka Marshal Dillon of the TV western *Gunsmoke*, regularly surfed on a long board. A local surfer told me Arness was a pilot and had traded in his twin-engine plane for a rugged bush plane so he could land on beaches in Baja and surf. He lived above the cliffs in San Clemente, and his son Rolf won the World Surfing Championship in 1970.

Trestles was not as crowded as most of California's surf spots because the marine base wasn't open to the public. My navy dependent ID card allowed me and one other person inside. For a few weeks, my friend and I hung out with two other surfers from Houston. One had a sister who was married to the editor of *Surfer Magazine*. On the drive south from our motel in Huntington Beach to Trestles, we routinely stopped at the magazine's office in Dana Point and plucked a few leaves from the marijuana plants growing in their outside garden.

Because I could only bring one guest with me into Camp Pendleton, we dropped two of the friends off at a spot along the chain-link fence before getting to the entrance gate. They crawled underneath and waited for us to pick them up. Between surf sessions, we were prone to getting high and exploring non-public areas. We discovered a deserted bamboo village with a sign that declared it Vietnam, but our tour in Nam was cut short when a helicopter appeared overhead and chased us back to the beach.

Upon leaving the base, we didn't hassle with dropping the two extra occupants off at the fence. It was fun to look back at the expressions on the marines' faces when they studied our pass and looked up to count the four of us driving away.

I didn't need to go to California to sell weed. Todd would sell it for me in Houston. But I wasn't destined to live in Texas forever, and I often thought about returning to California. I telephoned Ron, and he told me he'd be glad to take ten pounds off my hands at $400 a pound.

My Valiant had been faithful and honorable, but the time had come to step up to more comfort, more power, and air conditioning. A five-year-old purple El Camino at a car lot in Los Fresnos fit the bill, and it had the perfect hiding spot—a space behind the driver's seat that extended three feet under the bed. I installed wood paneling in front of the hidden space and along the back. Instead of a door, I put in a secret, removable section. The El Camino was also equipped with a seat belt.

I stashed ten pounds of rainbow weed behind the paneling, hid my vial of pollen and baggie of Especial under the dash, and headed west.

CHAPTER NINE

Saga of the El Camino

The fastest route to California was due north to San Antonio to intercept I-10. Instead, I cruised northwest on Highway 2 along the Rio Grande. The road climbed imperceptibly, and the more I drove, the more defined and brighter the desert's colors became. A sign for Langtry and the Jersey Lilly Saloon detoured me off the highway, and I paid homage to Judge Roy Bean. Above the bar, an authentic-looking plaque declared him, "The Only Law West of the Pecos River," but I doubted Judge Bean really had such a sign.

When the highway separated from the Rio Grande and continued north, I went west with the river through the Big Bend and Terlingua. I stopped for the night in Lajitas, a restored Old West town complete with old-fashioned saloon, hotel and raised wood-plank sidewalk. At the Hotel Rio Bravo, I got a room on the second floor looking east to the Chisos Mountains.

In the lobby, black and white photographs of Texas Rangers with long mustaches hung on the walls. Several of their desperado foes had also been photographed, but just the corpses—most of which were resting in fresh pine coffins.

I learned that Lajitas had been popular with smugglers and

other outlaws because of the clandestine passes through the nearby mountains that dropped straight into the Rio Grande. In the late 1800s, gold and silver had been the contraband of choice. Later, during the Mexican Revolution in the early 20th century, Pancho Villa hid in the passes and attacked the Mexican army, guerrilla-style. After that came the liquor smuggling of the Prohibition era. I wondered what was being smuggled these days.

I reached I-10 the next morning and turned west. At midnight, I got off the freeway just beyond El Paso and parked in the desert. After unrolling my sleeping bag in the El Camino's bed, I stared at the sky and tried to pick out the constellations I had learned in the Boy Scouts. So many stars filled the black night that Orion and the rest were hidden among the clutter. At three a.m., a cop woke me and politely told me it was too dangerous to sleep in the desert. I thanked him and drove away.

*

Ron and I met for breakfast at a log cabin restaurant near the summit of Highway 17 between San Jose and Santa Cruz. Redwood, cypress and pine trees towered all around, and I walked across the parking lot gazing up, in awe of their beauty and fragrance.

While we ate, I mentioned to Ron that I had been taking flying lessons. He told me he had gotten his private pilot license the year he graduated high school. I was astonished. He said he hadn't flown in a while, but we might be able to go up with an instructor in the morning. He needed to be back on the ground before noon to host a Super Bowl party.

I followed him to his house, and he weighed each pound. A few registered light. Several did. Ron played it down and said the weed must have dried on the trip, but I felt like I had gotten caught trying to cheat him. He was paying for the pounds in California, not Texas. Jack and I had weighed the pounds too close. Ron didn't say anything more about it, but I cut the total price by a few hundred bucks. I didn't like being a dealer. We smoked a little pollen, and I poured him some to keep.

Ron asked if I had brought any cassettes of the "outlaw country musicians" who performed and recorded in Austin, Texas; people like Jerry Jeff Walker, Waylon Jennings, David Bromberg and Willie Nelson. His local Tower Records didn't stock any of their music. I only had the Michael Murphey tape with "Cosmic Cowboy," which was more commercial than outlaw, but Ron was happy to receive it.

He told me about a shortcut to my motel, and I drove down from the summit through a redwood forest, listening to Pink Floyd's new album, *Wish You Were Here*. Sunlight streamed from above the ridge behind me, and diagonal beams cut between the trees like spotlights. I parked and walked across the carpet of leaves and needles and climbed onto a fallen redwood tree. So quiet, serene. Crows soon put an end to that. I sat and watched tiny flecks float around inside one of the light beams. When the particles hit the edge of the beam, they bounced back toward the center. That was how it looked anyway. As I drove away, "Shine On You Crazy Diamond" played.

The next morning, I took 101 south to a small airport near Morgan Hill. The Cessna 172 Ron had scheduled turned out to be a bigger, four-seat version of the Cessna 150 I had flown at Lakeside Airport in Houston. After takeoff, we climbed south with Ron in the back and his ex-instructor on my right. I leveled off at 1,500 feet, just below a layer of stratus clouds. Our three-dimensional world was bound by mountains all around, the valley floor below, and a ragged gray ceiling close above. Pockets of slanted rain were scattered about, adjoining the cloud ceiling to Earth.

Off the right wing, we paralleled mountains with their tops severed neatly by the overcast. As we passed over Gilroy, the instructor told me to turn right and follow a road to the west. I banked right but couldn't figure out where we were going. Only mountains and clouds appeared ahead. I kept the road below me as instructed.

"We thought you'd like to fly to Santa Cruz," Ron said from the back.

"Have you ever flown through a pass?" the instructor asked.

"No." I concentrated on the road and the mountains and my altitude. "I've only flown in Harlingen and Houston. It's flat there."

The land below us gradually rose, but if I climbed, we would be in the clouds.

"The highest mountain alongside Hecker Pass is two thousand feet above sea level," the instructor said.

He stuck his face against the windscreen and looked up.

"The cloud bases are around seventeen hundred feet, and the floor of the pass is a thousand. We have seven hundred feet of clear air to play with," he said.

It suddenly got bumpy. Mist coated the windshield and streamed back along the side windows.

"Keep it at sixteen hundred feet," the instructor said.

I glanced at the altimeter and saw I had been inching up.

Gray tentacles reached down from the overcast, and the wing sliced through them as if they were ghosts. A small circle of light appeared ahead and expanded as we flew toward it—Hecker Pass.

When we traveled through the aperture, the earth dropped away, the clouds became clear sky, and green and yellow fields spread ahead to a dark blue Pacific glistening in the sunlight. From one world to another, just like that.

We continued to the coast and looked down on surfers in wetsuits; black spots on blue water. They rode waves that peeled from the point and etched flowing white arcs behind them.

After circling a long pier and flying over an amusement park with a roller coaster, we landed at Watsonville Airport for a break. Ron flew the return leg to Morgan Hill while I sat in the back and stared below as we overtook northbound cars on Highway 101. You could make some distance in an airplane. It was just a matter of time until I would be flying everywhere instead of driving.

Even though watching spectator sports wasn't my thing, I followed Ron to his house for the Super Bowl party and met his friends. One of them broke the news that Peter Gabriel had left Genesis. I usually discussed important music issues with a friend I played guitar with in Houston. I found it interesting that someone who grew up in a completely different environment shared similar, somewhat-esoteric interests.

By the time the first quarter ended, I became antsy. On our flight back through the valley, I had noticed very little traffic on 101. Traveling on an empty freeway while everyone sat at home watching the Super Bowl—that was my thing. I clicked my seat belt around my waist and aimed the El Camino south.

*

An hour after crossing into Baja California, the turquoise waters of the Sea of Cortez appeared on my left. I had never seen a sea so calm. Barren cliffs rose straight out of the water and reflected perfectly on its mirror surface. Just before midnight, hordes of tarantulas moved across the road and reminded me of the psychedelic land crabs in Costa Rica. The tarantulas scurried faster than the crabs but, to my and their dismay, many weren't fast enough. I cringed each time one crunched beneath a tire.

Upon reaching La Paz, I drove into the hull of a ferry and spent most of the sixteen-hour boat trip to Mazatlan in my stateroom. There was a small desk under the porthole, and I made use of my downtime by updating my notebook and writing a letter to Sheryl.

After disembarking, I gradually climbed out of the coastal jungle and onto the western edge of the same plateau I drove when heading south during my usual runs. Cruise control came on, and I turned up the music and leaned back against the headrest.

*

Multi-colored cacti appeared ahead and into the desert, making no sense until I got closer and discovered that clothes were draped over them to dry, held in place by the needles. Mule-drawn carts plodded on the dirt alongside the highway. Dust devils made their way over the desert and spun across the road in front of me, pitching dirt and tumbleweeds.

Near Morelia, a cow lay dead and bloated on the road with a fraternity of four vultures and a dog feasting on its stomach. When I passed, the vultures flapped lazily a few feet away, but the dog continued to chow down, unfazed.

Several big trucks were loaded so unevenly, they looked ready to capsize. I sped up when I passed them. Many vehicles had mutated, and entire top sections of some were gone. Their occupants took advantage of the fresh air and sunlight. We waved to each other.

When I passed a truck driving within a cloud of feathers, I peered into a big cage behind the cab and saw chickens hovering inside, their wings flapping a mile a minute. More surreal cacti appeared, this time decorated with captured trash.

I avoided Mexico City by going through Toluca where I washed down lunch with a murky glass of pulque, a drink made from fermented maguey plants. Supposedly, pulque had been imbibed during ancient rituals and was rumored to impart knowledge, even visions. To me, it tasted sour or spoiled, and I didn't feel any different afterward, other than being concerned I might get sick.

At two army checkpoints, I was told "Pásale" and waved through. "El Camino" is Spanish for "the way" and "the road," and it held true for my trusty steed. I reached Oaxaca's vista overlook at three in the morning and laid out my sleeping bag on the Camino's bed.

The downshifting of trucks woke me before seven. I opened a can of Coke and sat on the low stone wall overlooking Oaxaca. Hanging out in the city wasn't good for anonymity. If I had to wait more than a couple of days for the oil, I would leave and return later. While I sat, the sun rose above the mountains, and the still, morning air began to warm.

I got in my car and coasted down the easy curves listening to Joni Mitchell. Halfway through an intersection at the outskirts of town, I was slammed hard. The El Camino flew left and I flew right as metal crunched, glass broke, tires squealed and things rolled on the asphalt. I don't know how long I had been lying sideways across the center console, but I suddenly straightened up and looked out the windshield. A yellow truck with a wrinkled left side and the letters SOP on the door had come to a halt on my right.

I turned my door handle and pushed. It didn't budge. I threw my shoulder against it. No go. When I banged harder, the door opened, but the seat belt held me back. As I unclicked it, I caught sight of my baggie of weed on the floorboard. Shit. I heard voices. I looked to the right and saw two men in ties and matching yellow shirts walking toward me. I snatched the baggie and pushed it back up under the dash. It dropped to the carpet. I tried again, taking time to shove it farther. It stayed. I reached under my seat and grabbed my roll of money.

I creaked my door open and got out.

"Cómo está?" one man asked.

"Pienso bien," I said. *I think okay.*

SOP was printed on the left pockets of their shirts.

We walked around the El Camino and over broken pieces of red and yellow plastic. The Camino's left side had made it through unscathed, but the right side was caved in from bumper to bumper except for the door. The hood had buckled, and part of it aimed skyward.

"La nuestra también es mala," the bald SOP man said. *Ours is bad, too.*

I scanned their truck. Its front left fender and rear panel were dented although not nearly as bad as the El Camino's.

"Por qué no paraste?" he asked. *Why didn't you stop?*

Even dazed, I knew where this might lead. I looked back from where I had driven and confirmed I had no stop sign.

"No tengo un rotulo alto." *I don't have a stop sign.* I forgot the past tense.

"No teníamos una señal de alta, tampoco," the other man said. He pointed behind their truck.

I turned and saw that they had no stop sign either. I also discovered why I hadn't seen their truck. The street they had been traveling was a boulevard, and a row of bushes over four feet high grew between the two directions of traffic. Not only did neither of us have stop signs, visibility had been blocked.

The driver reported our accident to the policia from a radio inside his truck. He tried to explain what SOP meant, but I only understood something about a government agency, which was enough. They wandered around their truck murmuring about the damage, and I walked back to the El Camino. In ten minutes, a police car arrived and a cop in a blue uniform got out. He asked me if I was okay, then walked over to the SOP guys.

He returned and said, "We must go to the oficina de policia and make the report."

I looked at the El Camino.

"What about my car?"

We spoke in Spanish.

"A tow truck will take your camioneta (*little truck*) to the police storage yard. After we finish the paperwork and determine the damages you will pay for the SOP truck, you can have your camioneta fixed."

"Repairs to their truck? There are no stop signs," I said.

"The road you drove is a lesser road. It is therefore your responsibility to yield," he said. "All drivers in Mexico know this. Is it not the same in your country?"

Well, I don't know. Maybe. I pointed to the row of bushes.

"But how can I see cars with those bushes there?" I didn't know the word for bushes, so I said trees.

The policeman stared at the bushes and said, "Los arbustos? They are there a long time. I am sorry but it is your fault. There is no problem. Your insurance will pay, and for your car too."

Fuck, fuck, fuck! For the first time in all my travels south of the border, I hadn't purchased Mexican auto insurance. U.S. insurance policies weren't valid in Mexico, so a temporary Mexican binder was necessary. I normally bought it in Houston, but sometimes I ordered a policy beforehand and picked it up at the border. I had been in a rush driving through San Diego. Fucking haste makes waste.

"No lo tengo aseguro," I told the cop. *I don't have insurance.*

The two SOP guys quit talking.

"You don't have automobile insurance?" he asked.

I shook my head. Insurance wasn't mandatory, but it was stupid not to buy it.

"No," I said.

What were the odds of getting into a crash the first time I didn't buy insurance?

"Why did you not obtain insurance?" the cop asked.

He was truly surprised. What gringo didn't buy Mexican auto insurance? The policeman had never heard of such a thing. Every tourist bought it. And wasn't I more than a tourist?

"I don't know," I said. Even if I had an answer, what difference would it make now? "How much do you think the repair will cost?" I asked. Perhaps a quick payoff would placate everyone and make a visit to the oficina de policia unnecessary.

"We need to determine. SOP will receive a repair estimate. We can go now to the station to make the report and wait for the estimate."

I walked to my car and took my passport and visa from the glove box. A tow truck arrived, and as the four of us drove away in the police car, I watched the front end of my El Camino being lifted. I thought about my weed under the dash.

The cop parked near the zocalo, and we followed him under an archway that connected two buildings. While we waited for a door to open, I looked beyond the arch to a red brick courtyard that ended at a cement wall with two gates of vertical steel bars. This was the city jail. I had walked past it often and never realized it.

Inside the office, I sat in front of a metal desk with the policeman sitting across from me. As he asked questions and filled out a form, I wondered if this might escalate into more than just a civil case. After all, I *had* broken the bigger road/lesser road law. What concerned me more was that my stash may have dropped back onto the floorboard during the towing. For all I knew, the police had already found it and were waiting until I paid for damages to the SOP truck before busting me and throwing me in the jail across the courtyard. What was the punishment for less than an ounce of marijuana? Could I bribe my way out of it?

"We only need to wait for the estimate now. Do you have money to pay for the damage?" asked the cop.

"Yes, but it is in my car, escondido." *Hidden.*

My roll of hundred-dollar bills was in the front right pocket of my jeans, but I wanted to make sure the pot was still under the dash before I shelled out any dinero.

"We can go to your car now while we are waiting," the policeman offered.

My request didn't surprise him, which made me suspicious. Were they setting me up or did everyone in Mexico keep money hidden in their vehicles?

One of the SOP guys left, and someone dressed in street clothes replaced him—maybe a plainclothes policeman. Not a good omen. As we drove to the car impound, the possible plainclothes cop and the bald SOP guy sat on each side of me in the back. Very little space separated us, but I seemed to be the only occupant uncomfortable. Why didn't one of them sit in front? What if they all accompanied me to my car?

At the impound lot, only the SOP official entered the yard with me. Near the back wall rested my crumpled El Camino, destined for the auto boneyard after not even one complete run. My escort followed closely.

"Momentito," I said, hoping he would understand that I didn't want him to see my escondido place. He nodded and removed a pack of cigarettes from his shirt pocket.

I held my breath as I looked through the Camino's right window. No baggie on the floor. Good. Maybe not. I scanned the yard as I walked around to the driver's door. My chaperone was leaning against another unfortunate car, smoking his cigarette and looking elsewhere. I opened the door and sat down. After a glance outside, I inhaled and reached behind the dash. My fingers touched plastic. Exhale. The baggie went into the left pocket of my pants. Nothing else came to mind.

We drove back to the police office in the same seating arrangement as before. At times, the weed in my pocket pressed against the thigh of the possible plainclothes cop. I tried to slide an inch or two without appearing impolite or nervous.

The estimate wasn't ready when we arrived at the station, so I sat and waited with the original policeman. I needed to get rid of the weed. I leaned back against the wall, relaxed and nonchalant, as the policeman read a newspaper spread across his desk.

"Hay un baño?" I asked. *Is there a bathroom?*

He looked up and gestured to his right. "There, then to the left," he said in Spanish.

The corridor turned left into a wider hall, and someone behind a window on the right glanced at me when I walked by. I spotted a trashcan and considered dumping the weed in it until I got a vision of a cleaning woman running through the hall, waving my baggie of Especial over her head.

The small bathroom at the end of the hall was painted official police blue like the building and everything in it. After emptying the baggie into the toilet bowl, I dabbed the pot into the water to make it soggy then flushed. I waited until the bowl refilled, and flushed again. No trace. I ripped the empty plastic bag into pieces and shoved them to the bottom of the wastebasket.

When I returned to the office, the cop folded his newspaper and told me the shop doing the estimate had closed for lunch. If I wanted to leave and get something to eat, I could. My escorts were nowhere in sight. I was being allowed out on my own.

"Voy a buscar por un hotel," I said. *I will look for a hotel.*

The policeman nodded and unfolded his newspaper.

Could I actually get out of this situation with my dinero? I walked while my mind ran. If I split, I would be out a totaled car and a few possessions that I could easily replace. I had $4,000 in my pocket, more money in the bank, and the remaining rainbow weed to sell in Laguna Vista. I hailed a taxi.

"Aeropuerto, por favor."

The ticket counter for all the airlines ran along my right. I walked its length and looked for a flight leaving soon, preferably to Texas. Mexicana had one bound for Brownsville, but it wouldn't depart until ten the next morning. I continued down the counter and broadened my search for anything that would get me out of Oaxaca pronto.

Someone walked in my direction, looking at me. Yes, he was looking at me and smiling. No way. It was the plainclothes cop who had sat next to me in the police car. I did a one-eighty and walked back toward the exit. Another man aimed directly for me, smiling. It was the bald SOP man who had also accompanied me to the car lot. How could this be? I had left the police station less than thirty minutes earlier. My head swiveled in search of escape. None. I slowed, then stopped. The SOP man held out his hand. I shook it.

"Buenas tardes," he said.

"Buenas tardes," I answered.

The plainclothes cop joined us from behind. He reached around me and rested his hand on my right shoulder like we were buddies.

"Going somewhere, amigo?" he asked.

"Checking flights for tomorrow," I said.

"Claro. Vamos. The estimate is ready." *Of course. Let's go.*

I walked outside to the police car with my buddy's arm over my shoulder, and we drove away, snug and cozy in the back like old times.

After shelling out $2,300 for damages to the SOP truck, I waited under the archway for my official receipt and release. Across the courtyard, a man in a suit stood in front of the steel bars, talking to someone on the inside. I couldn't see the prisoner in the shadows, but his forearms rested on a horizontal bar and his hands hung outside in the sunlight. An inmate and his lawyer.

My SOP amigo offered to drive me to my car. As we walked from the police station, I wondered what the people behind those bars were busted for. I had been lucky.

At the impound lot, I took a last look at my El Camino and told the guy in charge he could do whatever he wanted with it.

Un regalo. I filled my backpack with clothes and cassette tapes and got a ride back to the city center.

The next morning, I hopped the ten a.m. Mexicana flight to Brownsville and Jack picked me up. On the drive to Laguna Vista, I told him the saga of the El Camino and we made plans to head back down for the hash oil.

CHAPTER TEN

A New Era

Four days later, Jack and I crossed into Mexico in his girlfriend's Ford Courier mini-truck. If the Zapotecs had oil, great. If not, we would get it from William's people on the Pacific. That part of the coast was known for good surf, and after all my driving and crashing, a little ocean rejuvenation was in order. Our boards were in the back of the camper. As Jack drove from the twenty-kilometer checkpoint, I pushed in the cassette and "Already Gone" played through the Courier's four speakers.

A new era dawned. No more running weed. We couldn't do it if we wanted. The Courier had no back seat to stash kilos and no space under the bed to hang them (as if we would do that again).

"Nice pickup," I said. It was a definite upgrade from Jack's old Ford pickup, which had ceased to run again—the reason we were in the Courier.

"Didn't you tell me you were breaking up with Beth?" I asked.

Things might have changed between them during my drive to California and Mexico.

"Yeah, I still am." He kept his eyes on the road.

"Does she know?"

“I’m pretty sure.”

Although the three of us shared a house, I had been gone a lot, so I hadn’t gotten to know Beth well. For that matter, I hadn’t hung out with Jack much either. They did their thing, I did mine.

We cruised south on the central plateau, and I turned up the volume on Credence Clearwater. Jack reached into the front pocket of his jeans and pulled out a tiny brown vial. He handed it to me.

“There’s not much, but we can save it for when we’re tired,” he said. “And maybe a snort now to get us started.”

I had done cocaine a few times. A tiny spoon was attached to the cap of the bottle, and I dipped it inside and came up with a small white mound of coke. I held it below my right nostril and inhaled, then dipped it again and placed the spoon under Jack’s nose. After handing the vial back, I reached up under the dash for our baggie of pre-rolled joints.

*

When we got to Oaxaca, I pointed out my fateful intersection to Jack. Bits of glass and colored plastic shined along the curbs. In the afternoon, we met with William and asked if our friends in the mountains had oil.

“Es posible,” William said, “but is better the oil my amigos make.”

“On the Pacific?”

“Si. Aceite de oro.” *Gold oil.*

“It is made?”

“Si. Completo,” he said. “Por seguro. Vamonos.” *For sure. Let's go.*

The next morning, the three of us packed into the Courier’s small cab and headed down the mountains for the gold. Twenty minutes out of Oaxaca, the road turned to dirt. An hour later, it forked, and a sign for Puerto Escondido pointed to the right—the direction we needed to go for the hash oil. Escondido was renowned for good waves. Neither Jack nor I had surfed it, but we were ready and willing.

The long descent from Oaxaca terminated at a river.

Children and goats played on a beach in the shade of a steep cliff that rose from the opposite bank. We got out of the truck and walked toward the cliff. I took pictures.

"Buenos dias," I said to the kids.

They turned away. I looked around and didn't see any adults. When we started to walk back to the truck, they laughed. This was nothing new. Gringos were funny, especially to Mexican children. We assessed the river, and Jack backed up to cross at a better spot. After a few yards, the Courier's tires spun in the sand. Jack got on his knees and investigated.

"The differential is sitting on a rock," he said.

The children were watching. I waved an arm over my head.

"Venga," I yelled. *Come.*

Half a dozen boys marched in our direction.

"Hay una roca debajo," I said. "We need to lift the camioneta."

Three of the kids dropped to the sand and looked.

"Si," confirmed an eight-year-old.

After we raised the Courier off the rock, the other children wandered over to us. I grabbed my Polaroid from the glove box and took photos of the kids and handed them out.

Immediately, a dozen niños pawed me, wanting pictures of themselves. "Para mi, señor, para mi, por favor."

I shot more photos and gave them away. The children stood quietly in small groups and stared as the images slowly materialized. The moment they recognized themselves, they burst into laughter. I snapped a few of the kids looking at themselves in the pictures. We never saw their parents, but the niños would have a good story to tell—with proof.

The camera went back into the glove box, and Jack drove across the river. As the road climbed, we passed through fog wisps. When the wisps grew into solid gray, Jack switched on the headlights, leaned forward and concentrated.

We topped the summit and descended into daylight again. After another long descent, our road turned to mud and disappeared into a wide, fast-moving river. On the other side, the road emerged in mud and at a steep incline. The situation bore studying. As we stood gazing, a station wagon pulled up behind us. Its gringo driver rolled down his window and aimed a professional movie camera at the river. A woman sat beside him, and two kids were in the back.

"Is this the end of the road?" the driver asked.

I turned back to the river and saw tire ruts in the mud on the other side. Cars were either getting across or being swept away. I looked downstream.

"We stopped to check it out. It looks like cars have been making it across," I told him.

At that moment, a car with Mexican license plates plowed by on our right. It splashed into the river and zigzagged across, pushing water above its front bumper. On the other side, the car sprayed mud in its wake as it climbed the hill and disappeared.

Camera Man went next. His station wagon mimicked the previous car's jerky route, and he was across. Our turn. The Courier had a higher clearance than the other vehicles, and Jack drove slower. I watched the water gradually rise above the bottom of my door, then recede, and we were across. The station wagon was parked above the mud on the right, and we stopped alongside. The driver had his camera aimed at us, and his wife and kids were waving. We waved back.

A few kilometers before Pochutla, the road became asphalt, and we hit a military checkpoint. Green soldiers examined our papers and requested we vacate the truck. One looked inside the cab, and another opened the hatch of the camper shell and stared at our surfboards and everything else. They handed back our papers, and we drove away. We had stashed our few joints better than usual because William had warned us about possible checkpoints. The weed was still up under the dash, but way up.

Fifteen minutes later we came to another army stop. I had never before run into two checkpoints so close together. We might have been lured into a false sense of security. Ahead, a soldier with a rifle hanging from his shoulder stood to the right of Camera Man's station wagon. He held his hand up for us to wait. When the station wagon drove off, Jack moved up. The soldier stood a few feet away on my side and scoped out the truck from bumper to bumper. Mini-trucks were rare in Mexico.

He told William and me to get out, then sat in the passenger seat beside Jack with the barrel of his rifle pointing up through the open door. After hunching out of sight momentarily, the soldier straightened up and slid his hands over the top of the dash and around the air vents. He opened the glove box and pulled out my camera. When compacted, the SX-70 is just a solid rectangle less than an inch thick. I wondered if he knew it was a camera. He shook it, then searched through the glove box. For a couple more minutes, I couldn't see what the soldier was doing, then he got out and we drove away.

Jack told us the soldier had examined every cassette tape in the shoebox and had reached up under the dash. Jack said he tried to remain cool while his heart beat strong enough for his shirt to pulse at his chest. Good thing we were being extra cautious.

"There is another road to Oaxaca," William told us. "We will drive farther south to Puerto Angel to return to Oaxaca."

When we arrived in the hills above the Pacific, William's friends informed him the oil wouldn't be ready for a week. Shit. Por seguro was never por seguro. We were bummed. We drove to Puerto Escondido to surf and mull over our options.

Even though Escondido was famous for its big, hollow waves, the surf was almost flat when we got there. The next morning, the waves were still too small to ride. At breakfast, a gringo surfer informed us that shoulder-high surf had been breaking in the afternoon when the tide started filling in. Jack and I talked it over. Did we want to wait and try to get in some surfing? Maybe the Zapotecs had oil. If we departed soon, we could talk to them that night.

Jack drove us past the turnoff for the previous day's route and we made a left at Puerto Angel. There were no checkpoints on our drive up the mountains and we arrived in Oaxaca in time to take a nap.

In the evening, we picked up William and the mezcal, then maneuvered past the evil canine guardians of sleeping Mexican villages. Approaching our destination, Jack shut off the headlights and killed the engine. He made a sharp right and coasted to a stop between the shack and a sleeping burro.

Francisco greeted us at the door. He and William talked, and William told us they had oil.

Unbelievable.

We followed Francisco to the connection hut.

Gurtrek soon arrived with a small jar of liquid that did not resemble gold oil or even regular brown hash oil. It was a strange, chlorophyll-looking green and smelled like pot, not hash oil. Jack smeared the green goop onto a cigarette paper, and we smoked the joint as Francisco and Gurtrek watched. There was no hash oil taste or expansion, and I didn't get any higher than if I had smoked just the weed. Jack concurred. I felt bad we would have to reject the oil. The Zapotecs had gone to the trouble of getting it for us and most likely took pride in it. But business was business. I told them their oil wasn't what we wanted, but we would smoke it again in the morning to make sure. I didn't want to hurt their feelings. We returned to Oaxaca.

A few tokes after breakfast confirmed the oil was crap. Although Jack and I swore we wouldn't do it, we decided to make another weed run, but with only ten keys or less—and it had to be especial. We drove to a lumber store for materials and paneled the inside of the camper shell in three hours. Working construction in boomtown Houston had taught us a valuable craft.

When we returned to the mountains that night, I explained to Francisco and Santiago that the oil wouldn't work for us. Their smiles faded—not because they were losing a sale but because they had disappointed us.

"Tienen muy buena mota?" I asked. *Do you have good weed?*

Their smiles reappeared.

"Si," Santiago answered.

Santiago left the shack, and William, Jack and I sat on the dirt floor. Francisco walked to a portable radio under the mantel and turned it on, then sat down next to us and removed the cap from the mezcal.

"Born to Be Wild" by Steppenwolf played from the little radio, followed by a song in Spanish, then another classic rock tune. Between each song, a disc jockey shouted, "Radio Cinco en Oaxaca" from a deep, reverberating cavern. I wondered whether Francisco tuned in the station for us or if Zapotecs liked classic rock. We sat and waited for the mota, sipped mezcal, and listened to "Bye, Bye, Miss American Pie."

Santiago returned carrying two boxes of flower tops—with seeds; consemillan. If we were going to disregard our mandate not to smuggle weed, it would not be for consemillan. We told Francisco and Santiago the weed in the boxes would not do. But they must have already known that because Santiago immediately said another hombre would arrive in five minutes with mejor (*better*).

"El mejor, por favor," I said. *The best, please.*

Santiago left again and returned in fifteen minutes with a handful of flower tops without seeds. They looked good. Jack rolled a joint and we smoked it. Very good.

"You have kilos?"

"Si. Diez vienen." *Ten are coming.*

After another hour of mezcal and Radio Cinco en Oaxaca, ten keys arrived. But they were consemillan again. It was now after four a.m. We were tired of waiting, and just plain tired. Jack and I had been going nonstop since crossing into Mexico. We needed a good night's sleep. Francisco noticed our frustration and promised to have eight kilos of muy buena mota the next day, even better than what we had just smoked.

"Por seguro," Francisco said with a solemn nod.

That phrase did not instill confidence. We agreed to rendezvous with them off the highway at two in the afternoon. William took directions.

By the time Jack and I got back to our hotel, the sun was

above the mountains. I glanced up at the window of our room on the second floor and noticed the curtains were open. Hadn't we closed them? I pointed it out to Jack. Someone had been in the room. The maids? Where did we leave that oil sample? Would the maids have snitched to anyone? It was careless to have left everything out, but, in our defense, we hadn't expected to spend all night in the mountains or for the maids to come so early.

Abandoning our stuff wasn't an option, especially since we had hidden some cash in the base of a lamp. When I opened the door to our room, my eyes fell upon the neat beds. Maids. We discovered the jar of oil, our pot and an ashtray with two roaches tucked neatly inside the drawer of a nightstand. We flushed everything and slept until noon.

After leaving the maids a good tip, we checked out of the hotel and picked up William at the zocalo. As we drove past the road to Veracruz, I looked left and studied it. This time we were going to take the shortcut due east to the Gulf coast. It would shave at least eight hours off our run.

A few miles later, I saw that the truck-weighing station was deserted. Traffic breezed by in both directions. As usual, William reminded us of the bypass, but we wouldn't need to use it since the checkpoint was closed. We did not stop for mezcal.

As we drove south, a helicopter appeared ahead to the right. It was flying back toward Oaxaca, and I watched it out my side window until it disappeared behind us. William told Jack to turn right onto a dirt road, and we bounced along for ten minutes before rounding a hill and stopping.

Below us, figures moved under one of only a few trees growing on the dry, rocky terrain. We drove over, and Santiago guided us beneath the branches. Jack, William and I got out of the Courier and hiked down the slope with Francisco and Santiago, then across a dry riverbed. As we walked, our mountain friends kept glancing up at the sky. When they saw me look up, Santiago used gestures and Spanish to tell me they had seen a helicopter earlier, and that policia sometimes dropped down and burned their fields and took them to the carcel. I couldn't imagine these good-natured people in jail.

We hiked up the other side of the riverbed and found Gurtrek sitting in a Jeep under a tree. Francisco removed the burlap cover from a lone wooden crate in the back of the Jeep and revealed eight kilos of the limest-green weed I had ever seen. Bright red ribbons wound through each flower top. I picked up a kilo and inhaled. If marijuana ever became legal, scents like this would be marketed as perfume. Francisco had come through for us.

We carried the kilos across the riverbed and up to the Courier. Jack placed the box on the open tailgate as Santiago handed me a reddish-green semi-circle of something a quarter-inch thick. I stared at it.

"Achh," he said.

Hash.

"Un regalo. Podemos conseguir." *A gift. We can get.*

I put it to my nose. It smelled like mangoes. I handed it to Jack.

"Nice. Gracias," he said to Santiago and gave it back to me.

Jack jumped into the camper and began unscrewing the front ceiling panel. I gave William the money for the kilos, and he and Francisco walked away. I climbed into the back of the truck, and Jack and I put the kilos into two garbage bags, then stashed them behind the ceiling panel at the very front. Francisco and Santiago looked in.

"Muy bueno," said Santiago. "La policia—no hay problema."

That's the plan. I jumped down and inspected the paneling. My forte was rough framing, not finish work, but our job looked professional. The three-inch difference between the actual and false ceilings was not noticeable. Our lime-green kilos were concealed better than in any of my prior runs.

The Zapotecs kept looking up at the sky and appeared to want to get moving. We said goodbye, and they hiked back down the slope.

William asked to ride with us a little way north. After all our business together, I didn't mind him knowing which way we were going. At the main road, we turned left—toward Oaxaca. It felt strange not making the usual right turn to the south—away from the city—but the turnoff to Veracruz would come well before Oaxaca.

A Pleasant Valley Sunday prevailed, and clusters of people walked on the side of the road in the same direction we drove. William told us they were making their weekly pilgrimage to the Sunday market in Tlacolula. Muchos hombres with sombreros and mustaches marched northward. Women in dresses trailed behind, carrying baskets and holding hands with children who held hands with other children. Car traffic increased. It never hurt to get lost in the crowd, although our Texas plates somewhat impeded that.

I stared at the mountains ahead and tried to locate the pass we would soon be driving through, but clouds obscured the ridge. Sunlight warmed my right arm resting on the windowsill and made me drowsy. Lack of sleep was taking hold. Jack and I had thrown out our personal contraband the night before. Only the vial with enough coke for two decent hits remained—enough to jump start the run. I was anxious to get up that mountain and snort our last hit.

After passing the turnoff to Mitla and the Tree of Life, Jack pulled over to let William out. We shook hands for good business to come, and Jack and I continued north. Traffic became busier, and a big truck ahead of us slowed. Jack took his foot off the gas, but the truck continued to slow. We were soon driving in its shadow. Was there an accident?

The truck came to a complete stop, and so did we. Two soldiers with rifles appeared from around the front of the truck and stared at us. The checkpoint was active.

CHAPTER ELEVEN

Pop

A man in civilian clothes joined the two soldiers. He squinted at us as he said something to them. One of the soldiers pointed his rifle in front of the Courier and swept the barrel to our right. Jack pulled over to the inspection lane, and the men disappeared around the front of the big truck.

From the side, I saw that the checkpoint was in full force. Sawhorses blocked the northbound lane, and green soldiers with rifles walked between the cars, stopping to inspect documents and trunks. There was no way out of this.

How could they have activated the roadblock so quickly? Why? I reached into the glove box for our papers.

The truck drove away, and the man in plain clothes approached with the soldiers close behind. His pale-blue Guayabera shirt was stretched taut at his stomach.

"De dónde vienen?" he asked. *Where are you coming from?*

"Puerto Escondido," I answered. Maybe he knew it was a good surf spot, a reasonable getaway for a couple of college kids on break.

"What is your purpose in Mexico?" he asked in Spanish.

"A surfear."

"Papeles," he said.

I handed him our passports, visas and car papers through the window.

"Come out of the truck," he told us.

Jack and I got out, and the man sat down in the passenger seat. I walked around the front of the Courier to the driver's door where Jack stood. The two soldiers peered into the right window of the camper and continued behind the truck, where they stopped and stared through the back hatch. They were from the mountains, but taller and thinner than our Zapotec friends, and had no smiles. They circled the truck and passed by us with their rifles held close in front. One glanced quickly at my face, and in his eyes I saw bewilderment of foreigners who drove expensive camionetas with many precious things inside.

A man in a white sports coat came out of a small office on our right and walked to the Courier's passenger door. The guy sitting inside handed him our passports and visas. He flipped through them and glanced over the truck at Jack and me, then traced the soldiers' path around the Courier, also stopping to look into the rear of the camper. He continued up the left side to where Jack and I stood near the front fender.

His skin was lighter than mine or Jack's. At his open collar, a gold medallion hung from a thin chain. He wore white leather shoes with loose weaving that showed his beige socks. He opened our passports.

"Zhackson Antonee Cole." He turned to Jack.

"That's me," said Jack.

The man looked down at the other passport, then at me.

"Estephen Fraunkleen Walker."

I nodded.

He held both passports open and slapped them on his left palm a few times.

"What is your business in Mexico?" he asked in English.

"No business. We are students. College. We came to surf for vacation and are going back home to Texas," I answered.

The spring semester would have begun already, but how

would he know? The other agent handed him the truck's papers through the driver's window.

"Who is the owner of this truck?"

"It's my girlfriend's, but I have authorization to drive it in Mexico," Jack answered.

"College students," the agent repeated while looking at the car papers. "Bueno," he said and nodded.

Now he would return our passports and wish us a good education.

"Rafael," his partner called from inside the cab.

Rafael stuck his head in the driver's window. They talked for a minute, and Rafael turned back to Jack and me. He held out his right hand, clenched and facing up. When he opened it, two tiny green marijuana seeds lay in his palm. From where? The weed we got from the Zapotecs had no seeds, but the kilos were never in the cab anyway. They had gone straight into the paneling. Jack and I hadn't rolled any joints inside the car the whole trip. And we cleaned the truck this morning. Were we being set up?

Shit. William had rolled a joint at the beach—with pot that had seeds.

"Que es esa?" I asked, studying his palm. *What is that?*

"Seeds," he said. "Semillas de mota."

"Mota?" I repeated. He used the Mexican slang—slang that college students on a surf safari probably wouldn't be familiar with.

"Mota." He smiled. "Marijuana. Weed. Pot. Grass. Mary Jane." Rafael possessed a good English vocabulary.

"I don't know how it got there," I said. "It is not ours."

He looked over at Jack, who shook his head.

How much trouble could a couple of seeds get you in Mexico? Rafael walked over to the soldiers and said something, then followed them to the back of the camper. They opened the hatch and began taking our stuff out and laying it on the pavement. Fuck.

Rafael watched the soldiers for a couple of minutes before

returning to where Jack and I stood at the front of the truck. He stopped two feet in front of me, reached into the top pocket of my shirt and pulled out the tablet of hash. Fuck, fuck. I had forgotten all about it. How did he know it was there? It was at the bottom of the pocket. He couldn't have seen it.

Rafael put it to his nose.

"Muy bueno. From los Indios?" He pointed over my shoulder to the mountains where the Zapotecs lived.

I turned and looked in that direction.

"I don't understand," I said.

"The hashish is from los Indios. What else did you get from them?"

"I don't know about Indians. We drove through some mountains to go surfing in Puerto Escondido."

"Where did you get the hashish?"

I had to think. If I said we bought it in Mexico, he would hound us for the source. Jack listened.

"United States," I answered.

"How long have you been in Mexico?"

He could verify our entry into the country by looking at our visas.

"A week."

"A week," Rafael repeated. He held up the half circle of hash. "You did not smoke much for one week."

I said nothing. Rafael asked Jack if it was true we brought the hash from the United States. Jack said yes. As cars drove by, their occupants stared at the two long-haired gringos on the side of the road with four soldiers standing amid their possessions.

Rafael placed his arms over our shoulders and walked us around the front of the Courier to the right side. Maybe he thought we would try to make a break for it. Things *had* just taken a turn for the serious. I looked around again and saw no escape in our near future. They hadn't found the kilos yet, but this was unlike any previous search. Rafael stood next to the Courier's passenger door and opened the glove box. He pulled out my camera and photos.

"What is this?" he asked.

"A camera. Polaroid SX-70," I answered. He motioned for me to come closer.

"This takes these photos? Instant?" he asked, pointing to the photographs of the kids at the river.

"Yes. It is the newest Polaroid."

"Muy caro?" *Very expensive?*

"Más o menos."

He turned the camera over a few times. It was metal, not plastic like earlier models, and had a thin leather veneer on the front and back.

"How does it work?" he asked and handed it to me.

I pressed a button on the side, and the camera popped open into the familiar Polaroid shape. He looked through the viewfinder at me, then at Jack, who was watching the soldiers go through our stuff.

"Muy buena," he said and placed the camera gently into the glove box.

He picked up the photos again and looked at them.

"Where did you take these photographs?" he asked.

"On the road to Escondido," I said and added, "When we went surfing."

"What are the niños looking at in the photographs they hold?"

"Themselves."

"You gave these children photographs of themselves?"

"Si."

Rafael shuffled through the pictures and placed them back in the glove box. He picked up the SX-70 again and studied it. Rafael recognized quality.

"Muy buena," he said.

"You like it?" I asked.

He looked at me. "Si, of course."

"Es suya," I said. *It's yours*. "Un regalo."

"El mio? Muchas gracias." *Mine*. He paused and repeated, "El mio" as he gazed at his new camera.

It wouldn't hurt to offer a gift. We had only been caught with a little hash. Maybe now the soldiers would throw our stuff back in the truck and we could drive away.

I showed Rafael how to close the camera. When he slid it into an inside pocket of his coat, I glimpsed a pistol in a leather holster. He was some sort of plain clothes detective. His partner probably was, too.

Rafael seemed happy with his gift, but he had appeared happy during our whole encounter. He walked to the back of the truck, and Jack and I followed him. All our stuff was out of the camper and on the ground. Rafael picked up the Coleman lantern, then the stove, then Jack's tape player, and said, "el mio" with every new item in his hand. Was he saying that everything was his? The soldiers stood our surfboards up, and Rafael put an eye to each and tried to look through them.

Jack and I were directed to sit on a curb near the little office while the soldiers continued to rummage through our stuff. Rafael's partner came out of the building and walked past us holding a screwdriver.

"They're gonna remove the paneling," Jack whispered.

We had not been handcuffed or restrained. I scanned again for an escape and noticed Jack looking around too.

"Rafael has a gun," I said.

There was only open desert. We wouldn't get far.

"We can't say we got the weed from the Zapotecs," I told Jack. "We'd be snitching. And these guys will want to know where they live. They'll also try to get the person who took us to the Indians."

I thought about it.

"We bought the kilos in Salina Cruz," I said. "A connection that far away may not interest them. And this would be the route we'd have taken."

Salina Cruz was a town on the Pacific near the Isthmus of Tehuantepec. I knew it from my travels with Dan.

"We told them we were surfing in Escondido," Jack said.

"If they find the weed, it won't matter what we told them."

"Okay. Salina Cruz," said Jack.

"We bought it from a Mexican surfer we met on the beach."

Jack nodded.

I couldn't see much through the camper's windows, but a soldier appeared to be working on a side panel near the back. They would find no pot behind the side panels, of course. We had stashed the kilos in the ceiling at the very front. But it was just a matter of minutes before they found it—minutes before everything changed. I wasn't one for regrets, but I sure regretted not taking William's advice to use the bypass road.

Jack said, "In jail, if anyone tries to buttfuck us, we stick together."

What? His words jolted me. And they sounded strange coming from Jack. I only knew him as a peaceful guy, although I vaguely remembered him saying that he had been a juvenile delinquent before his parents moved to Houston. His experience might come in handy. I looked across the highway to the sand and cactus and mountains.

The soldier in the camper scooted up. He seemed to be unscrewing a ceiling panel. Rafael and the other agent stood behind the truck and watched. A flashlight came on. Another soldier was aiming it inside a ceiling panel. Shit.

What would their reaction be when they found our kilos? Calm, jubilant, victorious, angry, violent? So many ways we could have avoided this. If we had just gone the normal route south, or stuck to my night routine, or waited to surf at high tide in Escondido. Or taken the bypass. How could I have been so careless? Two fucking seeds.

We sat for another five minutes. The soldier jumped down from the camper and began throwing our things back inside. Rafael didn't even glance at us as he walked by and disappeared into the office.

"They didn't find it," Jack whispered.

I stared ahead in disbelief. Maybe they were playing a head game with us.

Soldiers continued to search cars while Jack and I sat waiting for verification—of what? No one seemed to be excited. Two soldiers wandered off, but our original Nazi youths remained close by, rifles in hand, ready for action. This could be their first bust. An ounce of hash might be something to them, but surely not to plainclothes federales.

The afternoon had progressed to sunset when Rafael put us in the back of an unmarked car. He sat in the front passenger seat, and I asked what would happen to the truck.

"Don't worry," Rafael answered. "It will be safe. I will look after it myself."

I believed him. After all, we had only been caught with an ounce of hash. And I had given him a nice camera.

Inside an office building in Oaxaca, Jack and I sat in front of a metal desk with Rafael and his partner opposite us. On the wall behind them hung a big, framed drawing of a marijuana leaf with Spanish text surrounding it. Our passports and visas lay on the desktop

"Name?" asked Rafael.

We told him our names and spelled them out.

"Age?"

"Twenty-two," I said.

"Twenty-three," said Jack.

When Jack was asked his date of birth, I was surprised his birthday had been a week earlier. He never said anything.

"Where did you get the hashish?"

"United States."

"Who is the owner of the hashish?"

"Both of us."

"What is your business in Mexico?"

"Surfing."

"What is your occupation?"

"Student."

"Do you want something from your truck for tonight?"

With those words came the reality that we were no longer free.

"Yes, por favor, sleeping bags and pillows."

Rafael and the other agent walked us to the Courier now parked on the street a block away. I was anxious to confirm our kilos had not been discovered. When Jack opened the camper's hatch, I saw the back end of a middle ceiling panel hanging down. It was where the soldier had shined his flashlight. I would have thought the kilos could be seen from inside the hanging panel. But if they had been discovered, the panel in front would have been removed. It appeared untouched.

Jack and I were driven to a military barracks somewhere in the city and assigned bunks. I threw my stuff on the top, and Jack took the bottom. Young soldiers walked to and from their bunks to the dining room and bathroom and ignored us. Many were people from the mountains.

In the morning, Jack and I were allowed to take cold showers and eat breakfast in the mess hall. When I occasionally made eye contact with a soldier, he immediately looked down at his plate as if he might be reprimanded for associating with us.

Rafael arrived around noon, and Jack and I accompanied him to a police office where our mug shots, fingerprints and palm prints were taken. When we returned to the military quartel, Rafael's partner removed two photos from his shirt pocket and handed them to him.

"Venga," Rafael said to Jack and me.

We walked over, and Rafael showed us photos of what seemed to be the heads and upper torsos of two mummies.

"Your American compadres," he said.

Rafael and the other agent laughed.

"They tried to take off in their airplane full of mota, but they were greedy and stupid and crashed down the mountain and burned," Rafael said.

I looked again. The figures in the photos didn't appear human, but I had never before seen burnt bodies. Were the agents fucking with us? They watched our expressions and laughed again.

*

Rafael showed up around two in the afternoon the next day

and told us we needed to make a formal declaration. Apparently, our previous declaration had been informal. We drove back to the Narcotics Office, and Jack and I were separated. I sat in front of the big desk again with Rafael and someone else opposite me. A translator from the American Embassy sat to my left. Rafael asked the same questions as before, and the person next to him wrote the answers on a pad of paper. Rafael told me that if Jack and I both confessed to possession of the hash, we would be declared addicts who had the legal right to possess a certain amount of it. We would be free in twenty-four hours.

The interpreter confirmed what Rafael said. I couldn't dispute the hash was mine. Rafael had plucked it from my pocket. I signed the paper.

Afterward, Jack told me he had also signed. From there, we were driven to the same jail I had visited during my SOP incident two weeks earlier. While we waited to be processed, someone in an office across the entranceway stared at me. He was the clerk who had given me the receipt and release documents after my El Camino crash. He began pointing me out to someone next to him. I turned away. The last thing I needed was for anyone to know I was a frequent visitor to Oaxaca, especially with eight kilos still in the back of the Courier.

Jack and I were led across the courtyard toward two cells. In the cell on the right, I saw two American-looking girls standing behind the steel bars, watching. The guards unlocked the gate on the left, and Jack and I entered. The gate clanked shut behind us.

Notes from Inside

CHAPTER TWELVE

La Carcel (Jail)

Feb 3, 1976

The cell felt cool and damp—like a cave. One yellow bulb hung from a wire attached to the cement ceiling thirty feet above, but most of the light now came from the courtyard through the bars. The walls were dingy brown, and marred with dirt, squashed mosquitoes, and what looked like dried blood. A bench ran almost the entire length of the back cement wall. Several men sat on it while a few others lay prone. Where the bench ended at the left, a porcelain sink tilted toward a cracked, dirty toilet with no seat. Green slime covered the cement floor surrounding its base.

A dozen Mexicans and Indians stood around the room; some in groups, some alone. Others sat on the floor. Two Indians who resembled our Zapotec friends were standing together talking quietly. They wore their customary white cotton garb, but dirty—and they weren't smiling. Another Indian sat by himself at the right end of the bench near the wall. His shirt was torn and blood-stained, and he had a cut across his left cheek. Three gringos stood near the center of the room, watching me and Jack. They walked over and introduced themselves.

Kimo looked to be of Asian descent with straight black hair to his shoulders. Tyler was thin with blond hair that reached the middle of his back. They were about the same age as Jack and me. Tyler told us they and the four girls with them had been driving back to Oaxaca from Zipolite Beach on the Pacific when Rafael discovered their stash under the front seat.

At the roadblock, Tyler and Kimo endured harsher treatment than what Jack and I had received. When Rafael wanted to know where they had gotten their pot, Tyler told him the truth—that they bought it from a young Mexican in Oaxaca. The answer wasn't satisfactory.

Rafael shook a bottle of orange soda with his thumb held over its opening while his partner punched Tyler in the solar plexus. When Tyler doubled over and gasped for air, Rafael placed the bottle under his nose and released its contents. Tyler couldn't help but inhale the soda into his lungs. He said he thought he was going to drown in the desert for an ounce of pot. After Kimo received the same treatment, they and the four girls were driven to the jail.

Tyler told us Rafael's name is Rafael Solas, and his partner is Carlos Garcia. They are federal judiciales—elite officers who don't answer to the federal police, municipal police or army. Wherever judiciales go, they are in charge.

"Watch out for Rafael," Tyler warned. "He's a snake."

Tyler led Jack and me to the side wall and introduced us to the girls in the adjacent cell. We couldn't see their faces, but they stuck out their hands and waved. Tyler's girlfriend is Lynette, Kimo's is Buffy, and the other two are Susan and Erica. They drove to Mexico from New York in Tyler's Chevy van.

The other American in our jail cell is 18-year-old Tony from southern California, and his story explained why the checkpoint had been activated so quickly. The burned pilots in the photos Rafael and Garcia had laughed at were Tony's friends. Their plane crashed two hours before Jack and I made our connection with the Zapotecs. Police immediately activated the roadblock to catch anyone involved.

Tony told us he and his friends had loaded and fueled their twin-engine Aero Commander on a plateau runway in the mountains. The plane lifted off during takeoff but never cleared the trees at the end of the runway. The Aero Commander disappeared off the plateau and down the mountain, followed by an explosion, smoke and screaming.

The screams came from only one of the pilots, Tony said, and he recognized the voice as his best friend's. Tony and the Indians ran to the edge of the plateau and tried to find a way down to the burning wreckage, but it was a sheer drop.

"I listened as my friend screamed and burned to death, and I couldn't do anything about it," Tony said.

I thought he might cry.

Fifteen minutes after the crash, a helicopter appeared above the smoke. Everyone had already split except Tony and one Zapotec. They ran, but the police dispatched cars and found them hiding in a shack a few kilometers away. Tony pointed to the Indian on the bench with the bloody shirt and told us his name was Nosario. I remembered the helicopter I had watched when we drove to make our connection.

Although I'm only a novice pilot, it seemed apparent that Tony's buddies had overloaded their plane. How could two experienced pilots ignore basic rules of flight—rules of physics? I'm no stickler for regulations in general, but even I consider laws of physics to be absolute. If Tony's friends had adhered to proper weight and balance, they would be enjoying the good life in California right now—and Jack and I would be doing the same in Texas.

The sun set, and the hanging bulb in our cell provided just enough light to see around the room. Most of the guests sat in small groups on the bench or on the floor and talked. A few, like Nosario, sat alone. Two Mexicans stood at the front of the cell, gripping the steel bars and staring outside. I looked past them across the courtyard and through the entrance to the street. Cars drove past; people walked by.

Three silhouettes appeared under the archway and came

across the courtyard. Rafael and two soldiers stopped at the bars near where Tony stood. Rafael looked around at all of us. He put his right hand through the bars and patted Tony's cheek three times progressively harder, then muttered something and sneered at him.

Tony could have backed away, but he held his place and endured Rafael's attention. I didn't understand what was going on, and I wondered if Tony did. He had told us that when the police caught him, they found only two joints in his pack of cigarettes, but Rafael kept hounding him to confess to being a smuggler, a contrabandista internacional. He said Rafael taunted him with the photos of his dead friends and kept repeating, "Too bad they didn't have room for you."

Rafael turned to me.

"Amigo," he said with both arms half-raised in Mexican welcoming fashion.

"Sale," he said and grinned. *You leave.*

"Salgo?" I asked. "Yo?" *I leave? Me?*

I looked around the cell. "Libre?" I asked Rafael. *Free?*

He smiled. "Hoy, no. Mañana libre." *Today, no. Tomorrow free.*

Tomorrow was better than nothing, although I wasn't looking forward to spending the night on the hard cement or using the disgusting community toilet. Our sleeping bags did not make the transition from the military quartel. Rafael pointed me out to the soldiers, and one opened the gate while the other stood a few feet away and aimed his rifle in front of the cell. I didn't see any of my fellow banditos ready to make a break, but I did notice Jack staring at me. He probably wondered where I was going with Rafael, and why. *Me, too.*

We walked out of the courtyard to Rafael's truck, or, rather, the confiscated truck he was using. It had California license plates. The soldiers hopped into the bed and we drove away. Rafael explained that he had forgotten to have me sign a document during my formal declaration.

Through my window, I looked at sidewalks illuminated by

streetlights. People strolled and gazed into storefront displays. A woman with serapes draped over her left shoulder talked to a man and woman eating at a sidewalk restaurant. I'm not a big fan of street vendors, but I wouldn't have minded being in that couple's shoes. I'd buy all the serapes the woman had.

"You are not like the others," Rafael said to me in English.

"What others?"

"The other gringos in the jail."

"I am the same as them."

"They are basura (*trash*). You are not."

Why was he saying this? Was he being a snake?

At a stoplight, I looked down the cross street to a small park with trees. In the dusk of a streetlight, two guys with long hair sat on a bench. The end of a cigarette glowed for a few seconds, then floated to the other person. Did they know how uncool that was?

"No son sus compañeros. They are Mejicanos," Rafael said.

I didn't reply.

"What do you think of Susan?" he asked as we drove from the intersection.

"I don't know her," I answered. "I don't know who is who."

"La rubia," said Rafael. "Es la mia."

Rubia means blond, but the term also refers to someone with pale or white skin. In fact, Tyler had told us Rafael's own nickname was El Rubio because his skin was lighter than most Mexicans. Rafael was telling me that Susan was his, just like when he called all our stuff "el mio" during the search at the roadblock. Apparently, everything was his, even an American girl.

"La suya?" I asked. *Yours?*

"Si. I fucked her," he said seriously, then laughed.

"You didn't fuck her," I said.

Did he?

"Si. I fucked her. And you know something?"

"What?"

"American women." He paused. "They are cold in bed."

I turned to him. "You know something?" I paused.

"American women are only cold in bed when they are with Mexican men," I said.

He stopped smiling and stared ahead. Did I cross the line?

"Ahhh, cabron," he burst and slapped me on the back.

The Courier was still parked near the Narcotics Office, and it appeared not to have been disturbed since Jack and I had taken our stuff out of it two nights earlier. Inside the office, a district attorney sat across the desk from me. Rafael sat to my right. The DA asked questions, and an interpreter from the American Embassy translated for me, then relayed my responses to the DA. A young pimply guy in civilian clothes sat at the far end of the table and typed.

During the questioning, Rafael interjected after several of my responses and altered them to sound less incriminating. That was how it seemed anyway. He changed one response to "he rarely buys it" and another to "it is only for personal use," referring to the hash he found in my shirt pocket. He also made sure that the document stated I was responsible for only half of the hash. Was this guy—who had administered the orange soda treatment to Tyler and Kimo—trying to help me?

We finished the declaration, and I followed the DA and Rafael into the courtyard and up metal stairs to another office. Inside, a portly army commandante sat behind a desk facing us. He laid down his miniature comic book, and the three of them talked while I looked up at a poster with photos of various drugs. Raphael removed a pack of cigarettes from his coat pocket and held it out to the DA and commandante. He offered me one, but I didn't accept it or put it behind my ear.

"No, gracias," I said.

"Quiere mota?" *Do you want marijuana?*

"Claro," I answered. *Of course.*

Rafael reached over to a metal filing cabinet where confiscated drugs were probably kept and began to slide a drawer open. He turned to me and laughed along with the DA and fat commandante.

"Pronto," he said. *Soon.* "When you are free."

They talked while I studied a map on the wall showing all the marijuana-growing regions in Mexico. I noticed the road from Oaxaca to Veracruz that Jack and I had planned to take. When we were released, we would most likely head home the quickest way—up the central plateau. What would we do with the kilos in the back? Toss them? There was no way we could complete the run.

On the drive back to the jail, Rafael asked if I wanted a beer. I answered yes, but only if I could take some back to my friends in the cell. He laughed and called me a cabron again. After parking in front of a little grocery store, he opened the glove box and removed the SX-70 camera I had given him, along with a cartridge of film that had undoubtedly once been mine.

"Amigo, will you show me how to replace the film?"

He handed me the camera, and I pressed a button in the front to unlock a door at the bottom. When the door swung open, I removed the used film cartridge and inserted the new one. I shut the door, and a motor activated and ejected the film's cardboard cover. I handed the camera back to Rafael. He smiled.

"Muy bueno. Gracias, amigo."

Yes. We are good friends.

He disappeared into the store and left me alone in the truck. I hadn't seen our two soldier chaperones since we went up the stairs at the Narcotics Office. I thought about making a break, then considered someone might be watching. It seemed too easy. It could be a trap. And if I did manage to escape, what would they do to Jack?

Rafael walked out of the store with a six-pack of Pilsner and got in the driver's seat.

"For you and your amigos," he said as he handed me the six-pack.

"Gracias."

"It is just one night. Tomorrow you will be free," he said and slapped me on the back again.

As we drove off, a car pulled away from the opposite side of the street and followed us. When Rafael parked in front of the jail, the car stopped nearby, and the two soldiers got out of the back. Had Rafael been testing me?

At the courtyard entrance, a police clerk stopped us and said I was not permitted to take alcohol into the jail. Rafael seemed surprised. He tried to persuade the clerk to let me take the beer inside, but apparently even a judiciale's power has limits. I was allowed to finish my beer and even chug another one as my jailmates watched through the bars.

Jack and I slept on the cement floor with only our jackets against the cold. During the night, street noise and cellmate noise interrupted my sleep, but the rats only woke me when their whiskers tickled my cheeks and lips.

Feb 4

This morning, a lawyer named Enrique Jimenez Ruiz approached our cell and offered to help me and Jack. We had already learned of his good reputation, and that he sometimes acted as a public defender. Kimo, Tyler and the girls had hired him. Enrique told us he had looked into our case and that we would not be getting out soon.

"The federal agents said we would be released today," I told him. "We're allowed to have hash for personal use."

"Even when you are declared addictos, it will take many days for freedom," he said. "And you do not have an appointment with the doctor yet. To be declared addictos marijuanos, you must go to the Centro de Salud, the Health Center. Nurses or doctors will ask questions and test you."

"Test us?" I asked.

"Don't worry," Enrique said. "You will not fail."

Enrique said his fee would be $1,000 for both of us, and we could think about it. He'd be back after lunch.

When Rafael didn't show by late afternoon to set us free, Jack and I began to believe Enrique. When he returned, we hired him. Enrique immediately obtained authorization for us to make a phone call. Guards escorted me to a small room where I called my parents in Houston. My father was at his law office, so I explained to my mother that I had gotten in a car wreck and needed $1,000 for repairs. She said she would have my father send it right away. Enrique requested the money be wired to him, but we compromised and had it sent to me in care of Enrique.

Feb 5

I slept better the second night because I was more tired, but also because Jack had come up with a solution for our rat-somnia. The rodents were entering the cell from the courtyard, so Jack put food scraps on the other side of the bars. They dined on the outside while we slept rat-free on the inside.

When Enrique returned in the afternoon, he informed Jack and me that we had been declared contrabandistas internacionales—international smugglers. *What*? He said we had confessed to smuggling hash into Mexico from the United States. *That didn't go as planned.* However, the charge would be removed after the doctor confirmed our addicto status. Enrique told us Tyler, Kimo and the girls had an appointment for addicto tests tomorrow, and that Jack and I would tag along.

Feb 6

After another rat-free night, the eight of us were ushered into a van bound for the Centro de Salud. We wore no handcuffs or other restraints. No one had changed clothes or showered for several days, but nobody seemed to notice. We were all upbeat about being declared marijuana addicts because freedom would soon follow.

Benches ran along the van's sides in the back, and I sat across from Susan. She said she was from Syracuse in upstate New York, and I told her I only knew New York from movies and television shows. Susan described the rivers with boulders and waterfalls where everyone hung out on the weekends, and told me people actually surfed on Lake Ontario. I was surprised so much nature existed in New York. Her brown hair was parted in the middle and fell straight and simple past her shoulders. Freckles spotted her pale face, and she looked cute in a wholesome country girl way. There was no way Rafael fucked her.

At the Centro de Salud, our group climbed an outside stairway and entered a large sterile-looking room with white walls. Four metal desks occupied the back left corner, but only one had a nurse sitting behind it. The room had apparently been reserved just for us criminal addictos. A row of 1950s-style chairs with chrome frames and green plastic upholstery ran along the back wall on the right. We sat down in them and waited for the nurse to call our names. A guard remained near the door in case we tried any funny business.

When my turn came, I sat at the side of the desk while the nurse in a blue uniform and matching bonnet asked questions.

"How long have you been taking marijuana?" she asked.

"Since I was ten years old." (Not really.)

"How long has it been since you last smoked marijuana?"

"A week." (Really.)

While the nurse wrote down my answers, I acted a little jittery and nervous—how I imagined she thought an addict might feel when deprived of marijuana or hash. After the questions, she asked me to walk a twenty-foot straight line of masking tape on the linoleum floor. I almost lost my balance a couple of times, but I didn't want to overdo it.

When we returned to the van, Jack and I were briefly out of the guards' sight while they walked around to the driver's side. We whispered about making a break but decided not to risk it. We'd be getting out as soon as our addicto papers went through.

In the afternoon, the girls were escorted from their cell, across the courtyard and through the exit. Susan looked back and gave me a thumbs-up. Two hours later, they reappeared in the courtyard. All four had been cut loose; released. Tyler, Kimo and Jack talked with the other three girls while Susan and I had our own conversation off to the side. Shortly after the girls departed, two guards came for Tyler and Kimo.

"We'll be back later and tell you how it went if we have time," Tyler said as they left. "Otherwise, we'll come tomorrow. And bring you something to eat."

Jack and I were happy for them, and for us too, because we were next in line.

When Tyler and Kimo didn't return, Jack and I considered it a good omen until Enrique came and informed us they were in the state penitentiary.

"What about their addicto status?" I asked.

"Do not worry. I will help them go free, and you too," he answered.

CHAPTER THIRTEEN

Kilos

Feb 7

I sat up. My back ached. Most of the other jailbirds were already awake and talking. Some drank coffee; some spooned avena from metal bowls. Jack was still asleep on the cement a few feet away. He and I had no one to bring us food from the outside, so the watery oatmeal would be our breakfast too. Last night, we dined on rice and beans. So did the rats.

Mid-morning, a guard approached and pointed to Jack and me. Two guards led us across the courtyard and into the back of a windowless van. Our trip to the courtroom would result in either freedom or a reunion with Tyler and Kimo in the state penitentiary.

Instead, the van door opened in front of the same Oficina de Narcoticos where Jack and I had made our declarations. When we entered the building, one guard directed Jack through a door on the right, and the other took me up a stairway and into an empty room. I sat in a folding metal chair against the wall and waited.

Thirty minutes later, my guard and I went back down the stairs as Jack climbed up with his escort. He and I exchanged glances as we passed, but his eyes were glazed, and it appeared that I hadn't even registered with him. The guard followed me into the room and shut the door. Rafael and Carlos Garcia sat behind the familiar long table. Rafael gestured for me to sit.

"Mucho problema," Rafael said and shook his head, obviously upset.

I maintained eye contact and waited to hear about the big problem.

"Mira," he said. *Look*, and he pointed behind me. I swiveled to the left and saw our eight kilos of lime-green flower tops lined up against the wall. My eyes focused on the weed, but I was stalling while I thought.

"Que es esa?" I asked after I turned back. *What is that?*

Rafael shook his head. Garcia stared at me. Neither appeared happy.

"It is your marijuana," Rafael answered. "From inside your truck."

I stared back at them.

Garcia removed a small glass vial from the desk drawer and placed it upright on the desktop with a loud tap.

"También cocaina."

I had forgotten about the coke. There was only enough for two hits in the vial.

"Eight kilos of marijuana," Garcia said in Spanish. "And one-tenth of a gram of cocaina discovered in the glove box of your truck."

It was in the glove box, and they didn't find it for a week? Jack and I weren't the only ones who were sloppy.

"Your compañero confessed that the marijuana is both of yours, but that the cocaina is only his," said Rafael.

It was good of Jack to take the blame for the coke, but why did he admit to anything? Had Rafael and Carlos used the orange soda method on him? How could I be sure Jack confessed. I couldn't trust Rafael. He was a snake. I shook my head.

"It is not ours," I said.

Of course they wouldn't believe me, but I had rights, didn't I? While I argued for a lawyer for twenty minutes, Rafael kept telling me it was useless and for me to confess.

Useless?

"It will be better for both of you," he said.

He told me that if I admitted the eight kilos were mine as well as Jack's, we would split the guilt and be deported. If I did not confess, the consequences for both of us would be much worse. I wasn't convinced Jack had confessed.

Rafael opened a law book and pointed out two paragraphs to prove what he said was true. I read the first one slowly and understood that persons found with an illegal substance would be charged with possession of equal shares. I remembered that during my "formal" declaration, Rafael made sure they wrote down I was responsible for only half the hash, so the legal passage was believable. He turned to another page and showed me a paragraph stating that deportation would occur for persons convicted of possession of fewer than five kilos. It would have been good to hear an interpreter's translation, but I really couldn't trust an interpreter. The last time I did, I ended up a narcotraficante internacional of hashish.

Rafael told me that my alternative would be to present my case while inside the penitentiary. I opted for deportation with Jack and signed the confession. Rafael pointed to our sleeping bags and backpacks against the wall near the kilos, and told me we could take them to the jail. Jack and I didn't talk on the drive back because a guard sat nearby. I wanted to know if the agents had forced him to confess.

"What happened with Rafael?" I asked once we were back in jail.

Jack's eyes glazed again.

"When I saw the pot, my heart fell to my stomach," he said. "I knew we had just entered hell. My heart was pumping so fast I couldn't think. I was fucking scared."

He paused, then continued.

"I remembered that as soon as we got busted, you said, 'If they find the weed, we say we bought it from a guy on the beach in Salina Cruz, that's the story—to keep the heat off the Indians.' That's what I told them."

"You're right. That's what I said."

Rafael had told Jack the same thing about splitting the guilt and being deported, but Jack said no one had shown him any law book passages.

Jack's confession threw me off, but when I thought about it, he had probably saved us from the torture our compañeros had experienced. And I'm not a fan of pain. I sat on the bench and looked inside my returned backpack. Inside were clothes, shampoo, a toothbrush, photos, paperbacks and my Piper Flite Manual. And we now have our sleeping bags to cushion the cement.

Feb 8

This morning, we were allowed to use the phone again. Up until now, Jack and I hadn't thought we needed help from the outside. We expected to be free as soon as our addicto status was confirmed. Discovery of the kilos changed matters.

I considered calling my parents again. My father's law practice is just a one-man, retired naval officer operation, but he's smart and might be able to help. However, he hasn't gotten over my quitting college, and I didn't think my current situation would impress him. I telephoned William instead. He said he'd come to the jail in the afternoon. When I returned to the cell, Tony and his Zapotec friend, Nosario, were gone—presumably to a hearing.

Susan arrived in the afternoon and brought chicken empanadas and other pastries. She confirmed that Tyler and Kimo were in the penitentiary south of Oaxaca near Tlacolula. The other girls were there visiting.

When I told Susan about the police finding the kilos in our truck, she just stared at me. Jack and I hadn't mentioned the hidden weed to anyone, of course. I explained that we were going to be deported. She hung out for a while, and we held hands and kissed when the guards weren't watching.

An hour later, William arrived with a young, skinny guy wearing a suit way too big for him.

"Why did you not take the bypass?" were William's first words—words I didn't need to hear.

His pale friend was a lawyer named Arturo, who told us he had already learned which judge was handling our case. He said he and the judge had a good relationship, which was important. If we wanted, Arturo would review the charges and our declarations.

Jack and I liked Enrique, but Tyler and Kimo's incarceration in the state penitentiary didn't instill us with confidence. I trusted William, and Arturo sounded like he knew what he was talking about. We signed a document naming Arturo as our lawyer and agreed to pay 10,500 pesos [$840] for our defense.

Tony and Nosario did not return from their hearing or wherever they were taken. We suspect they are now in the state penitentiary.

Feb 9

When Enrique showed up this morning, we handed him 1,300 pesos [$104] and told him we had hired Arturo. He said he already knew we switched to Arturo because he had run into him at the courthouse. Enrique didn't seem upset with us. As a matter of fact, he informed us we would be going before the judge tomorrow.

"I am no longer your lawyer, but let me give you some advice," he said. "Do not admit to anything. Deny everything. Your truck was parked on the street one week before they discovered the marijuana. Any person may have tampered with it, even the police."

"Why would they do that?" Jack asked.

"That is not important. Perhaps to keep the truck and the things inside. It would not be the first time. More important is that when the police searched your truck at the roadblock, they found nothing. The documents even declare the police removed the panels. They found the marijuana a week after. Your confessions, however, will make complications."

"But if we deny the kilos are ours, will that affect our deportation?" I asked.

"Deportation? Who said you will be deported?"

I told Enrique about the legal passages Rafael had shown me.

"That is not true. Persons caught with marijuana are not deported. I am advising you so the entire case will be dropped here in Mexico," he said. "You must tell the judge the marijuana is not yours, and you know nothing about it. Tell him they made you confess."

"What is the sentence for someone convicted of eight kilos?" I asked.

"The minimum time for that amount of marijuana is five years, three months. There is no lesser punishment. An addict is permitted to have in his possession only fifty-six grams. But if the judge decides against you, there can be an appeal."

I held the bars in both hands and watched Enrique disappear through the archway. Five years, three months. I left college to live. Five years in a Mexican prison wasn't living. Suddenly, I felt heavy—dragged down. Instead of flying through mountain passes, I'd be looking out from the inside of a Mexican prison. I stared through the bars and focused on nothing, my life.

Feb 10

Guards arrived before noon and told Jack and me to bring our things. We were driven across town and deposited inside a courtroom where a judge in a black robe sat at a raised pulpit in the front. Jack and I stood behind a short wooden fence with an interpreter and typist to our left.

The judge spoke Spanish, and his questions were translated into English for us. When we were asked to confirm our confessions of two days prior, Jack and I denied any knowledge of the kilos. The judge asked me how the marijuana had gotten inside the panels of our truck.

"I don't know," I answered. "The truck was searched thoroughly at the checkpoint and they found nothing. Maybe the policia put the kilos there later."

It appeared the judge understood English because he started taking notes before the Spanish translation began. He asked me why I had confessed to possession of the marijuana, and I told him I had been coerced.

"In what manner were you coerced?" he asked.

After I explained about the orange soda treatment, the judge scanned the room. I had already noticed that neither Rafael nor his partner was in attendance. He asked Jack the same questions, and Jack corroborated the story. The judge seemed to be genuinely concerned with our plight. When it was over, we thanked his honor, and I left the hearing with a good feeling. The guards walked us to the van, and we were driven straight to the Oaxaca State Penitentiary.

*

Jack and I stepped out of the van and stood before a high cement wall with towers at both ends. Brown, barren land surrounded the prison, and mountains stretched along the horizon. An immense metal door replaced a section of wall at the right end. Within that door was a smaller door, and Jack and I were escorted through it. We walked twenty feet along a covered walkway and came to a tall gate of vertical steel bars.

A guard searched my backpack and Jack's duffel bag, then unrolled our sleeping bags and felt all around the padding. The gate opened, and the guard told us to wait inside for our cell assignment. Jack and I passed through, and the gate shut.

Inside was not the Mexican penitentiary I had imagined. Jack and I stood at the front corner of a big, sunny courtyard. Straight ahead, in the center of the yard, inmates played volleyball. Near the back wall, smoke rose from small concession stands. I smelled food cooking. It smelled good. People waited in lines in front of the food stands. Others stood nearby, holding plates and eating. More inmates sat on wooden benches set along the perimeter of the yard.

To the left of the food stands, four people played basketball on a half court. Behind them, mountaintops poked above the back wall. Across the yard in front of us, a two-story building ran most of the length of the courtyard. Behind us, another long building lined the other side of the yard. I heard a constant drumming and scanned the courtyard for its source. In the very back, to the left of the basketball game, men sat on chairs and pounded something between their knees. The sound and rhythm reminded me of the African war drums in Tarzan movies.

"Hey, Jack. Hey, Steve."

Tony walked toward us along the front of the courtyard.

"Welcome to the peni. We're in that dorm on the second floor."

He turned and pointed to the building across the yard. Two rows of windows lined its plain facade; one row halfway up, and another row just below the roof overhang. I looked back at the other long building behind us, and saw they were identical.

"Robert has a corner room at the end of the hall by himself. You guys are across from him. I'm about halfway down. Me and Nosario."

"You call them dorms?" I asked.

"Yep. Come on. Your room isn't ready yet. Someone is moving out but you can meet Robert. He's from New York City. He's a heavy dude. I told him you guys were cool."

I wondered what Tony meant by "heavy dude."

"How did you know we were coming?" Jack asked.

"I told Robert your story, and he said you'd most likely be arriving soon. He talked to the guy in charge of room assignments and got you a room with us. We didn't know when you'd get here exactly."

Tony seemed like a different person—upbeat, revitalized. Jack and I picked up our stuff and followed him across the yard. We climbed the wide cement steps at the front end of the building and entered the upper dorm through a metal door held open with a padlock at the top. A long hallway extended in front, and a shorter one ran ninety degrees to our right. As we continued straight ahead, Tony pointed to a bathroom on the left. Through a wide, door-less opening, I saw several sinks and the beginning of a line of toilets. The toilets had no seats or partitions, but they would be an improvement over the facilities in our jail cell.

On both sides of the hall, doors were spaced every ten feet

or so. The hallway's walls were only six feet high, and I looked above them to the building's perimeter walls and high ceiling. Fluorescent lights hung from above, but most of the light was coming in through the high glass windows facing the courtyard. The rooms on our left were against the other side wall of the building. Above those rooms, a row of smaller, open-air windows with two vertical bars stretched the length of the dorm.

"There are three more halls to the right with rooms on both sides," Tony said as he pointed toward the courtyard windows.

Tony's cell was halfway down the corridor on the right. Its door opened onto a four-foot floor space separating two narrow beds along each side wall. The head and side of the beds' metal frames were mounted into the cement walls, and thin mattresses with blankets lay on top of each. Their belongings were stowed underneath. Between the beds, a piece of plywood sat atop a wooden crate—their nightstand. The room had no ceiling. I could have looked into the adjacent cells by standing on my toes.

"You have to buy your own mattresses, but I know where you can get a couple," Tony told us.

We continued to Robert's cubicle, the last one on the left at the back corner of the building. Tony pointed to a door across the hall.

"That's your room," he said.

Our cell was second to last on the right. The door was ajar, and I saw someone placing things into a basket. Tony knocked on Robert's door, and a voice said to come in. Tony pushed the door open, and an older guy about thirty years old with curly brown hair sat flossing his teeth on a bed against the back wall.

"Robert," he said and put down the floss. We shook hands.

Jack and I sat on small chairs, and Tony sat down on the edge of the bed. Led Zeppelin played from a boom box on a nightstand. Snapshots of a woman holding a baby decorated the wall at the foot of the bed. I looked up at the barred window directly above Robert.

"How about a smoke," he said.

Before Jack or I could tell him we didn't smoke, Robert

opened a box containing pot and cigarette papers. I looked at Jack and saw him smile for the first time in a while—like me.

"It's pretty good stuff for the peni," Robert said as he rolled a joint. "Tony told me they charged you guys with eight kilos."

Jack answered, "Well, they got us first for less than two ounces of hash. They didn't find the kilos until a week later."

"That's a good thing," Robert said.

Robert lit the joint with a match and handed it to me. The smoke soaked into my blood and instantly relaxed me. Maybe the Centro de Salud was onto something about us being addictos.

While we waited for our room, Robert told us he and his wife Janet had been caught with 400 pounds of weed. They had hand-pressed the flower tops into bread-loaf-size bricks and hid them behind a fake floor and wall of their truck's camper. Janet was pregnant at the time, and the feds held her a few days before releasing her. That was eight months ago and the baby is now five months old. Robert said Janet and the baby are living in Oaxaca while she oversees his appeal.

After we smoked another joint, someone tapped on the door and said our room was ready. When I stood, I had to hold on to the doorjamb to keep my balance. Was Robert's pot that good? Or was I that tired?

We crossed the hall and entered our modest eight- by ten-foot new home. Jack dropped his sleeping bag and duffel on the wire mesh of the bunk to the right, and I put my stuff on the left. We both sat down. I didn't feel too bad. The despair that had swept over me in jail yesterday had faded. Maybe I was getting used to the loss of freedom, or it may have had something to do with more space and sunlight in the penitentiary. Or maybe the weed put me in a good mood.

If the judge dismisses the kilos, only the charges of the hash and one-tenth gram of cocaine will remain. Our confirmed marijuana addiction will void the hash charge, and the coke should disappear since the police discovered it a week after the initial search, like the weed. Freedom is within grasp.

Tony came into our room. "Let's go to the courtyard. I'll

give you the tour."

"There's no lock on our door," said Jack.

"No one has locks," Tony answered. "Robert says we don't have to worry about thieves. A thief is as bad as a snitch in here."

We walked down the steps, and Tony pointed to the volleyball game in the middle of the yard on our left.

"There's Tyler," he said.

Tyler stood at the front of the net and gave us a quick wave. His teammates were three other gringos. Their opponents were four Mexicans.

"His dorm is the one below ours," said Tony.

"Where's Kimo?" I asked.

"Kimo was cut loose this morning."

"Really? That's good news."

"Sure is."

We continued along the front of the courtyard where high vertical bars separated the yard from an area on the other side.

"That's the sala de la visita, the visiting area," Tony said.

The tall steel bars were embedded into a three-foot cement wall that ran across the front of the yard and ended behind a dilapidated Coca-Cola stand at the far right, close to our dorm. The visitors' section behind the low wall and bars extended fifteen feet to a windowless building. A wide counter capped the short wall, and people sat on both sides. A woman in the visitors' area pushed a basket through an opening in the bars, and a prisoner sitting on our side reached in and removed a tamale. Children played behind them.

"Visiting hours are from 8:30 to 10:30 in the morning and 1:30 to 3:30 in the afternoon," Tony said. "On Saturday afternoons, wives and families come in and spend the night."

"Spend the night inside the prison?" I asked.

"Wives, girlfriends, kids; they all stay Saturday night. Robert said Janet and the baby usually come."

We continued to the dormitory opposite the yard from ours, then made our way toward the back wall. I glanced around and was happy to see that no one appeared interested in the new gringos. In front of one of the food stands at the back corner, an inmate stood eating a small pizza. Inside another stand, a vendor squeezed oranges with a manual press.

"Is this food for sale?" I asked Tony.

"Yep. That's mostly how we eat."

He led us to the black bean soup stand where a Mexican in his early thirties with thick black hair and spooky black eyes stared at us from inside. Tony ordered three bowls of the soup, and Jack paid. The soup came with a miniature French bread called a bolillo.

"That's Reynaldo," Tony said as we walked away to eat. "He stabbed his father."

Three buildings connected at their ends stood close to the back wall. Tony told us they were inmate workshops. The African drum-beating emanated from in front of the workshops. More than a dozen men sat hunched on stools while they swung mallets over their heads. I watched as they banged sheets of leather draped over one-legged wooden supports held upright between their legs.

"They're making soccer balls," Tony said. "It's how they support themselves and their families on the outside."

I looked across the yard to where the front wall stood above the visiting area. It was the same height as the back wall—about twenty feet tall. Only the rear portions of the side walls were visible because of the dorms, and they were the same height.

At each corner of the yard, guard towers rose an additional twenty feet above the walls. Stairs led up to a room at the top, and one guard occupied each tower. The two guards in the front towers sat behind wide openings and looked down into the courtyard with their rifles resting on the window ledge. In one of the back towers, a guard stood without his rifle. The guard in the other back tower was looking behind the prison toward the mountains.

"AK-47s," Jack said.

CHAPTER FOURTEEN

La Casa Grande

Feb 10 (cont'd)

I spread my sleeping bag over the wire mesh of my bunk and lay back in luxury. Afternoon sun entered through the windows across the hall and gave the dorm a surge of warmth. I put down the flight manual and closed my eyes.

"Lista, Lista, Lista," blared from a loudspeaker high on the nearby end wall. Doors opened and shut. People talked and moved through the hall. I looked above our cubicle to the window over Robert's room and saw it was dark outside. Someone knocked on our door.

"Lista, Lista, muchachos," Robert said. "Roll call twice a day, seven in the morning and eight in the evening. Vamonos."

Jack and I followed Robert and everyone else through the corridor and down the steps. He told us the guards had locked the dorm entrance an hour and a half earlier and had re-opened it for evening roll call. We shuffled into one of several parallel rows facing the courtyard. Residents of the dorm below us formed lines to our left, and inmates from the dorms across the yard lined up near their building. Tony showed up almost last and cut through other lines to get to us.

Someone stood in front of our platoon with a clipboard and began reading names. Inmates responded with "Si." The name-caller spoke fast, and I worried I wouldn't recognize my name when he tried to pronounce it. I didn't want to stand out.

Because the sun had set behind our dorm, I knew we were facing east. Jack's name came second to last, and mine was last. We responded with only slight delays. The Spanish versions of our names were becoming familiar. After we filed back up the steps to the dorm, guards locked the door behind us.

We got high in Robert's room while he told us more about life in the peni. He said the prison provides two free cups of avena a day to each prisoner. The Mexican oatmeal is just an emergency or supplemental ration and would not keep anyone alive for long. Inmates normally purchase their meals at the concession stands or eat food brought in by visitors. The stands sell tamales, bananas, eggs, refritos, mangoes, black bean soup, and more. The pizza I saw earlier had been a grilled corn tortilla with tomato paste and cheese melted on top. On occasion, chorizo or another meat could be added for a peso.

The food concessions are private enterprises, and so is the manufacture of soccer balls. Robert said many inmate-entrepreneurs earn more on the inside than they had on the outside. Prisoners with little or no money perform menial tasks to earn enough to eat: sweeping the courtyard, mopping floors, cleaning bathrooms.

Someone tapped on the door, and Robert nodded to me. I opened it to a skinny, shirtless guy in his mid-twenties. Dark, stringy hair hung to his shoulders, and a black, wiry beard covered his lower face and continued down into two pirate-like points. I closed the door as he sat down on the bed between Robert and Tony.

"Hey," he said. "The new guys." He grinned and pointed his thumb to his chest. "Scorpio."

Jack and I introduced ourselves, and Robert rolled another joint. I had seen Scorpio walking across the yard earlier, shirtless and swinging his arms all around. I figured he was a crazy Mexican. Now I considered that his arm-swinging routine might come in handy for getting people not to mess with you.

The police busted Scorpio with a few ounces of weed in Oaxaca, and he is waiting for his appeal. All judicial decisions are apparently made in Puebla, a major city halfway between Veracruz and Mexico City. After we finished smoking the joint, Scorpio disappeared down the hall.

"Scorp's alright," Robert said. "He got here right after me, but the peni's doing a number on him. They caught him with less than the legal addicto limit but charged him with smuggling. That's what his appeal is about. He gets hardly any money from the outside, so I turn him on now and then and share food that Janet brings. I hope his appeal goes through soon because I don't think he's gonna last."

"Scorpio's been in as long as you? Eight months?" I asked.

"Yep. Almost."

In the jail, Jack and I had heard about an agreement between the U.S. and Mexico to keep all Americans caught with drugs imprisoned in Mexico—part of the Keep America Beautiful campaign, most likely. And every experienced traveler knows that the DEA and American Embassies share the same office in many countries.

Robert put Crosby, Stills and Nash in his boom box and "Suite: Judy Blue Eyes" came through the small speakers. We smoked another joint, and I learned how to play Gin Rummy.

Feb 11

In the morning, "Lista, Lista, Lista" blared again from the loudspeaker above our room and interrupted my best sleep in a week. When the lista part stopped, an enthusiastic voice continued through the speaker with a long spiel beginning with "Those children who have lost their way." I only understood a few words after that. When the admonishment ceased, someone in the dorm started up with his own "Lista, Lista, Lista," accompanied by the ringing of a bell. I opened our door and looked. A short, stout Mexican with a handlebar mustache stood in the hall chanting "Lista" and shaking a small bell. He stopped in mid-ring and grinned at me, then began walking toward our room. I shut the door.

Everyone lined up in the yard again and listened for their names. Prison officials apparently wanted to make sure no one had died or escaped during the night. As we waited, the sun rose above the dormitory across the yard. Jack's name came early, and mine was called close to the end but not last. Our names had been placed into the alphabetical order. We were part of the family.

After lista, I decided to take a shower since my last one had been at the military quartel over a week ago. With a bar of soap and shampoo, I walked down the steps, then back along the front of our dorm to the shower room. Instead of actual showers, several of us stood in one large room and bathed by emptying buckets of cold water over our heads—ice-cold water that had to have come straight from the mountains. Although in shock, I felt like a new man.

The morning sun warmed the courtyard, and I walked across to the concession stands in the back corner. A glass of fresh orange juice cost three pesos (24 cents). I sat down at one of the benches along the yard's perimeter and enjoyed the peace. Volleyball and basketball had not yet commenced, nor had the soccer ball war drums. A Mexican sat at the opposite end of my bench. He nodded to me and sipped his own orange juice. Afterward, I walked to another stand and bought a plate of huevos revueltos Mexicana with tomatoes, peppers and onions. Not bad. I finished as Jack and Tyler walked over.

"Lynette and the girls are coming at one thirty," said Jack.

"They visit almost every day," Tyler said. "And they bring food. You're both invited. Susan usually comes."

But only Lynette and Erica showed up. From the other side of the bars, Lynette spread out corn tortillas topped with sliced tomatoes, avocados, peppers and string cheese. Tyler, Jack, Tony and I sat on stools anchored into the courtyard's asphalt and dined. Erica told us Kimo and Buffy were flying back to the States tomorrow, but that Kimo would return if Tyler started getting the runaround. Lynette said she expected to hear from Puebla soon regarding Tyler's case.

Feb 12

Just before noon today, Jack and I heard our names called over the loudspeaker, then "Visita, visita, a la sala de visita." We looked at each other. Robert knocked on our door and said someone was waiting for us in the visitors' area. We walked down and found Arturo standing on the other side of the bars, smiling.

"The charges of the eight kilograms of marijuana are removed," he told us.

Did I hear right?

Arturo continued, "But the charges of the hashish and the cocaina remain. It is not a problem with the hashish. It will be dismissed because the court has declared you addictos."

"If they dropped the marijuana, why didn't they drop the cocaine?" Jack asked. "It was discovered a week after the initial search, like the kilos."

Arturo shrugged his narrow shoulders.

"I will learn. Do not worry. The marijuana is the more important thing."

That was right. No more kilos. What a relief.

Lynette and Erica came to visit in the afternoon, and Susan was with them. She and I sat together, and I explained how we had told the judge we knew nothing about the weed in the truck's paneling, and he must have believed us because the eight kilos had been dropped. We held hands, and I told her I didn't know when we'd be released—that it seemed everything hinged on a measly one-tenth of a gram of coke.

Susan said she planned to stay in Oaxaca with Lynette and Erica at least until Tyler was free, which would be in about a week. We kissed between the bars, and I felt pretty good when I returned to the room.

Feb 13

As I lay reading on my bunk this afternoon, the loudspeaker broadcast only my name, followed by words I did not recognize. Robert and Jack had both gone to the yard, so I walked down the steps and looked inside the visiting area. I didn't recognize anyone, so I continued to the prison entrance. A guard asked my name, then escorted me through a door near the gate. We walked past the telephone booths, and he left me in the middle of a hall. There was an open window to my left. I turned to it and came face to face with my father.

He stood neat and formal in his sports coat and tie. I looked at him, waiting to hear something like, "So this is what you quit college for."

Instead, he simply said, "You bastard."

Why had he come, and how did he know where to find me?

"It's normal not to hear from you for long periods, but we've never had to wire you money before. When your mother and I didn't hear anything afterward, I telephoned the lawyer we sent the money to—Enrique. He told me someone named Arturo was now handling your case and gave me his telephone number." He paused. "Your case. Not a car accident."

I nodded.

"I met with Arturo. We discussed your situation and the eight kilograms of marijuana found in the back of the truck."

"The kilos were dismissed," I said. "The police found them after the truck was parked on the street for a week."

He gave me an impatient look—one I was not unfamiliar with.

"Arturo explained it to me. He said you are still charged with hashish and cocaine. We're going over everything this afternoon, and we'll meet with you and Jack here tomorrow."

He shook my hand through the open window, and I was escorted back to the yard.

Feb 14

At the sala de visita this morning, Arturo hit us all with the news that Jack and I would have to wait a month for our appeal to go through.

"Appeal?" I asked.

"For the cocaine," Arturo said.

"Why didn't you mention this before?"

"It is the normal procedure," he told us. "There must be time for both sides to prepare."

Arturo said he had finished the paperwork for our defense and would mail it to Puebla right away. He and my father agreed to meet again, and Jack and I would talk with them after the weekend. When they left, I walked to my bench in the back corner of the yard and sat down. Jack and I were now stuck in the same situation as Robert and Scorpio—hopefully not for eight months.

*

Conjugal weekend arrived, and the yard filled with women carrying baskets and boxes and babies. Some families sat on benches and the steps to the upper dorms. Others strolled the perimeter of the courtyard as if it were the zocalo in downtown Oaxaca. Niños and niñas held hands with their errant padres. When I returned to the room, I had to work my way through the familial throngs in the corridor. Jack lay on his bed, reading.

"Have you seen what's out there?" I asked.

"Just came back up. There are so many kids and women in the bathroom, I had to wait in line just to take a leak. And someone strung a sheet up to divide the toilets into his and hers."

I flopped down on my luxurious, ten-dollar mattress and stared at the ceiling.

The girls didn't visit today because Lynette planned to come inside the prison and spend the night with Tyler. A half hour before sunset, Jack and I walked down to the food stands. We didn't have to wait in line because most inmates were enjoying home-cooked meals with their families around the courtyard and in their rooms. Jack dined on black bean soup with chili verdes, and I indulged in a tortilla pizza with slices of chorizo.

The black bean soup chef, Reynaldo, isn't friendly with anyone and always seems to be in a bad mood. Robert told us Reynaldo was convicted of stabbing his father, who had lived to testify against him. Reynaldo also tends several rabbit hutches and sells their fur and meat to inmates. Sometimes he makes a special stew. Jack and I once watched him raise a rabbit skull from the broth with his fingers and suck the brains out of it.

That's about when I lost my appetite for black bean soup.

Feb 15

I got very little sleep last night. Weekend conjugalers talked all night, slammed doors and played music from battery-powered radios. Children ran through the halls, and when everything finally eased at midnight, babies cried until dawn. In the morning, the filth and stench in the bathroom were unbearable.

After morning lista, I dragged myself across the empty courtyard for a glass of orange juice and quiet sunshine. At noon I was trying to catch up on my sleep in the room when the annoying, bell-ringing hall monitor knocked on the door and told me that prisoners without visitors were not allowed to be inside the dorm from one to three in the afternoon on Sundays. I returned to my bench in the courtyard and read a little, then played volleyball with Jack and some other gringos. As the last of the visitors dribbled out of the dorm in the late afternoon, I returned to the room and dozed under sunbeams coming in from the windows across the hall.

Feb 16

When Arturo and my father returned this morning, they filled us in on their agreement; $3,000 up front, and $3,000 when Jack and I were free. Arturo will also hold an additional thousand dollars to dole out for our expenses. It should be enough to keep us fed until our papers come back from Puebla and we are released. Arturo exited the sala de visita, and Jack walked away. My father and I faced each other through the bars.

"I left you something that had to go through extra inspections," he said. "The guards said you could collect it anytime."

"Okay. Thanks."

He still appeared neat and clean, and I'm sure I looked scroungy to him. I had no reason to shave, especially with ice water from a bucket. The hair on my face has grown unrestrained for as long as I have been restrained.

We shook hands, and I told him thanks for coming down to

help. He looked me over then said he'd see me in Houston in a month. After he turned toward the exit, I walked beyond the visiting area to a window near the entrance gate. A guard handed me an acoustic guitar and a brown paper bag through the window. Inside the bag were science fiction paperbacks and a classical guitar instruction book. Gripping the guitar by its neck as I walked away imparted a strong memory of how life used to be.

Feb 23

It's been a week since Arturo and my father signed the agreement, and the days have become routine as Jack and I await almighty Puebla's decision. Mornings for me begin with orange juice and early tranquility. During the day, I read, play guitar and stroll the courtyard, talking with new acquaintances. I join in a volleyball game now and then, but often I watch Jack and his gringo team play while I read or write in my notebook. From the top of the dorm steps, I occasionally stare out at the mountains and watch cumulus clouds build in the afternoon and drift toward the prison, sometimes bringing rain.

Prisoners talk about escape all the time, and most ideas involve going over the wall. Jack and I will be released soon, so we listen only out of curiosity. There's also a rumor going around that the U.S. has finalized a prisoner exchange program, and all the gringos will be transferred to prisons in the States. I certainly hope it's just a rumor because I don't want to go to a U.S. prison. Jack and I will be free in less than two weeks. Who knows what the U.S. would do to us?

The girls continue their almost daily pilgrimages, and Jack and I remain grateful participants of their picnics. We contribute money for the food and take leftovers back to our room. While Susan and I talked and kissed a few days ago, she mentioned she would never come inside the prison to spend the night. I didn't expect her to. Susan and I aren't Tyler and Lynette, who have been together for years. Also, our timing is slipping. Tyler will be out any day now, and Jack and I still have another two weeks before our appeal. By then, Tyler and the girls will probably be back in upstate New York. If Susan changed her mind about coming inside, though, I wouldn't object. Yesterday, she gave me a small black-and-white picture of her.

*

Jack and I have encountered no problems whatsoever with any inmates, nor have we seen any violence. Everyone minds their own business. Most of the inmates we've met were busted for petty theft or drugs. A 17-year-old campesino kid is inside because he ran off with the daughter of a well-to-do Mexican who didn't approve. The father got the kid convicted of something, and, without money for defense, he ended up here. His story is not the only one like that.

Murderers, rapists and gun runners live in a separate, maximum security building between the front wall and the visiting area—the exception being Javier (Ha-vee-air), a dapper, gentleman murderer. Javier is friendly with everyone and always travels the courtyard with two quiet buddies. He might be the Godfather of something on the outside—maybe on the inside too. Javier stopped Jack and me in the yard recently to introduce himself and ask about our case. When we told him we were now only charged with the hash and a tiny bit of coke, he assured us we would be out soon. Javier has the best attitude of any murderer I know. His sentence is fourteen years, the standard for murder.

The crazies are housed in another building, but I don't know exactly where it is. I've never seen any of them. Supposedly, they roam the space between the prison buildings and the outside walls during their recess.

Jack and I have met several Americans from other dorms, and new gringos arrive from the jail every few days as if on a production line. Many of those who were here when we checked in have gone free, and Enrique had been the lawyer of several of them.

The gringos are all in their twenties except Tony, who is 18 years old. Tyler is 23; Scorpio, Jessie, Rick, Crombie and George are 25; Apache is 26; I'm 22 and Jack is 23. The three

Houstonians who arrived five days ago are also in their early twenties, and I feel sorry for them. They're not hardened criminals like Jack and me. They had just graduated college and got caught celebrating with a little weed on the beach. They were persuaded to confess their source by the application of an electric cattle prod to their testicles. The police laughed every time they screamed and jumped.

We don't understand why many of our fellow gringos are in the peni. Jack and I were busted for eight kilos, so we understand that. But why haven't the three guys from Houston been released on the addicto marijuana defense? They are certified addicts like almost every gringo busted for a small amount of pot. Why is Tyler still here when his friends were released? We can't even count on our lawyers to tell us the truth. Why hadn't Arturo mentioned the month-long wait for our appeal right away?

Three older 29-year-old gringos reside in the prison. Tall Bob is one of them. We met him when he was delivered to the jail the day before our transfer to the peni. When he arrived here a week after us, he said a young Mexican in the jail had been harassing two Zapotecs minding their own business. Tall Bob, who is 6'4", grabbed the guy by the shoulders and shook him and told him to lay off. When he let go, the Mexican bent himself over the bench at the back wall and pulled his pants down, yelling something to the effect of "punish me." Tall Bob punished him by smashing a mango into his face and smearing it all around.

Ben and Glen are the other two 29-year-old gringos. They live in the lower dorm across the courtyard and appear to be long-time friends. You never see them apart, and they present an interesting sight as they walk the yard together. Ben's height does not match Tall Bob's, but he's taller than the rest of us, and Glen is short and pudgy. Whenever we talk with them, they pause before saying anything and speak reservedly. They meet with a friend every day at the visitors' area and always return to their dorm carrying a basket or two.

The rumor is they're connected to a big smuggling

operation—something in the realm of 1,000 pounds at a time by air. They supposedly have very good pot, although no one we know has been invited to smoke with them—as if we would visit those smug guys just to get stoned. I might.

Ben and Glen seem out of place running drugs, as old as they are. I can relate to searching for life and adventure in your early to mid-twenties and trying to make a few bucks in the process. But I certainly don't plan to be doing it when I'm their age. By thirty, people should have gotten their shit together and have a direction in life. Was smuggling their life's goal? Ben and Glen cast an air of superiority and mystery, but to me, they're losers grasping for something late in life. I vow not to follow in similar footsteps.

Bob Denver and Cat Stevens are Mexicans in their early twenties who live in a room caddy-corner to ours. They are the only gay inmates in our dorm, although we're not absolutely certain they're gay. Those aren't their real names, of course. Bob Denver resembles the actor who starred as Gilligan in *Gilligan's Island,* and his roommate plays guitar and sings—and his favorite song is Cat Stevens' "Moon Shadow." How many times must we listen to "Moon Shadow?" Now we're talking torture. One evening, Jack stood on his bed, glared down into their room and courteously requested that Cat play a different tune or shut the fuck up. Other than "Moon Shadow," our dorm is pretty peaceful during the week.

A Mexican named Machista satisfies our addicto appetite. He lives in the upper dorm across the yard and sells pot in palomas—little triangular envelopes made from newsprint. The packet with the flower tops Dan and I bought in Veracruz a lifetime ago had been a paloma. Machista's palomas contain only enough weed for three meager joints and aren't red-hair sinsemilla, but no one complains.

We're not sure how Machista gets his pot. We heard it might be thrown over the back wall—maybe when a guard is conveniently looking the other way.

For the first couple of weeks on the inside, I felt light-headed after getting high, and sometimes lost my balance. Jack told me he felt the same way. It was like we were drunk. We wondered if someone had soaked the pot in alcohol so it would seem stronger. Or maybe the weed had been sprayed with paraquat while still in the fields. I hate to think what effect that would have on our health. Robert settled the issue by informing us the high altitude was the culprit, and we would soon acclimate. We have, and now I rarely bump into walls.

Except for the filthy bathrooms and crying babies on the weekends, and not taking a shower every day, the peni isn't so bad. Jack and I shouldn't have a problem holding out for two more weeks. In the evenings after lista, we usually meet in Robert's room with Tony and Scorpio to play Gin Rummy.

Feb 25

As Susan and her friends continue to visit, we are all losing steam. The delays in Tyler's case and the forty-minute bus rides to the prison, along with the searches, are draining the girls. It has become painfully clear nothing in Puebla gets resolved in a week or two or three. Puebla is a judicial black hole. Susan and I kiss as usual, but the enthusiasm is waning. You can't just kiss forever—and between bars.

Arturo came to the sala this afternoon and said he had just sent our papers to Puebla.

"You said you were going to send them last week," Jack said, pissed—like me.

"No importa. The papers are ready and will be available when the judge reviews your case. It is on his itinerary."

It may not have been important to Arturo, but it was to Jack and me. Arturo doled out 500 pesos of our expense money, and I returned to the room.

Feb 28

Lynette showed up at the sala de visita alone today and told me that Susan had flown back to New York with Erica. She handed me a note, and I put it in my pocket for later.

Susan wrote she was sorry she didn't tell me in person about leaving. She had only decided the previous night to fly home after Erica convinced her. She included her New York telephone number and told me to call her when I got out.

I pulled my cardboard box from under my bunk and placed the picture Susan had given me inside the folded note. Among other pictures in the box was a snapshot of Sheryl on the beach at Surfside. I've now written her two letters and haven't received anything from her or anyone else, and neither has Jack. I wonder what our friends in Houston are thinking about Jack and me, or if they are thinking anything about us at all.

March 1

Jack and I were sitting on a bench this afternoon when Robert walked over and said he had a special treat. He told us to meet him in his room in fifteen minutes and asked if we'd seen Tyler or Scorpio. We told him no, and he walked away in search of them.

In the room, Robert sat on his bed and dangled a handwritten letter from his fingertips. We all stared at it. Scorpio leaned forward. His long black hair hung down the sides of his face and merged with his pirate beard.

Nobody said anything. Did the letter contain good news?

"Look," Robert said.

The elegant cursive writing was impressive. I can barely read my own.

"Here," Robert said, pointing to several amoeba shapes outlined in ink.

"LSD," he said. "Liquid blotter."

Short phrases with arrows pointed to the dark blotches on the paper: "Take This," "Eat Me," "Lick This."

Robert used a knife to cut enough paper acid to go around. We hung out in his room while Jefferson Airplane played on the boombox, then ventured down the steps to explore an alternative courtyard—a field trip without leaving the premises.

CHAPTER FIFTEEN

Escape

March 4

Jack and I have now been incarcerated for a month and four days. It's easy to keep track of because we got popped on the first day of February. Although Jack and I have lost the all-important *basic* freedom, we rely on lesser freedoms to make us feel we have some control over our lives, like choosing what to eat, when to take a nap, which book to read, whether to play volleyball, not to cut our hair. Freedom gets stretched out. It's relative.

Earlier today, Jack and I were lounging in our room when someone knocked on the door. Jesse and Rick entered—good guys from the upper dorm across the yard. They had never been to our room before. I scooted back against the wall, and they sat down at the ends of our beds.

"How's your case going?" asked Jesse.

Jack answered, "Our appeal is in ten days. So as long as it stays on schedule, we should be out a little after that."

"Is that right?" Rick looked at me.

"Yes," I answered.

It was strange that he wanted my opinion too.

"The kilos got dropped, but what about the cocaine?" he asked.

"According to our lawyer, it's a technicality and the coke should have been dropped with the kilos. He said when the judge gets the new paperwork, it will be dismissed," I said.

"Robert told us to talk to you," Jesse said. He paused. "We're making a break. Do you want to come with us?"

I was stunned. Inmates only talked about escaping.

"When?" Jack asked.

"Soon."

Jack and I expected to vacate the prison legally, but the possibility of an earlier exit made me think. In Mexico, escape from prison is legal as long as no one gets hurt in the process. But the escape isn't complete until the escapee makes it across the border. Any time before that, the hunt was on.

"How're you doing it?" I asked.

"If you're going with us, we'll tell you."

"What about getting to the border?" Jack asked.

"It's taken care of. You'll be included."

I looked at Jack. "What do you think?"

He took off his glasses and rubbed the bridge of his nose.

"We'll be out legally in two weeks. Why chance it?"

I nodded and looked at Jesse and Rick, envisioning them on the outside, going anywhere they wanted and doing whatever they felt like.

"Is Robert going with you?" I asked.

"No, he's gonna wait for his appeal. He said it'll go through in two weeks, like yours."

If Robert's lawyer got his charges dropped, it would be a miracle. It's not like the feds found the 400 pounds of weed after his truck was parked on the street for a week.

"Something else to consider," Rick said. "After we get out, there'll probably be a lot of heat on you guys. We want you to know that."

Jack and I nodded. If that was the cost of freedom for four

gringos, I'm sure we could manage.

"If either of you change your mind about going, tell us soon," said Jesse.

March 7

Another awful night with the screaming, crying kids and babies. I muted the noise by chewing up toilet paper and jamming the wads into my ears. To avoid the crowd in the bathroom, I went in late last night then waited until after this morning's rush hour to go back.

At noon, Arturo gave me and Jack another 500 pesos expense money and told us he had received the Courier's release papers in the mail. He handed the documents through the bars, but we couldn't decipher the Mexican legal jargon. The papers were supposedly part of the process to return the truck to Jack when we are released. Arturo gave Jack a letter from Beth. Nothing for me. Arturo said our chances of getting out in March were good, and he would know the date of our audiencia in the evening.

Our chances were good? Jack and I planned to be free in a week—around the 14th of March.

Arturo explained that an audiencia is when the judge listens to arguments from the defense and prosecution, reviews all documents, then makes a decision. To me, audiencia implies Jack and me in the audience. Apparently, the term loses something in translation. Arturo said he would telephone our parents later and return in the morning with the date of our audiencia.

I bought an orange juice, then sat and watched as families exited the dorms and filled the yard. All the men who used to live in the mountains were wearing clean white shirts and white pants. Their wives wore simple dresses with embroidery. Many of the Mexican inmates had on cowboy hats, and their Sunday shirts and bellies were tucked behind silver belt buckles. Most of the children stayed close to their parents, but some chased each other across the courtyard as if it were a playground. After finishing my orange juice, I removed a notebook from my back pocket and wrote.

Later, as I made my way back to the room, conjugalers crowded the hall. Robert stood at our doorway with Janet next to him, holding their baby. I said hello and squeezed past two Mexican women standing just inside our room. I sat down on my bed and looked up at the women. Who were they and why were they in our room? Friends of Robert? I looked over at Jack sitting on his bunk. He gave me a weird smile. I turned back to the women. They stared at me. I opened my mouth to say hola, and it hit me that they weren't women. They were Jesse and Rick.

"Fuck," I said.

Their shiny red lips grinned. They had on dresses, brown wigs, makeup and mascara. Jesse's beard was gone, and nylons covered their legs.

"We're going now," Jesse said. "Are you sure you don't want to come? There's time. We're going into the sala de visita, and we're gonna walk out with the visitors. Crombie and Apache are going next. You two can go after them. We've got two more wigs."

Wives and families who enter the actual prison yard through the main gate must go through inspections and identification verification before being issued plastic tags which are returned when leaving. But visitors in the sala de visita aren't subject to the same scrutiny. When departing the sala, visitors only file past a guard sitting near the exit.

Jack turned to me. "I told them our audiencia is still happening."

"Jack's right. But I appreciate the offer," I said.

"Okay, good luck," said Jesse.

They were the ones who needed the luck. Jesse and Rick both seemed calm—as if their entire futures weren't going to be determined within minutes. They would require that calm while walking past the guards.

"Buena suerte to you," I said.

"Can you guys do something for us?" asked Jesse. "We need

people to move around the back of the yard to help keep attention off us. No distractions or anything abnormal, just walk around. The guards in the front towers can't see down into the sala de visita, and with all the visitors in the yard, the guards in the back towers shouldn't be paying attention to the sala."

"We filled the sala with friends," Rick said. "Robert and Janet are going to distract the guard at the front of the yard. Only one of the back towers is manned right now, so we're gonna get moving."

Robert listened quietly as Janet rocked the baby in her arms. Jack and I departed for our mission. Near the bottom of the stairs, I looked into the visitors' area on my right. It was definitely packed. Jack and I walked to the back of the yard, and I noticed the Sunday popcorn stand was open. I waited in line, and Jack continued walking. I looked up at the rear towers and saw that one was still unmanned, which wasn't unusual. Three guards still kept watch from the other towers, and one or two guards always roamed the yard.

I caught up with Jack, and we strolled along the back and paused where the soccer ball malleteers usually sat. They had Sundays off. Jack and I alternated glances toward the front. Inside the sala de visita, everything looked normal; visitors and inmates sat on both sides of the bars and picnicked. Several women visitors congregated around the lone guard inside the sala at the left, near the exit.

"Do you know how they're going to do it?" I asked Jack.

"Just that they're going into the visitors' area from near our dorm."

At the bottom of our dorm steps, Robert and his wife talked to a guard in the courtyard as she held their baby. They were positioned so that the guard faced away from the dorm.

I saw rapid movement at the top of the steps. A second later, someone was crouching on the roof of the unused Coke stand. The figure vaulted the upper four feet of the sala's bars and landed on the narrow tin roof above the visitor benches. A second later, he descended into the sala de visita and disappeared in the crowd. It was Jesse. He was the smaller of the two. The visitors and inmates sitting under the roof where he had landed never looked up or behind. Conspirators. The guard inside the sala turned and stared through the bars into the courtyard. I thought he may have heard Jesse land on the roof, but he turned back to the woman he'd been talking to, and she handed him something from her food basket.

"Unfucking real," said Jack. We kept walking.

With quick glances, I watched another figure, stockier, jump from the steps of our dorm onto the roof of the Coke stand, then over the bars. When he landed on the narrow roof, he stumbled. It looked like he was about to go head first into the sala, but he caught his balance and landed on his feet. The crowd immediately engulfed him.

The guard inside the sala de visita walked to the bars and stared into the yard again. This time, he heard something. He looked up at the two towers behind Jack and me, then walked along the bars, studying the courtyard. As he tried to figure out what he had heard, a large group of visitors funneled through the exit behind him. I looked up at the front wall and its two towers and counted off the seconds—one thousand one, one thousand two, one thousand three. At thirty, Jessie and Rick had to have made it out.

The sala guard ended his survey and walked back for another tamale. Oh, man, was he going to be in trouble. There was no indication Jesse and Rick had been caught—no alarm or yelling or lista. Hopefully, they didn't quietly get the shit beat out of them. Jack and I sat on a bench, and I finished my popcorn. Two down, two to go. Robert and family were still engaging the guard near our dorm steps.

"Coke stand," said Jack.

Someone crouched on top of the stand again. Three seconds later, he descended into the sala. Jack and I resumed walking. I glanced up at the rear towers. One was still vacant. I turned in time to see another figure leap onto the Coke stand, over the bars and into the sala in one fluid movement. A few seconds later, another crowd of visitors exited the sala de visita en masse.

Jack and I sat down on a bench. There were no sirens or alarms or gunshots or screams. We waited twenty minutes. They made it. All four.

Surprise Lista

The loudspeaker blared the usual evening lista spiel, but at six o'clock—two hours early. They knew. How did they know so soon? We streamed out the door and lined up in the courtyard—everyone except four gringos. The surprise lista confirmed it.

*

The morning after the breakout, we awoke to a new and not-better peni world. The prison director and everyone working under him were pissed off, to say the least. It didn't help that newspapers in Oaxaca and Puebla and probably Mexico City carried front page headlines about the "Escape from Oaxaca Penitentiary by Four Narcotraficantes Americanos." Visitors smuggled in the papers, and we took them to the dorm and translated them.

Jesse was right about the heat coming down. In the week following the escape, new lights have been installed in the towers, and structures not being used, i.e., the Coke stand, have been demolished. Officials must have somehow figured out how they escaped. And all towers are now manned at all times.

The rules for entering the sala de visita have become harsh. All female visitors, including elderly women and young girls, are now subject to unpleasant body searches by unpleasant women prison employees. Guards examine every item of food entering the prison and visiting area, and, if brought in by a gringo visitor, it often doesn't pass whatever criteria the guards decide for the day. Scrutiny of everyone exiting the visitors' area has become thorough.

An emergency junta supposedly convened in Mexico City to determine whether all gringos should be placed in security cells. I don't know what a security cell is, but I'm sure I'd prefer to keep the room I'm in now.

Male visitors with long hair are prohibited from entering the sala de visita, and all gringo inmates were ordered to cut their hair. Didn't the idiots know the guys who escaped wore wigs? They probably knew and just wanted to punish the gringos.

After the haircut edict, most of us became invisible. Jack and I thought we might make it to our audiencia without having to cut ours, but good old Scorp doesn't always think ahead. He was out walking the yard, swinging his arms all around like they were trying to escape on their own, and the guards began yelling at him. They had always harassed Scorpio, but after the escape, it was no longer friendly harassment. In his endearing manner, Scorpio told them to fuck off and shot them the bird with both hands. The guards held him down on the asphalt and gave him a buzz cut with an electric razor.

Scorp's buzz job reminded me of the baldie haircuts the deputy sheriff in Kingsville gave our surfer friends. Deputy Bubba would be proud of his Mexican counterparts and their successful effort to Keep Mexico Beautiful.

Unfortunately, the loudspeakers eventually demanded all Americanos report to the yard for haircuts. The guards allowed us the option of cutting our own hair or they would use the clippers on us. We were handed scissors, and I cut Jack's shoulder-length hair to a straight block, level with the bottom of his ears. He did the same to mine. It was a pain washing my hair in ice water anyway. A gringo in another dorm was forced to cut his hair even though officials knew he was going to be released the next day. The prison was exacting revenge.

For some reason, the new grooming policy includes beards. Jack didn't have one, but mine had been growing for six weeks. I couldn't allow those fuckers the last word, so I left a Fu Manchu mustache that hung an inch or so below my chin. Jack told me it made me look mean, but I didn't feel mean—just pissed. Scorpio still walks the yard swinging his arms, and now the guards laugh and yell "pinche pelon," which means fucking baldie.

All the Mexican inmates resent the gringos for causing

trouble. We had polluted the atmosphere, affected the status quo, violated the prime directive. But none of us resent the gringo escapees for the new prison sanctions. Our American brothers had beaten them.

CHAPTER SIXTEEN

Kilos Again

March 15

The wives and children of our indigenous dorm mates coughed and sniffled throughout their last sleepover. The following morning, trash bins in the bathroom overflowed with toilet paper smeared with green phlegm. Inmates in the yard have been coughing and hocking loogies onto the asphalt ever since. Flies feast, and I don't want to think about where they land afterward. My sinuses are stuffy, and I have pressure under my eyes.

It's been over a week since the escape, and everyone hates the gringos—especially the guards. And more of them and their rifles now patrol the yard. The break made it tough on them, and they're neither happy nor friendly with the group responsible—los marijuanos, as we're known. The guards no longer greet us with smiles and a "Buenas tardes." They suck their cheap Delicado cigarettes and stare at the gringos with looks that dare us to try something so they can prove who's the boss.

We're not going to try anything. We're peace-loving hippies—just like the four marijuanos who made fools of you.

Tyler was finally cut loose. As much as we will miss him, we'll also miss the picnics and information about the outside world that Lynette provided.

In the yard recently, Javier the murderer walked toward me. I stopped and waited. He might have been mad because of the escape, but he was, after all, Javier. He shook my hand and asked about our appeal and held out his pack of cigarettes. I removed one and put it behind my ear. Scorpio or Tony would appreciate it. I told Javier our audiencia was in a few days, and that we would depart soon after. He never mentioned the break. Later, I saw him talking to Robert, and I wondered if his public cordiality was an attempt to smooth things between the gringos and the Mexicans.

Almost all requests by gringos are now ignored. When Tony experienced stomach pains recently, the guards refused to let him into the infirmary. He continued to pester them until they finally gave in. Two days later, Tony complained to me about blood in his stools. He said the guards wouldn't let him see the doctor again, so I followed him to the front gate and translated his request.

"Hay sangre en su mierda," I said. "El necesita un medico." *There is blood in his shit. He needs a doctor.* I work with the vocabulary I know.

The guard responded by pointing his rifle at my feet and swinging it toward the courtyard. Tony had bothered them enough.

Tony first made himself known to the prison staff when he complained of bedbugs a couple of weeks after he arrived. He came into Robert's room and showed us red marks on his calves and upper arms—bites of some sort. As proof, he held up a small bottle filled with yellow liquid. Immersed in the fluid were half a dozen pale, bloated dead bugs with pincher mouths. A few were almost the size of a mezcal worm. We followed Tony to his room, and he pointed to the broken cement where the bed frames attached to the walls.

"That's where they live," he said.

I thought bedbugs were almost microscopic. And how could bugs the size in his bottle be in those cracks without us seeing them? Tony said the whole dorm needed to be fumigated. I sympathized with him, but no one else was getting bit. Tony marched across the yard and presented his proof to the guards. We figured they would tell him to get lost. Instead, they gave him a spray can of kerosene. Tony coated his walls and bed frame, and that's the last we heard about bedbugs.

One morning after the escape, Tony's name was called several times for lista before he emerged from the dorm wrapped in a blanket. As he walked down the steps, inmates turned to watch. A few whistled. Tony's eyes were half closed when he took his place next to us. He was our dorm mate and fellow American, but he was becoming an embarrassment to the gringos. Everyone else tried to go unnoticed.

At the end of lista, a guard walked to Tony and poked a finger into his shoulder. He told Tony if he was late again, he would be sent to El Toro.

"Una más vez," the guard said. *One more time.*

He held his index finger close to Tony's face while Tony stood silent, wrapped in his blanket like an Indian chief.

It was the first time I had heard anyone threatened with El Toro, the peni's solitary confinement cell. With the guards' animosity toward the gringos, I wondered why Tony hadn't been punished right then. Maybe they cut him some slack because of his age.

Although we believed Tony about his stomach problems, we were growing weary of the scenes he made. Showing up late for lista draped in a blanket was the last straw for Robert. While we played Gin that evening, Robert told Tony he was making it bad for the rest of us, and he better cut the shit out. Tony said it wasn't his fault. He was having trouble waking up because of the Valium he was taking for his stomach pain. *Valium*? Robert asked how he got the Valium, and Tony said from the doctor. He'd only gone to the infirmary once as far as we knew, and that visit lasted fifteen minutes. We were skeptical that the prison doctor would dole out Valium to an inmate, and wondered where Tony really got it.

Since Robert's admonishment, Tony hasn't been late for lista, but he often lines up wearing his blanket-cape. His nickname is now Prince Valium.

Arturo didn't show last week with the date of our audiencia like he said he would. Jack and I figured it had something to do with the prison's stricter visiting procedures. But Arturo didn't make it the next day either. Or the next week. Our first lawyer, Enrique, comes to the sala de visita every few days to talk with his clients. Even though we fired him, he's still friendly. Enrique is the one who told us our audiencia is March 17th, in two days. Finally.

Jack and I are almost out of money. To stretch what little we have, we've only been eating when we're very hungry. I occasionally splurge on my morning orange juice, but we cannot afford huevos rancheros. Instead, Jack and I opt for the more economical rice and refried beans with a corn tortilla. We are ready to be out of here.

March 18

The Zapotecan Mountain Flu has spread through the peni like an apocalypse, and I feel like shit. I cough green phlegm, my nose runs nonstop and I have a fever. There's no need for a thermometer. My head spins, and I sweat one minute and freeze the next. The crazy dreams at night are the only consolation. Tony's cellmate, Nosario, told me this sickness comes to the mountains every year, and that I will be better in a week. Nosario is not sick, and neither is Jack.

Our audiencia supposedly took place in Puebla yesterday, and Jack and I listened all afternoon for our names to be called over the speaker. They never were. Robert reminded us that Arturo had been in Puebla to argue our case and may not have made it back to Oaxaca yet.

Today as I lay in bed trying to ignore my aching sinuses, Jack's name and mine finally came through the speaker. I rose slowly and followed Jack to the visitors' area. We looked for Arturo and instead saw his freckled, pale, red-haired assistant, Luis. He handed Jack an envelope from Beth. Nothing for me.

"Dónde está Arturo?" I asked. Each word banged my skull.

"Está en Puebla, presentando su caso." *He is in Puebla, presenting your case.*

Jack looked up from his letter.

"What about the audiencia? It was yesterday. We had to find out from Enrique," said Jack.

Luis didn't understand a lot of English, but Jack's anger registered. He stared at Jack and me through the bars.

I asked in Spanish, "Why is Arturo presenting our case now? What happened yesterday?" I pulled a rag from the pocket of my blue jeans and wiped my nose. I was dizzy, and my head expanded with each heartbeat.

"Arturo did not agree with the decision of the judge," Luis said in Spanish. "He is in Puebla today to discuss this with him."

"What decision?" Jack asked. He clenched his jaw.

"Arturo will talk to the judge in Puebla," Luis said.

"Que. Decisión," Jack asked again, enunciating each syllable in Spanish.

"The judge did not remove the cocaina," Luis answered meekly.

How was that possible? A pissant tenth of a gram of coke—found a week after the initial search. Yet eight kilos had been dismissed.

"What do you mean?" I asked.

"Arturo says that you will stay here no longer than six months. Possibly less."

"Six months?"

I had been holding out a month and a half for our audiencia—for when the judge was supposed to remove the cocaine—the only charge keeping us in this menagerie. Now Jack and I had to be here another six months? For one-tenth of a gram of coke found illegally? Nothing made sense.

"Arturo will come tomorrow. No later than the next day when he returns from Puebla. I have only the information he told me on the telephone."

Jack spoke slowly in English. "We need our money. Arturo

hasn't come for two weeks. We are broke, and we are hungry."

Even though Luis had watched Arturo hand us money twice, he pretended to have no idea what Jack was talking about.

"Arturo did not tell me anything about money. I do not have any for you," he said.

"What do you mean you don't have our money?" Jack asked. He moved closer to the bars, fists clenched at his sides. Luis backed away.

"We are broke. Comprende? Arturo tiene our fucking dinero. You tell him to get his scrawny ass here tomorrow and bring our money," Jack demanded.

"How many pesos do you have?" I asked Luis. "You can get it back from Arturo."

Luis shook his head and said, "Arturo will come tomorrow. He will bring information on your case and also money. I promise you."

Luis couldn't promise shit. Didn't he just say that Arturo might not return until the day after tomorrow? Luis is a liar like Arturo and probably every lawyer in Mexico.

"Mañana," said Jack, and we walked away.

March 21

The Zapotecan Mountain Flu was the worst flu of my life. I still don't feel great, but I'm pretty sure I'm on the back side. My sleeping bag wasn't drenched when I woke this morning, and my brain didn't pound my skull when I descended the steps for lista.

So far, the Mexican penal system has allowed me to experience fifty consecutive sunrises. Is that a punishment or some sort of religion? The sun always rises into a clear sky, and clouds often build during the day and bring rain to wash away the courtyard's dust and dirt and phlegm.

Arturo didn't come yesterday as Luis promised, and Jack and I have no faith he will come today. The news that we might be here for six months has hit us hard. Jack and I still can't believe it. This is the only time in my life that I remember feeling helpless. We need to do something. Accepting whatever the

Mexican government and our lawyers decide for us is not a desirable reality. I am used to being the creator of my fate, not the victim of it.

*

After my first bucket shower in over a week, I walked across the yard and sat on my bench. The sun beamed its energy across my skin and into my body. I could feel the cells regenerating. Other inmates stood nearby, enjoying fresh orange juice. With no money, I got up and went to the avena stand for my free oatmeal.

In the afternoon, as Enrique talked with a client at the sala de visita, he held up an index finger to me and Jack. We waited, then walked over when his client left.

"Your case," Enrique said. "What do you know about it?"

Jack explained about the cocaine and the possibility of six months. Enrique nodded, then shook his head.

"You are charged with the cocaine because the eight kilos of marijuana still remain against you."

Although he spoke English, I must have misunderstood.

"The kilograms of marijuana were never dismissed," said Enrique. "The documents still declare that you are narcotraficantes of ocho kilos of marijuana."

"They were dropped a month ago," Jack said.

That's right. Enrique must have read an old document.

"Arturo presented a defense that a person could have placed the kilos in the truck after the initial search," Enrique told us. "But when the judge here in Oaxaca reviewed the documents last month, he decided there was not enough evidence to dismiss the charge. He allowed it to go to Puebla for a decision."

"The judge in Oaxaca didn't drop the kilos?" I asked.

"The audiencia in Puebla was to attempt to remove the kilos. The cocaine is only part of it."

None of this made sense. Did Arturo fabricate everything? Why?

"Have we been sentenced?" Jack asked.

"No. No sentence. The judge in Puebla reviewed the

arguments and decided to allow the charges of the prosecution—the same as the judge in Oaxaca. Arturo is now able to appeal."

I shook my head. The pounding returned. Did Arturo screw up or was this part of Mexico's regular, fucked-up legal process? How can we tell what's real and what isn't? We're broke. That's real. And we're trapped in a judicial pinball machine.

Jack and I climbed the steps to our dorm and lay down. We didn't have energy for anything else. Cat Stevens was singing John Denver's "Rocky Mountain High." I picked up my guitar and walked down the hall and around to his cell. He had asked me two weeks ago if he could buy it when we were released. I sold Cat my guitar for 200 pesos [$16]. He handed me his old guitar and said I could play it until he found a buyer.

With our new wealth, I ordered a tortilla pizza, and Jack had a bowl of Reynaldo's black bean soup with chili verdes. The next morning, we feasted on huevos revueltos washed down with fresh-squeezed orange juice.

March 25

It has been two and a half weeks since Arturo last came with news or money. Except for the proceeds from the sale of my guitar, Jack and I have been completely broke for over a week. We exist on two bowls of avena a day, bananas, and occasional handouts from fellow gringos. Keeping our stomachs full of tap water helps us from feeling so hungry. On the plus side, my flu is gone, and I'm coughing up less and less residual phlegm.

Somehow, Prince Valium manages to finagle his way to the telephones more than anyone else. Lately, his being a pest has worked in our favor. Tony called Arturo's office yesterday and asked the secretary to tell him we needed money and information about our case. She said Arturo was in town, and she would relay the message. When visiting hours ended, Tony telephoned again. The secretary said Arturo would be at the prison the next day with our money. He didn't show.

With the runaround and all the lies we've been getting, Jack and I have come to the conclusion that everyone knows we're not getting out of here, including our parents, but no one wants to break the news to us. Robert's appeal has come and gone, and his charge of smuggling 400 pounds of weed remains. His lawyer filed another appeal. The topic of escape has evolved from talk to planning.

Jack, Tony and I met in Robert's room after evening lista to discuss options. Scorpio is too loose a cannon to be included for now. Robert put in a cassette and rolled a joint. He said he had been considering escape ever since he got here.

Approximately twenty feet of dirt known as No Man's Land separates the prison buildings from the twenty-foot-high outside walls. Guards in the towers have the ability to aim their searchlights and AK 47s into almost every area of No Man's Land as well as outside the walls. The lights, however, would not be a concern, Robert said. He'd get to that later.

One plan we talked about is to climb down a rope from a bathroom window, cross to the outside wall, then throw up another rope with angle iron and climb over. To fit through the window, we would need to remove only one of the vertical bars, which could be accomplished while everyone slept. Robert estimated it would take two nights to loosen the cement.

The second idea is a variation of the first. The windows in our dorm are higher than the outside walls. We could attach a cable or rope to one of the bars in the bathroom window and have someone on the outside connect the end to something on the other side of the wall—either a tree or a vehicle. Freedom would then be just a slide away. Securing the cable to a vehicle would be preferable because the car or truck could be parked at a precise spot, and the rope or cable kept taut by positioning the vehicle. Robert's wife has already explored the outside area adjacent our dorm.

"We'll shoot a thin line over the wall from the window," Robert told us. "Someone on the other side will attach a thick rope or cable to the line, and we'll pull it back over the wall and tie the cable to the remaining bar in the window."

A third option is to do the same thing through the window above Robert's bed. If we employ this plan, we need to erect a tent above his room while we loosen the cement around the steel bar. Several rooms in our dorm already have canopy roofs, so another one over Robert's room shouldn't create suspicion for the short-term. Noise during removal of the cement would be our main concern. We'd probably do the work before lights-out and use music from Robert's boom box to mask the sound.

Another possibility (the one we're tending toward) is to tunnel thirty feet under the back wall from one of the workshops near the food stands. The workshops are housed in three separate buildings, which any inmate can use with authorization. When several prisoners work on the same project, they are allowed exclusive use of a workshop. We discussed how to camouflage the tunnel entrance and where to hide the dirt.

Jack reminded Robert to explain why the search lights wouldn't be a concern.

"Thunderstorms," he said. "The electricity goes out sometimes during thunderstorms, right? We'll wait until there's a thunderstorm or heavy rain and shut off electricity to the whole peni."

CHAPTER SEVENTEEN

The Judge

March 27

Other than going down to the courtyard for lista and our two free cups of avena, Jack and I spend most of the time on our beds reading, sleeping and conserving energy. I don't know what I weigh, but I'm skinnier than when I flew back from Costa Rica with jaundice. Jack is just as thin.

After morning lista yesterday, the three Houstonians lent us a hundred pesos ($8). We'll spread that over several days to supplement our avena. Everyone inside depends on someone on the outside for money, and the Houstonians were generous to lend it to us. We didn't ask for it, and we have no idea when we can pay them back. Yesterday afternoon, Tony actually got hold of Arturo on the phone. He said he would come to the prison in the afternoon. He didn't.

On our way back from an oatmeal run this morning, Enrique gestured from the sala de visita. When we sat down, he told us he had looked into our case and that Arturo had done nothing to help us go free. The papers Arturo filed were full of inconsistencies and errors. Enrique spoke with anger and disgust. He said he could file a grievance against Arturo and present it to the judge. Enrique would also explain how Arturo had not given us money or information in over a month.

"You can do that?" I asked.

"Yes. It is a procedure. Not common, but it happens."

"Let's do it," Jack said.

Enrique said he would return after the weekend for our signatures.

This evening, Robert told us he had received permission to use one of the workshops. Robert knows how to get things done, and it doesn't hurt that he is a model prisoner. We're going to tunnel our way out of here.

March 29

Jack sold his green jacket today for six dollars so we could eat. If we're thrifty, we can stretch the money for several days. After that, I don't know what more we have to sell.

Robert told us a friend of his who he calls G.O. had arrived in Oaxaca and was here to help with our escape. Because of G.O., we have switched to the over-the-wall plan. It will take less time to prepare, and less time means less chance of getting caught. Sliding down a cable attached to the window above Robert's room will be our ride to freedom.

This afternoon at the sala, Enrique handed us a document describing Arturo's mishandling of our case. We signed it, and Enrique said he would present the grievance to the judge tomorrow. We are beginning to trust Enrique, but not enough to get fooled again. The grievance won't affect our case, but it might get us our dinero. Before Enrique left, he told us in plain English that Arturo had fucked us good.

In the evening, Robert informed Jack that G.O. had gotten in touch with Beth in Texas, and she said she'd be down in the next few days. Also, G.O. located the peni's main circuit box and plans to test it soon. We aren't ready to go, though, Robert said. Details for our trek to the border still need to be worked out, and we have to come up with leather gloves or straps for sliding down the cable.

Robert asked Jack and me if we would be interested in making a weed run on our way to the States. He said G.O. was talking to their connection in the mountains about getting a big load ready. We told him that we wanted to know more about the plan before deciding.

March 31

When Enrique returned today, he said he had presented the grievance to the judge and explained our situation to him. The judge immediately telephoned Arturo's boss, who said he knew nothing about our money. Then he called Arturo, who denied receiving $3,000 for the case but admitted to having our expense money. The judge ordered Arturo to come to the penitentiary immediately with the money.

Enrique also informed us that the judge would be arriving at the prison in two days for an informal audiencia with many of the prisoners. The meeting would take place inside the prison, and Jack and I were specifically on his agenda.

A judge here on the inside, and an audiencia we would attend?

The judge told Enrique that he expected us to have received our money by then, and was considering summoning Arturo and Luis to the meeting inside the prison so we could discuss the matter together. This was hard to fathom. Or was Enrique feeding us more lawyer bullshit?

April Fool's Day 1976

Jack and I never believed Arturo would come. We were waiting to use the phone to report to the judge's office that Arturo had ignored his orders when Arturo showed his lying ass in the visitors' area. He moped in, hunched over in his wrinkled, over-sized suit, looking like he hadn't slept in days. I was hungry and weak, but his pathetic appearance lifted me.

We sat down on our respective sides of freedom, and Arturo removed a document from his briefcase with no apology or excuse—not that we would have accepted either. He handed the paper through the bars without saying anything. Jack and I turned toward the courtyard and read it slowly. It stated that Arturo only owed us 4,000 pesos expense money, and after receiving the 4,000, we could not claim any more. We turned back around, and Jack slid the document to him.

"Are you crazy?" asked Jack. "We want all our pesos now."

Jack and I had starved for a month. We could last another day—long enough to tell the judge what Arturo was still trying to pull. He owed us 8,000 pesos. We weren't beggars anymore. Apparently, we had a judge on our side. After a lot of arguing, Arturo finally admitted that he owed us 8,000 pesos, but he had told the judge he only owed us 4,000. He needed us to sign the receipt so he wouldn't be disbarred.

We didn't give a shit if he was disbarred. Not only should he be disbarred, he should be locked up in here with no money or food.

We told him we would sign a document saying we had received 4,000 pesos today if it also stated we would receive the other 4,000 within two days. His appearance instantly worsened—as if his inner decrepit self had been lurking just below the surface. He looked like he had been crying all night. We had no pity for his miserable soul. Arturo is a liar and a thief and who knows what else. Jack and I might be narcotraficantes internacionales, but we don't steal and we have never forced anyone to starve in a Mexican prison.

Arturo said he could not write up the document like that. It would end his career because it would appear that he had lied to the judge.

Did he think we didn't understand that?

For two hours, we went back and forth with him pleading for his career and Jack and I refusing to budge. Arturo finally handed us 4,000 pesos without getting our signatures on anything, and he must show up with the other 4,000 before the judge arrives at two o'clock tomorrow. Only then will we sign off that he has paid us in full. Jack and I don't care what total amount is written on the document as long as we receive all our money. We can't eat vengeance, and I have faith that karma will catch up with Arturo sooner than later.

There was also the $3,000 my father had paid him. Arturo argued that he was still our lawyer and had a contract with my father. Jack and I will talk to Enrique about that.

Afterward, Arturo filled us in on our case as if he hadn't just screwed us over for a month and a half. Jack and I were starved for information as well as food, so we listened. He said Luis didn't work for the firm anymore. *Was Arturo trying to blame Luis for everything?* Arturo also confirmed the eight kilos were still on our charges but offered no explanation for his lie about them being dismissed. He said his boss, Jose Morales, had just hired a lawyer who had good vibes with the judge. Arturo suggested we shift our case to this new lawyer. I remembered when we first met Arturo, and he told us that *he* had a good relationship with the judge.

No more money would be needed to finish our case because it was now political, Arturo said. Ten minutes later, he told us he needed money to use politically. Jack and I listened to his bullshit, but we weren't going to be sucked in. He had no letters for us. I haven't received a single letter the entire two months I've been here, and Jack has gotten only two. Arturo closed his briefcase, and Jack and I walked away.

Money! Dinero! Four thousand pesos. Over three hundred dollars. We were on top of the world. Jack and I walked past the volleyball game to the food stands and ate real food. The soccer ball malleteers banged away in celebration.

In the evening, rain pounded the roof, and the dorm lights went out for half a minute. I went across the hall to Robert's room and asked if that had been the electricity test.

"Not that I know of," he answered, but before I closed his door, he said, "I'll check with G.O."

April 2

Beth arrived at the sala de visita today. As she and Jack talked, I watched her lay out tortillas with sliced tomatoes, avocados and peppers. Lynette had always brought string cheese. Robert and Tony joined us.

Beth said she had met with Arturo yesterday, and he started transferring the Courier's title to her, which would take a week. Before she left, Beth slid some pesos to Jack, and he and I carried the meal leftovers to our room. Jack reached into his front pocket, counted the pesos and gave me half. He said the money came from sales of our rainbow weed. Friday was shaping up nicely. Would a judge actually show at two o'clock?

Arturo arrived with the new document, but, unfortunately for him, it was not what we had agreed on. Arturo was still a lying, sniveling perro, and Jack and I didn't waste time arguing with him again. He told us he'd return with an acceptable receipt and our remaining 4,000 pesos within the hour. He didn't.

The time for our meeting with the judge approached, and whether or not it would really happen, I shaved with cold water and put on a shirt with a collar. Jack and I met in the courtyard and walked to the recreation room near the back wall. No announcements for the meeting had been made. Anyone who was supposed to attend knew about it from their lawyer. We made our way through the crowded doorway and stood in the back of the room. Jack and I are both only an inch under six feet tall, but we would have no problem seeing the judge above the inmates standing in front of us.

A few minutes after two, the judge walked through the door and past the crowd to the front of the room. Two guards with rifles followed. He looked different in a sports coat and tie, but I recognized him as the same judge who had asked Jack and me why we had confessed to the eight kilos of marijuana, then sent us here. He laid down a stack of yellow legal pads on the desk.

"Good afternoon, I am Judge Felipe Garcia Martinez," he said in Spanish. "I am here to talk with you about the progress of your cases. I have your names and notes on each case. Please be patient. I will try to answer all your questions."

Judge Martinez looked down at his notepads and called the first name. As he worked through the list, I caught only parts of the conversations in Spanish and became concerned Jack and I wouldn't be able to present our situation accurately.

After an hour, the judge looked up from his notes, directly at me and Jack, and spoke our names. We raised our hands halfway and nodded.

"Has your lawyer brought you your money?" he asked in English. The inmates in front of us turned around to look.

"No," I said. Jack shook his head in agreement.

Arturo had returned a portion of our money but not all of it. We weren't about to cut him any slack.

The judge shook his head. "If your lawyer does not return your money by tomorrow, the next time you converse with him will be here in the penitentiary while he is also an inmate."

The judge told us he could release the truck in a day if the title and registration were translated to Spanish. The Courier seems to have a higher priority than Jack and me. Why would they transfer the truck to Beth before Puebla decides our fate? Wouldn't they keep it if we're convicted?

An hour after our meeting with the judge, Arturo and Luis returned to the sala de visita. Didn't Arturo tell us that Luis no longer worked for the firm? Arturo handed over our other 4,000 pesos, and we signed his receipt.

Beth came to visit again later, and I finally received letters; one from Sheryl and one from my mother. As Beth spread out our picnic, inmates I didn't know hovered about. She began to serve them and I went back up to the room.

In her letter, Sheryl quoted lyrics from "Nights in White Satin" by the Moody Blues and explained how the words related to her situation. "Gazing at people, some hand in hand, just what I'm going through, they can't understand." She also wrote that everyone had told her to forget about me—that I was a lost cause. At least now I know what people in Houston are thinking. But I'm not sure what to think regarding Sheryl's concern about her predicament. I have my own problems to deal with.

My mother wrote that my brother and sister were doing fine, and that everyone expected me back by Easter. She is a typical housewife, and I'm sure my father has shielded her from what is actually happening down here. Inside the envelope were some coins and bills from Costa Rica that she must have found in my room. Thankfully I didn't need money anymore. I smiled.

April 3

Jack and I met with Enrique at the sala in the morning and filled him in on our meeting with the judge. We thanked him for making it happen and asked if it would complicate our case if we switched lawyers. Enrique said it would be better to have no lawyer at all than Arturo, and that he would return with a formal document for us to change lawyers.

In preparation for Beth's sleepover, Jack and I rigged a line between our beds and hung clothes and towels on it. I'm sure Jack and Beth don't plan to have sex while I'm in the room, but it will give them a semblance of privacy. They'll also have the room to themselves during my banishment from the dorm tomorrow afternoon.

After lunch, Jack walked back down to the yard to wait for Beth, and I went with him. Inmates were gathered near the front gate waiting for wives, children, babies and baskets of food. I noticed Robert talking to G.O. at the sala de visita, and he waved us over.

"There's a problem," said Robert. "Ben and Glen are planning a break."

It took a few moments to realize how serious that could be. The next escape would be the last. Subsequent sanctions would be a nightmare. All the gringos could end up in security cells or be shipped to a hardcore prison near Mexico City. We couldn't invite Ben and Glen to come with us, even if we wanted. We're going out Robert's window at night, and they live in another dorm.

"How're they doing it?" asked Jack.

"I don't know, but it's gonna be at night," said G.O.

Jack kept his eye on the front gate for Beth.

"They're the ones who shut off the electricity two nights ago," Robert said, "and they know we're planning an escape."

"How do they know that?" I asked.

"The same reason I know about them," G.O. said. "I was parked on the road to the circuit box, checking out the area like I've been doing, and I saw the prison lights go off. A minute later, Ben and Glen's friends drove past me."

"They saw you for sure?"

"No, not for sure. But I saw them, so they probably saw me."

Jack had disappeared. I looked around and spotted him carrying a basket on his way to the dorm with Beth.

After evening lista, I went across the hall and played cards with Robert, Tony and Scorpio. Tony was also making himself scarce. Nosario's wife and three children had traveled by bus from the mountains to spend the night. Tony's blanket and pillow were piled in a corner.

April 4

Sunday banishment doesn't bother me. I'd rather be in the yard than inside with the kids and crying babies and cigarettes and dirty bathroom. The only time I minded was when I was waylaid by the Zapotecan Mountain Flu. This afternoon, I sat on my bench and soaked up rays while eating popcorn. Three Mexicans were shooting hoops near the workshops. I removed my notebook and pen from my back pocket and placed them beside me.

The distinct silhouettes of Ben and Glen appeared on my left. I ate my popcorn and hoped they would go away. They sat down.

"Hey, Steve," said Ben. He was tall, even when sitting.

"Hey."

"Where's Jack?" asked Glen—as if we were always together like them.

"With his girlfriend."

"Oh, Beth came in?"

"Yep."

Ben and Glen knew about Beth because their friends had talked with her while waiting in line to enter the visitors' area. They had also run into each other in Oaxaca. It was one big happy family on the outside.

Ben looked at his watch. "We can go back to our dorm now. We're gonna get loaded. You wanna join us?"

What? Me get high with you two losers?

"Sure," I said.

I grabbed my notebook and tossed the empty popcorn bag into a trash can.

It was the first time I'd been inside the lower dorm across the yard from our building. The ceiling was not as high, and the only windows faced the courtyard. Their room was identical to ours except for all their stuff. I sat in a chair and put my notebook on a stool. Ben and Glen sat down on their beds, and Ben opened a wooden cigar box and removed a joint.

There had to be a reason they invited me to smoke with them, and it had to have something to do with our escape.

"Your judge came inside to talk to you. Any good news?" asked Ben.

They probably knew all about our case.

"The judge talked to a lot of guys. He seemed to want to help us. We're going to change lawyers," I said.

I didn't care to give them details, but I wanted to be positive enough to throw them off the idea we were planning an escape. We smoked the doobie. The rumors about their pot were true. It was good—very good. Their room was stuffy, though, and I felt claustrophobic with the chairs and boxes and clothes. There was very little free floor space.

"How about your case?" I asked. Prison small talk. I knew they wouldn't tell me anything.

"Another month for our appeal, maybe less."

Yeah, you don't need to escape either.

Ben passed me the joint, and I took a long hit. I coughed. They laughed. I held it out to Glen, and he nodded for me to keep it. I puffed away. Make hay while the sun shines.

We talked about the guards and how the Mexicans' attitude toward the gringos seemed to be softening. The doobie made it around and around and I got fucked up. Glen stood and brushed past me. He looked through some clothes that were piled on top of a cardboard box. When he returned to his bed, he dropped a shirt over my notebook on the stool.

As if I wasn't getting high enough, Ben rolled another joint. The weed was red-hair sinsemilla, and I wondered if it had come from the Zapotecs. Ben stood up and handed the joint to Glen. He lit it while Ben sifted through his clothes, mentioning he had been cold last night. He grabbed a jacket and held it up like he was considering putting it on even though it was warm in the room. He placed the jacket over Glen's shirt on the stool and sat back down on his bed.

I got it. They were getting me stoned because they thought I had written something in my notebook about our escape plans. They wanted me to leave it behind. Now that I solved the mystery, I could enjoy the weed even more.

They each placed another article of clothing on the stool as we smoked a third joint. A foot-high pile of clothes sat atop my notebook. Would getting this stoned affect others enough to make them forget their notebooks?

After the third joint, I decided not to waste my best high in the peni by sitting in a stuffy cubicle, talking with people I didn't want to talk to. I said I needed to go. I stood up and reached under all the clothing for my notebook then walked slowly but not surely down the corridor and out into the courtyard. There were no references to our escape in the notebook. Ben and Glen had wasted a lot of good smoke on me.

The sun was above the west dormitories, and its beams wove between tall cumulus clouds and warmed the bustling courtyard. Through the outside speakers, songs from records that families had brought from home played across the yard. It was not an unpleasant prison Sunday.

CHAPTER EIGHTEEN

You Will Be Free

April 4 (cont'd)

"They're gonna fuck with our break," Robert said when I told him how Ben and Glen got me stoned so they could steal my notebook. "If we go first, it'll be impossible for them to go. They're gonna try to stop us."

He opened his stash box and began rolling a joint.

"They probably think our escape has something to do with the workshop," he added.

Ever since we received permission to use the workshop, we've been hanging out there so we don't lose access to it. Although we scrapped the tunnel idea, we plan to use the tools in the shop to fashion a bow to shoot a line over the wall. And if we can't get good gloves, we'll have to cut leather straps for the slide down.

"If we don't stop 'em, they'll stop us," Robert said.

We discussed planting tools in their room and having someone snitch to their dorm's attendee (the equivalent of our mustachioed, bell-ringing lista reveler). No one wants to put fellow gringos in El Toro, but Ben and Glen are planning a similar strategy against us, most likely.

April 6

Yesterday Enrique brought the request to change lawyers. Jack and I signed.

"I have looked at your case," Enrique told us. "I believe the kilos and cocaine should have been dismissed. What holds you here is your confession to the federal agents. When the court in Puebla schedules another audiencia, the federal agents who arrested you will be requested to testify. They will deny your accusations of torture, but the judge expects this. What is important is that he will ask the agents if they inspected your truck thoroughly at the roadblock. How can they answer without looking bad?"

This morning, Jack's and my names were called over the speaker, and we trudged down to the yard. A guard at the front gate escorted us through the corridor where I had met my father two months earlier. But instead of standing in the hall and talking through the window, a door opened and we entered a room where three people sat at a round table. I only recognized Beth.

A stocky man in a brown suit stood up and shook Jack's hand. It took me several seconds to realize the man was Jack's father. Mr. Cole turned to me and we shook hands. I didn't know what to say. He introduced us to Olga, who sat quietly in a white dress with a matching purse on her lap. She would be Mr. Cole's interpreter and guide during his stay in Oaxaca.

After the introductions, Mr. Cole turned and stared directly at both Jack and me. His smile disappeared.

"I'm here to bring you home," he stated absolutely. "Olga and I are working with a lawyer in Mexico City."

I had met Mr. Cole years earlier in Houston, and I knew him as well as I knew most friends' fathers—brief encounters before we headed to the beach. Jack filled him in on our month without money or food, and Mr. Cole told us he had spoken yesterday with Arturo and his boss, Jose Morales. He said Arturo had sat mute and pale while Morales chewed him out.

When Jack and I returned to the yard, Jack was noticeably happy—not only his smile but in his posture and gait. I could see he believed his father would rescue us. Mr. Cole didn't seem the hero-type to me—with his round face, slicked hair and thick eyeglasses, but he was savvy enough to hire an interpreter right away and had already met with Arturo and his boss.

In the afternoon, Mr. Cole, Olga and Beth came to the sala de visita, and Beth laid food out for Jack and me. They had all eaten earlier at a restaurant in Oaxaca. Mr. Cole said that since Arturo had started the Courier's title transfer, he was going to let the process continue. Why so much attention was focused on the truck while Jack and I remained behind bars still baffled me.

It rained in the evening, and the lights went off for a couple of minutes. Robert came to our room and told us G.O. had successfully tested the peni's circuit box. Freedom is one step closer.

April 7

When Mr. Cole came to visit in the morning, he confirmed that the decision to dismiss the eight kilos rests with the appellate court in Puebla. He also mentioned that he and Olga had talked with the Supreme Court President and Judge Martinez about getting our case on track.

Only one week ago, Jack and I had no money, food, or hope in the Mexican judicial system.

In the afternoon, Jack met with his father and Beth while I stayed in the room and finished two letters. I didn't need to be at every reunion with Jack and his father and once-again girlfriend. After sealing the envelopes, I read until the end of visiting hours, then walked down and handed them to Mr. Cole.

Jack told me later that Judge Martinez had told his father he liked "the boys," and that he couldn't sleep nights thinking about our situation. The judge promised Mr. Cole he would do everything he legally could to free us as soon as possible. He also showed his father our alleged eight kilos, which Mr. Cole referred to as "the junk evidence."

When the judge told Mr. Cole he needed a notarized Texas

title to get the truck released from the impound, Beth said the Courier wasn't impounded—that she had seen a nicely dressed woman driving it around town. Judge Martinez had Beth write out a complaint, and decreed that anyone caught driving the vehicle from then on would be jailed. Mr. Cole plans to fly back to Houston in the morning to obtain a notarized title.

This evening, Robert told us the person helping Ben and Glen had returned to the States. Their escape was on hold, so we didn't need to rush our own break or get Ben and Glen thrown in El Toro. Robert also said his lawyer was optimistic about his new appeal, and he wanted to see how that played out. Jack and I were cool with the postponement. We supposedly had a judge and a Supreme Court president looking into our case at least for now.

Scorpio doesn't want to wait, though. He's been itching to go over the wall ever since Robert put up the canopy above his room and told him about our escape plan. Scorp now wears a red bandanna around his stubbled head, and his beard is growing back. He doesn't resemble Charles Manson anymore, but he still looks a little insane.

"They're never going to appeal your sentence," he said to Robert. "A quarter ton is too much. They ain't ever goin' to let you out. When we splittin'?"

Robert passed him the joint.

April 11

Mr. Cole returned from Houston, and when he came to the visitors' area this morning, Jack's mother was with him. She didn't break down and cry or anything, but there was dismay on her face when she saw poor Jack behind bars. Jack forced a smile, and they held hands through the bars. Mr. Cole told us he had obtained the notarized title and had driven to another office in Houston for an "authenticated" notarized title. Jack's father understood the importance of being a Man of Papers. He said he was going to present both copies to Judge Martinez during lunch with the judge and his wife.

Lunch with the judge and his wife?

When they returned in the afternoon, Beth pulled food from her basket and fed anyone who came around. It was a nice gesture, but everything she bought was with the proceeds of the sale of our rainbow weed. Half my money was feeding inmates who didn't need our help—people I don't remember offering me or Jack anything when we were broke. Subsisting on two cups of oatmeal a day for a month is not easy to forget.

April 13

Mr. and Mrs. Cole and Beth often visit twice a day, and I feel like an outsider. Sometimes I get the impression they blame me for getting their son in trouble. Maybe I am to blame, but it's not like Jack was an angel before we partnered up. And Beth bothers me when she talks about restaurants where she and her new friends eat, and about the things she buys in Oaxaca. She acts like she is on a paid vacation. Lately, I've been leaving them alone to their family picnics.

When I stopped by to say hello yesterday, Mr. Cole said that Arturo's boss had proposed a new contract. He and Olga were going to review it. I couldn't believe they were considering using Arturo's firm. I told Mr. Cole and Olga that I had no faith in Arturo or anyone associated with his office, and that Jack and I had signed a document to switch to Enrique a week ago. What happened to that?

This morning, however, Mr. Cole told us they favored Enrique's proposal, and were going to his office in the afternoon to sign a contract. *Finally.*

April 15

A little before noon today, our names were called over the speaker. Jack and I went down and found Enrique standing inside the sala de visita with a document in his hand. Mr. and Mrs. Cole were behind him to the right. Everyone was smiling. Enrique handed us the two pages. I saw "Puebla Judiciaria" at the top of the first page. Jack stood next to me, and we tried to translate it.

"The kilos are dismissed," Enrique said impatiently. "And no more cocaina."

I looked up at Enrique. I had developed some faith in him, but he was still a Mexican lawyer. Jack's father nodded to us. So did his mother. At the top of the second page, I read Jack's name and mine followed by "desestimó el caso de ocho kilogramos de marijuana y .095 gramos de cocaina por falta de pruebas."

"What does desestimó mean?" I asked Enrique.

"Dismisses," said Jack's mother.

Enrique translated the rest. "Dismisses the case of eight kilograms of marijuana and .095 grams of cocaine for lack of evidence."

"The decision arrived from Puebla this morning while we were in the judge's office," Mr. Cole said. "It's real."

Rafael's testimony crossed my mind. I scanned the pages and found a reference to Rafael Solas and Carlos Garcia at the bottom of the first page. I handed it to Enrique.

"It states that the arresting Federal Judiciales Rafael Solas and Carlos Garcia each acknowledged the request to testify but were absent at the hearing."

Rafael didn't show up? Was he otherwise engaged applying a cattle prod to the testicles of gringo hippies? Did he remember me giving him a camera? (He would have taken it anyway.) Had someone been paid off? Enrique handed the document back to me, and I read through it again. I was in a daze. After all the conflicting information we'd received during our lifetime in the peni, it was hard to believe Jack and I were getting out legally.

"You will be free," Enrique said, perhaps noticing my non-reaction.

"What about the hash?" I asked.

"You are addictos," he answered, raising his hands, palms up.

Jack stayed at the sala and talked with his parents while I returned to the room. Were we actually going to leave this place through the front gate? It seemed like I'd been locked up a lot longer than two and a half months. Although I could now make plans, no image of the future came into focus. I sure wouldn't be flying around in my own airplane, or even driving through

Mexico or the States. I reached under my bed for the flight manual.

April 16

This morning Enrique returned to the sala and told us, "There is a problem in the removal of the hashish."

Of course.

"In your declarations, you and the agents spoke the words hash and hashish. But when the district attorney created the documents, he wrote THC."

Jack and I listened.

"THC is tetrahydrocannabidinol, which is a pure extract from marijuana. The law does not have allowance for a person to be addicted to this. The judge cannot free you with THC written in the document."

Of course not.

"But the district attorney is in error. THC requires refining in a laboratory and arrives as capsules or liquid. Hashish is only concentrated marijuana. I will present this fact to the judge. You will be out in fifteen days with a chemist's and doctor's affirmation that the hashish is for personal use."

"I thought we were already declared addictos," I asked.

"Since hashish is concentrated marijuana, the doctors will determine that the amount you possessed was for personal use only."

April 17

The judge told Jack's father today that he would approve Enrique's argument about the hash being marijuana, not THC.

Beth flew back to Texas, but before leaving, she and Jack's father attained a document that allows him to drive the Courier in Mexico. He's going to fly home tomorrow and return before our release.

*

Everyone believes we're getting out. I lay on my bed and stared up at the metal beams and hanging lights. What could possibly derail our freedom? Maybe the doctors or chemists will decide we were caught with too much hash for personal use. Surely the judge would have already considered that. Surely.

Another Saturday night, and a baby is crying. But it sounds distant. Cat is playing "Peace Train" and singing in English as usual. When I am finally out of here, I won't be able to listen to the real Cat Stevens without thinking of our Cat. I'm already reminiscing. That has to be a positive sign. Cat's guitar picking is pretty good, and his voice isn't bad. Does he know the meaning of the songs he sings? I remember Sylvia singing along with Bob Dylan in Costa Rica—the good old days.

April 18 Easter Sunday

Today was a Pleasant Prison Sunday, and with Beth gone, Jack joined me in afternoon dorm banishment. All the conjugalers wore their best clothes, not just because it was Sunday, but because it was Easter Sunday. Imprisonment has not shaken their faith. American and English rock tunes played over the outdoor speakers, along with Mexican pop and religious songs. I figured the songs were religious because I recognized words like Jesus (Heysoos), Dios (aka El Señor) and Maria (Mother Mary, Let it Be).

I enjoyed my hopefully last Sunday popcorn in the peni while Jack and I sat on a bench watching families stroll the yard. I snapped a mental picture—not for the fond memory, but because it was something I would never see again. I won't miss any of it.

"Our last Sunday," I said.

"Yep." Jack nodded as he looked across the courtyard.

"What are you going to do when we get out?" I asked.

"Back to Laguna Vista," he said after a few moments.

I didn't need to ask if Beth was included in his plans.

He looked around the yard, then at me.

"I'll probably enroll in the fall semester," he said.

"In the valley or the University of Houston?"

"Probably the valley. I don't want to go back to Houston."

Me neither. But it was plain to see I wouldn't be returning to the house in Laguna Vista. Jack didn't ask about my plans, which was fine because I didn't have any.

April 26

Our connection to the outside has faded again, but this time we have money and food, not to mention freedom on the horizon. Hunger, lies and despair have been replaced by boredom and waiting. It helps that we can again afford palomas of weed from Machista.

It's been ten days since the kilos were dismissed, and Jack and I still await the judge's approval of Enrique's definition of hash. Didn't the judge tell Mr. Cole last week that he would accept it? I thought for sure we'd be out of here before this weekend.

"Is there a possibility he won't approve it?" I asked Enrique a couple days ago.

"It will not be a problem," he answered.

This afternoon I sat on a bench and looked above the back wall. I was too close to the wall to see the mountains, but I watched a hawk circling below the clouds with a small bird shadowing it. I thought about everyone telling Sheryl to forget about me. I was a lost cause.

April 27

When Enrique came today, Jack and I expected to learn the date of our doctor's appointment. Instead, he told us the judge had rejected the document regarding his changes to the definition of the hash.

Back to the judicial pinball machine.

"Do not worry," he added quickly. "It is a technicality and is a good sign. The judge wants everything to be without error because this final approval will bring your release."

Enrique said the judge was very disappointed he could not approve the document as it was written. *Me, too.*

So we wait.

Jack came into the room in the afternoon to try to get me to join in a volleyball game. I haven't been in the mood for extracurricular activities lately.

"Put down that damn flight manual and play ball," he said.

"Maybe in a little while."

I don't feel like I'm part of this anymore. I don't know what I'm a part of.

April 29

This afternoon Enrique told us, "The judge has approved the documents. Now, you only await your appointment at the health center."

"When will that be?" I asked.

"Pronto. Afterward, there is only the final audiencia with the judge. Then your release."

Another fucking audiencia?

"Another audiencia?" Jack asked.

"It is just a formality. You will not attend. The judge will do everything for you to be released. This audiencia is only a signing of documents. If completed early, you will have libertad the same day."

With the way things go in the peni, we'll be lucky to get out the day after. But I am finally convinced we will go free.

May 7

A long week passed before Jack and I caught a ride to the Centro de Salud to update our addictos status. After being incarcerated for over three months, supposedly with no access to marijuana or hash, we were going to be declared addicts. How did that make sense?

Mountains paralleled us on both sides as we drove up the valley to Oaxaca. Campesinos and burros with and without sticks on their backs walked alongside the road. A pretty girl in a pale blue dress swept the front porch of a store. I watched a man riding a motorized bicycle with a woman seated behind him. She had one arm around his large waist and the other around a baby. We drove by the turnoff for where I used to buy mezcal for the Zapotecs, and past the truck checkpoint where we met Rafael and life came to a halt.

At the health center, Jack and I answered the same stupid questions as before but were not asked to walk a straight line. I wasn't in the mood for it anyway. A prison guard stayed close, rifle-ready.

Five days later, Enrique told us the doctor and chemist had confirmed that our hash was for personal use, and the judge would schedule our final audiencia for next week.

Next week? One more conjugal weekend—my last, por seguro. I hope.

In anticipation of our release, Mr. Cole has returned to Oaxaca. This afternoon, Jack was telling him we were waiting to learn the date of our audiencia when Enrique arrived and reported it would be in four days.

May 17 Libertad

One might think that with freedom due today or tomorrow, Jack and I would have had a problem sleeping. I am so worn down mentally, I've been sleeping like a baby (and not a conjugal Saturday-night crying baby). I don't believe Jack has had any difficulty either.

For lunch, I went down for a tortilla pizza, then returned to the room to lie on my bed. What could go wrong? At one thirty, our names were called over the speaker. I followed Jack through the hall and down the steps. He looked quite thin from behind, but his posture was erect, and he held his bony shoulders upright. I straightened my slouch.

Enrique and Jack's father were waiting inside the visitors' area.

"It is complete," said Enrique. "You are free."

Enrique looked genuinely happy for us, but I was still behind bars. Once I was out, I'd jump for joy, I guess.

"Pack your things," said Enrique.

"Today?" I asked.

"As soon as the penitentiary processes the documents."

Jack and I returned to the dorm and told Robert to give our mattresses, sleeping bags and pillows to anyone he thought needed them. We got our "things" together—it took less than a minute. We lay down on our bare mattresses and waited. Tony came in, excited for us. He put dibs on one of our mattresses. His had a kerosene smell, he said.

An hour and a half later, our names were called over the speakers, followed by unfamiliar words. One word I did recognize was “libertad,” which means liberty; freedom. Murmuring started up in the dorm. So much for slipping out incognito. Robert opened our door and said, “Lista, Lista, Lista. No more Lista.” I picked up my backpack, sleeping bag and box, and Jack grabbed his stuff. We walked with Robert through the hall, down the steps and past the sala de visita where Tony and Scorpio joined us.

Gringos and Mexicans were waiting for us at the gate: the three Houstonians (who we finally paid back), Tall Bob, Nosario, Machista, even Javier, as well as several Mexicans I didn’t recognize. Quite a sendoff, but I missed my buddies, Ben and Glen. So much for fair weather friends. Everyone circled around to say goodbye and shake our hands. I told a few that I wouldn’t forget about them—that I would check on their cases, although in the back of my mind I was pretty sure the peni would begin to fade as soon as I walked out the gate. It's how the brain works; repression of bad memories—self-preservation. I had my notebooks with their words, names, events and dates, but that’s probably all they would soon be.

Enrique and Jack’s father stood on the other side of the gate and watched. Two guards unstrapped the rifles from their shoulders. The gate swung open, and Jack and I walked through to the outside.

Rehabilitation

CHAPTER NINETEEN

Disco Sucks

As we walked to Mr. Cole's rental car, I looked back at the visitors disappearing into the portal through which Jack and I had emerged. The corner tower with its guard and AK-47 rose above the entrance. I was looking at it from the outside.

"Shit," Jack said. "They ripped me off."

I turned. The car's trunk was open.

"Who ripped you off?"

"Someone took my jacket and some other clothes."

Jack had been able to buy back his green jacket when we got our money from Arturo. I lifted my box into the trunk and noticed a few items missing.

"They got me too," I said. "Just some shirts, I think."

That was why people we didn't know had given us a sendoff. I turned to the peni entrance. I had freedom. Why didn't I give all my things to those still trapped inside?

Enrique said he'd see us in town and walked across the dirt to his car. I sat in the back as Mr. Cole drove us to Oaxaca. Jack sat in front. We were both quiet. His father looked at me in the rearview mirror.

"The Courier is stored at a car lot. Jack and I will pick it up tomorrow and start for Texas. You've got a plane ticket to Houston, leaving in the morning."

To consider I might have hung out in Mexico while pondering my situation would have been a fantasy. I had re-attained the big freedom but lost a smaller one (or two).

We stopped at the Narcotics Office, and Jack and I sat on a bench in the hall while Enrique and Mr. Cole went to retrieve our passports and visas. The room where Rafael had confronted us with the kilos was just around the corner. I expected him to walk into view any minute. Thankfully, he didn't. As I looked around, I became aware of my shifting reality. Time spent on the inside had already begun to compress.

Enrique returned with our passports and two green garbage bags of forgotten belongings.

"Your surfboards are in the back of the Courier," Mr. Cole said.

Surfboards.

Our visas had long expired, so the next stop was the immigration office. Jack's father handed the agent our passports with a document from Enrique. A few minutes later, the passports were returned with new visas. Mr. Cole placed them in his coat pocket.

At the Hotel Calesa in downtown Oaxaca, Jack and I were given keys to a room down the hall from his father. Jack showered as I sat on a real mattress and looked around. There was a television on top of the dresser; framed paintings hung on walls that went all the way to the ceiling; windows opened to the outside world; and we had our own private bathroom. I took my first hot shower in a long time. As usual in Mexican hotels, there were no washcloths, so I scrubbed off my tan with a white sock. In the hotel restaurant, Jack's father told us to order anything we wanted. I turned the plastic pages and stared. So much food. I ordered spaghetti and meatballs—what my mother cooks on my birthday.

During dinner, Jack and his father spoke a little, but no one said much. They would have plenty of time for conversation on the drive to Texas. When I got up to go to the room, Mr. Cole told me not to leave the hotel. In the morning, we would meet for breakfast, then drive to the airport.

I sat on my bed and opened one of the garbage bags the police had returned. The sweet, fermented aroma of colitas rose from within and brought back olden times. Inside the bag were paperbacks, clothes, photos and my shoebox of cassette tapes. All of a sudden, my stomach ached. I headed for the bathroom. Had the spaghetti been bad, or too rich for my prison palate, or did I just eat too much? Afterward, I lay back on the bed, propped my head on two pillows and stared at the blank TV screen.

By the time I got out of bed in the morning, Jack had gone downstairs. I stood on my bed and looked through a high window to the rooftops and mountains. In an hour, I would be taken to the airport and shipped straight to Houston. *Don't leave the hotel*.

Outside the window was Mexico—not the travesty I had endured for three and a half months—but the jungles, deserts, colorful cacti, stupid burros, warm surf, cinnamon girls and mountain islands that floated on oceans of white fog. I wouldn't get to see any of it. The peni would be my last memory of Mexico.

At the end of the hallway, stairs led both down and up. I took the ones going up and went through a metal door. Beyond the flat tar and gravel roof, a cathedral rose above colonial buildings with red tile roofs. Behind me, the sun was already above the mountains. I had missed morning lista.

I walked to the edge of the roof. A short wall separated the hotel from another building, and I sat down with my legs dangling over it. Below me, blackbirds swarmed the tops of trees at a little park and made a racket. Motorcycles shifted gears and roosters crowed. I got up. Bells began to ring from the cathedral. I sat back down. Bells from other churches echoed.

As I made my way back across the roof, it hit me that the

door may have locked when it shut. Why hadn't I thought about that? Jack's father would be sitting at the breakfast table wondering what the hell I was up to now. But the door opened, and I made it to the dining room where Jack and his father were waiting. While we ate, they discussed their route to Texas. No one asked for my input. I had only driven that route more than a half dozen times. Jack and his father planned to drop off the rental car and pick up the Courier after taking me to the airport. The Courier was fueled and ready to go.

At the Mexicana Airlines ticket counter, Mr. Cole handed me my passport and visa and said my father would pick me up at Houston Intercontinental. When I changed planes in Mexico City, I stood at Mexican customs while the agent examined my papers. He looked up at me. I waited for him to ask why I had been in Mexico so long and why my visa had just been issued in Oaxaca. He handed back my passport, and I moved to the gate area with everyone else.

During the flight, I sat next to a window on the right side and watched the central plateau's volcanoes, highways and cities pass underneath. As we flew near Brownsville and Matamoros, I traced the Rio Grande to the Gulf and focused on the river mouth until it disappeared behind the wing—most likely, my last view of it.

While I waited in line at U.S. customs in Houston, I wondered about communications between the U.S. and Mexico. Jack and I had ultimately been declared not guilty, but I'm sure the embassy translator at our "formal" declaration had returned to his joint DEA office and filed a report about the two young narcotraficantes internacionales.

When my turn came, Immigration Man asked, "What was your purpose in Mexico?"

"Surfing. Spring break."

"Welcome home."

*

My mother was waiting for me outside the terminal in her white Buick station wagon.

"Your brother still has classes in Austin," she told me. "He'll be back in two weeks for summer vacation. You'll have the room to yourself until then."

My younger brother studied electrical engineering at the University of Texas. My older sister was also in Austin, finishing her certified public accountant courses.

"Did you get the money I sent you? I found it in the top drawer of your desk," my mother asked.

"Yes. Thanks."

The Costa Rican money was inside my backpack. I had written a letter thanking her, but it was still in my notebook. I hadn't mailed it because I mistakenly thought we would be free shortly.

"You're thin," she said. "And your hair is shorter. It looks good."

I nodded and stared out at all the traffic, billboards and shiny new cars parked at the dealerships along I-45.

"Were you treated okay? Your father said it was like a country club with volleyball and basketball and lots of sun."

"It was alright."

*

The bathroom scale read 128 pounds—the same as when I returned from Costa Rica with jaundice. Jack and I had made up some of our weight loss. My mother came into my room and cheerfully announced we would be having my favorite meal—spaghetti. I hoped my stomach fared better than the day before.

The subject of Mexico did not surface at the dinner table.

"You are certainly welcome to stay here as long as you want," my father told me. "When your brother gets back, you two can share the room. He'll be happy to see you, and I'm sure the tight quarters won't be a problem for you."

He grinned as if he had said something funny.

*

My assets amounted to $436 in the bank and a 1966 Plymouth Valiant parked in the grass of my parents' back yard. At the moment, I didn't even have a surfboard.

Sheryl dropped by the second day, and we locked the bedroom door.

"Do you have any plans?" she asked as we lay together in the twin bed.

"To get out of here."

"Out of where?"

"This house."

She may have thought I meant Houston.

"I'll work construction. Save money," I said.

Boomtown Houston.

Jack remained in the Rio Grande Valley, so I became the first to tell our story to friends—basically, "It wasn't terrible, it's not what you think, no we didn't have to fight, no—no one tried to make us their bitches." It seemed that time had passed a lot quicker for our friends on the outside than it had for Jack and me.

My guitar-playing buddy, Alan, asked if it was true I had sold my Madeira acoustic guitar in prison so Jack and I could eat. Alan and I had bought identical blond guitars four years earlier. I told him it was a different guitar I had to sell. Everyone knew something about us, but the knowledge was distorted.

Dan stopped doing runs when he found out Jack and I got busted. He asked more about prison and the bust than my other friends, but he seemed to consider it just another adventure.

Alan worked while he finished college, and he hired me to run wood roof trusses at an apartment complex in southwest Houston. In May, Houston had not yet heated up, and it wasn't bad to be on top of a three-story building in the fresh air. My worn leather nail bag felt familiar around my waist as I ran on top of an outside wall with the end of a thirty-foot truss in my hands. Alan's partner, Lance, had graduated from our high school two years after us.

"You ready for the good life?" Lance asked during a break. His accent was pure Texan. Life was "laff."

We sat on top of the building near the water cooler. Around us, steel skeletons of high-rises stretched into the sky. Cranes swiveled at their tops, and I heard the tapping of steel workers.

"What good life?" I asked.

"The good laff. Party. Dranks, daincin, disco."

While I had resided in the peni, or surfed in El Salvador, or drove through Mexico and swam the Rio Grande, a travesty of music called disco had infiltrated society. Lance meant well.

"I don't like disco," I told him.

"It's naht just the music, it's the bait, the daincin', the partyin'. Don't knawk it 'til ya trah it."

There was no way I could listen to that shit. The rhythm was monotonous, and the lyrics had no meaning. As far as the good "laff," I didn't mind having a drink or two, but getting drunk and losing half the next day because of a hangover didn't appeal to me.

*

Sheryl and I moved into an apartment in northwest Houston. She worked as a cocktail waitress at the Hyatt on the Southwest Freeway and normally got home after midnight. I almost always left for work before she stirred in the morning.

Jack drove up from the valley two months after our release and brought my surfboard and Madeira guitar. Robert's wife, Janet, had written Jack that Robert and Tony tried to escape and failed. They climbed through Robert's window like we had planned but shimmied down into No Man's Land instead of sliding over the wall on a cable. Robert threw another rope over the outer wall and climbed up. When he reached the top, Tony called his name. Robert climbed back down into No Man's Land to help him, and the guards pounced on them both and beat the shit out of them.

I wrote a letter to Robert and Tony and said that nothing had changed on the outside, and not to let six months or a year in the peni get them down. And if they weren't out in a year, I should be in a better financial position to help them with a real break.

I didn't send the letter—not only because I didn't have Janet's address, but because what I wrote was bullshit. I was minimizing their situation so I wouldn't feel guilty about not thinking about them. They weren't getting out in a year—not after trying to escape.

News of their failed breakout reminded me how strange it felt to eat at restaurants, go to the movies, drive to the beach, and do all the things everyone takes for granted. What I predicted had become truer than I imagined. Prison memories faded, and fast. I still remembered everything that happened, but the actual sensory memories were dissipating as if it had all been a dream—a bad one.

Janet also told Jack that Scorpio had been released a month after us. Two days later, police arrested him in the Oaxaca zocalo for being drunk and disorderly. Scorp resisted arrest, of course, and it took several cops to drag him to jail. When they discovered who he was and where he had been for a year, they transported him to the U.S. border. Did the Mexican police have a heart or did they just not want to bother with Scorpio again?

CHAPTER TWENTY

What's Your Purpose?

Under "Flight Instruction" in the yellow pages, I spotted a one-line ad for Harold Smith. I drove to Collier Airfield and found a stocky man wearing jean overalls and a goatee standing next to a Cessna 150 inside a hangar.

"I'm looking for Harold Smith," I said.

"That's me. Grab aholt of the other side of this cowling."

I walked to the front of the plane and helped Harold lift the sheet-metal cowling and place it on top of the engine.

"What do ya need?" he asked as he secured the right side of the cowling with screws.

"I'd like to get my private pilot license. I have sixteen and a half hours. I soloed in a Piper Warrior in Harlingen and then got checked out in a Cessna 150 like this one."

"Sixteen and a half hours," Harold repeated, still busy with the screws.

"What's the approach speed with forty degrees of flaps?"

He walked around me to the left side and continued screwing.

"Fifty miles an hour?" I couldn't remember exactly. I'd been through a few things since I last flew. If I'd known Harold taught in a 150, I would have studied the manual I had bought at Lakeside Airport the year before.

He turned and looked me over.

"You got your logbook?"

"Yes, sir."

"Let's push her back. You do the preflight, and I'll be right out."

Harold came out of the hangar and sat down next to me in the right seat. I started the engine according to the checklist, and we taxied to the end of the runway. He watched as I accomplished the before-takeoff items.

"Have you done short-field takeoffs?" he asked.

"No, but I read about 'em."

Tall pine trees bordered the runway's right side and departure end.

"Hold the control wheel midway for the least amount of drag and accelerate to sixty miles per hour. Rotate and climb at sixty-five until you're above the trees, then let the nose down a little and climb normally."

After clearing the trees, I lowered the nose to the horizon, and we climbed at 500 feet per minute.

"Climb to twenty-five hundred feet," Harold instructed.

When we leveled off, he ran me through almost all the maneuvers I had learned before soloing the first time, including stalls. Rather than correct me verbally, Harold tapped the glass faces of the instruments with the eraser end of a pencil. The more urgent, the faster and harder he tapped. The hour lesson cost me only twenty-one dollars; fifteen for the plane and six for the instruction. Lakeside Airport had charged twenty-four and ten.

Harold appeared to be a no-nonsense guy, and I felt good about finding an instructor who seemed to care about teaching me to fly. That evening, I dug up my Cessna 150 manual and reread its fifty-four pages. I lay on the sofa, puffed a joint and contemplated the sky.

After two more lessons and fifteen short-field takeoffs and landings, Harold signed me off for solo flight. When I arrived a few days later, excited to go up alone, the plane needed fuel.

Collier Airfield had no gas pumps, so Harold usually got fuel at nearby Weiser Air Park.

"Give me a minute, and we can fly over," he said.

"Why don't I go by myself?" I asked.

He and I had done touch-and-go landings on Weiser's long grass runway. He squinted at me.

"You remember where it is?"

"Just off Highway 290," I answered. "North side," I quickly added.

"Okay. Don't mess around. Go directly there and top off. And only fly an hour afterward." He wrote an authorization in my logbook, and I taxied away.

While I ran the checklist at the end of the runway, Harold stood in front of the hangar, smoking his pipe and watching me. I climbed out over the trees and leveled off at 1,000 feet before turning due west. In ten minutes, Weiser Air Park did not appear where it should have. I continued up Highway 290 and still didn't see it. Nothing looked familiar. I turned back to Collier and flew for a little over ten minutes.

Collier, too, had disappeared. It was right down there when I took off. A rectangle of black asphalt surrounded by houses and trees shouldn't be that hard to spot. I circled twice and looked all around, then decided Weiser Air Park would be easier to find since it was adjacent Highway 290. Also, the surrounding rice fields would make for a softer emergency landing than houses and trees. Maybe I hadn't flown far enough the first time. I turned west again.

In five minutes, I came to a cluster of white, round storage tanks and remembered Harold telling me Collier Airfield was exactly ninety degrees from the tanks. I turned around and headed east again. In a few minutes, Collier magically appeared. I landed and taxied to the hangar.

"That was quick," Harold said. "I thought you were going to fly an hour."

"I couldn't find Weiser," I told him.

He lowered his pipe.

"You mean to tell me you've been flying all this time, and you never got gas?"

"Yes, sir."

Harold disappeared into the hangar and returned with a stepladder. He placed it in front of the right wing, then climbed up and removed the gas cap on top of the wing. I watched as he inserted a slim clear tube into the tank. When he pulled it out, he studied it, then repeated the procedure on the left wing. Harold climbed down and walked to me. He held up his plastic tube.

"Do you know what this is?"

"No, sir."

"It's a dipstick like you use to check the oil in your car. It shows how much gasoline is actually in the fuel tanks. Gauges aren't accurate, as I'm sure you've been taught."

I nodded. He examined the tube again.

"You just landed with one gallon of fuel. Total. Less than ten minutes of flying, and that's if the wings were perfectly level. You were flying on fumes, boy."

I screwed up. My fear was not that I had almost run out of fuel. I would never do that again. My fear was that Harold wouldn't allow me to fly his plane anymore. He stared at me.

"You and me are going up," he finally said. "Do another preflight." He walked back to his hangar and returned with a red, five-gallon gasoline can.

As the months rolled by, Sheryl and I spent less time together. It seemed like whenever I waited up for her, she'd come home even later. And on her one weekday off, she liked to go dancing. I wasn't a big dancer, so it became a girls' night out for her. Whenever I brought up her nocturnal life, she countered that I was aloof. Maybe I was aloof because she chose to hang out with her restaurant and bar friends rather than coming home. But I didn't say anything.

I used my spare cash to fly Harold's Cessna 150 on the weekends and occasionally after work. To satisfy the FAA's requirements for a private pilot's license, I needed to log ten hours of cross country flights. In preparation for my first trip with Harold, I drew a straight line on the chart from Collier Airfield to a small airport near Huntsville, about fifty miles north. I highlighted the route in yellow and circled distinctive landmarks: roads, lakes, railroad tracks, power lines.

"Always keep a finger at your location on the chart," Harold instructed as we flew the course. One by one, the landmarks on my chart appeared on the ground, and I jotted down the time at each.

My cross country training had just begun when Sheryl told me she thought we should live in separate apartments. She caught me off guard, although I should have seen it coming. We weren't breaking up, she said, it was just that we could afford our own places. Being the efficient person she was, Sheryl found me an apartment in a week.

We drove over to check out my new home in a convertible she had borrowed from someone at work. Her purse rested against the center console, and I noticed a driver's license at the top. I picked it up. She glanced at me but remained silent as I read the license. It belonged to some guy twelve years older than her and nine years older than me.

"Who's this?" I asked.

She admitted it was someone she had been seeing but told me she hadn't slept with him. He owned a restaurant in Aspen, and she met him at her job at the Hyatt. He liked to gamble, she told me with a hint of a smile. I looked around at the car's leather upholstery, faux wood instrument panel and quadraphonic stereo system.

"This is his car?" I asked.

"Yes."

I didn't blame her. What could an aimless 23-year-old construction worker offer her compared to a sophisticated restaurateur/gambler?

After I moved into my new apartment, Sheryl became history. I worked and flew and had Sunday dinners with my parents. College brochures still lay on tables for my perusal, and neither my mother nor father ever mentioned Mexico. They probably thought it would either depress me or give me ideas.

On Thursday nights, I met the gang at Richie's house to get high and watch a sitcom called MASH about doctors during the Korean War. The characters' wit and dialog made the show different from any other program on the air, and the parallels to the Vietnam war were poignant and plentiful. None of our immediate crowd had gone to Vietnam, but we had all grown up during its eleven, television-showcased gruesome years. I was ten years old in 1964 when the U.S. involvement in Vietnam began and twenty-one when it ended in 1975. Vietnam had been a part of life for everyone.

As far as dating went, I was a recluse. Clubbing was not my thing, especially with the current popular music. Girls in Houston sparkled in glitter make-up and flashy clothes and were interested in guys who sparkled in dollars and Trans Ams and Porsches.

I surfed, played guitar, watched movies, read, and studied for the private pilot written exam. For a night out, Dan or Alan and I headed to Anderson Fair or Fitzgerald's to listen to Vince Bell, Don Sanders and others perform their unique folk styles.

*

In January of 1977, one year and three months after my first flying lesson, I passed my private pilot checkride. Although the minimum required flight time for the license was forty hours, it took me sixty-four. Considering life's distractions, I was quite happy to have finally become a certified pilot. I worked construction through the winter and began renting Cessna 172s at Andrau Airpark in southwest Houston—the same type plane I had flown through Hecker Pass in California.

As the anniversary of my prison graduation approached, I still drifted over Houston without a vision of the future. The idea of finishing college surfaced now and then.

When I mentioned to Alan that I was considering returning to college, he said, "I thought you were attending the university of the sky."

It may have been just a quick comment, or maybe not. Before

I exchanged my dreams for a role in a Oaxaca cage, my plan had been to buy a plane and fly wherever and whenever I wanted. Alan's remark made me think. Maybe I could fly for a living. I researched possibilities and even visited an army recruiter who told me that chief warrant officers were taught to fly. But they flew helicopters.

*

The apartment project in southwest Houston ended, and I took a job as a lead framer in a new upscale subdivision. I replaced my old Plymouth Valiant with an old VW Bug, and that was how I became friends with Tom, a grunt laborer. Tom had ventured from Rochester, New York, to take advantage of Houston's boom, and a red, turbo-charged 1974 VW Super Beetle was his pride and joy. I admired it too. Tom enjoyed my stories about Mexico, and I figured to a New Yorker, they must have been like *Grimm's Fairy Tales*.

After hanging out together for a few weeks, he suggested we buy Quaaludes in Houston and drive to Daytona Beach to sell them at a profit. I could use the cash to continue flying, and Tom's idea sounded risk-free compared to my previous endeavors. We drove I-10 East to Daytona in his Super Beetle.

At Daytona Beach, Tom revealed his secret identity as a successful racing hustler. Drag racing on the beach after sunset was apparently a popular thing to do, and Tom knew about it. We cruised the hard sand nightly and waited for drivers of muscle cars to challenge Tom's meager VW Bug. He never lost.

After our third night of racing, we returned to the motel and discovered someone had ripped us off. Our Quaaludes were gone. The door to our room was still locked, but the bathroom window was open. We had kept it latched. Outside the window, a ladder was leaning against the wall. The guy who had been to our room in the afternoon to buy some Quays had apparently unlocked the window under the pretense of taking a leak. While we were gone, he came in through the bathroom window.

Tom and I were pissed off, but we didn't waste time crying over spilt Quaaludes. We drove across Florida the next day to catch Pink Floyd at Tampa Bay Stadium. A cosmic pink sunset opened the show, and the evening became more cosmic as the mescaline Tom won the day before took effect. Pink Floyd performed the entire *Wish You Were Here* album and their new one, *Animals*.

An immense oval screen hung above the stage, and we sat close to the field, mesmerized by the surreal, animated video that accompanied "Welcome to the Machine." Skyscrapers cracked and bled and flooded the streets. The blood tide rose higher and higher, and waves emerged and pulsed to the rhythm of the music. The waves transformed into blood people whose arms reached into the sky and swayed with the music while moving in mass toward a high-rise obelisk that separated from the sea of red and spun into the sky.

During the performance of *Animals*, huge inflated farm animals (in particular, a gargantuan pig) roamed the sky above the stadium.

*

We got on I-10 for Houston the next day.

"Ever thought of going back to Mexico and doing a run again?" Tom asked.

"No," I said.

But I *had* thought about it.

"You said the reason you got busted was because you made mistakes. What if you didn't make those mistakes? What if you did it like you did in the beginning? It's a pity to waste everything you learned."

It was night as I drove Tom's Bug across Louisiana and blue-and-white lights flashed in the rearview mirror. We weren't speeding. I pulled over.

"Where y'all headed?" asked the Louisiana sheriff.

"Houston."

He looked at my driver's license and the car registration. My hair had grown since Oaxaca but was shorter than it used to be. My face had just a two-day stubble, and my mustache went only to the bottom of my chin. Tom wore his hair relatively short, although he hadn't shaved either. We may have appeared scroungy to the officer.

"Where y'all coming from?"

"Florida."

"And your purpose in Florida?"

Why must there always be a purpose? Our purpose had been to sell Quaaludes, but we got ripped off by a smarter criminal, so our purpose became Pink Floyd and mescaline.

"Just a break from work," I answered.

"What type of work?"

"Construction."

"You know why I stopped you?"

To give us haircuts? Because we have New York license plates?

"No, sir," I answered.

"Your right taillight is out. I don't know what they'all allow up in New Yawk, but here in Looziana, 'at's a violation."

I looked at Tom.

"We didn't know it wasn't working. We'll get it fixed," I said.

"Y'all gettin' a break today. I won't give ya a ticket as long as ya keep goin' straight ahead and cross the state line with no dee-lay."

We drove off with no dee-lay.

"Maybe you should get Texas plates," I suggested to Tom.

A week later, we attended a repeat performance of Pink Floyd at the University of Houston's Jeppesen Stadium, my almost alma mater. Our mescaline perspective was replaced by a hash oil perspective.

"How much money would it take to buy forty pounds down in Mexico?" Tom asked.

CHAPTER TWENTY-ONE

Southbound with Our Ears On

"Fifty or sixty bucks a kilo," I answered.

Tom drove west on I-10, back to Spring Branch.

"It's not the money. We could save enough for that in a month. I'm not going back to Oaxaca."

"What about where you bought your first pot in Mexico when you lived in that village?" he asked.

Tom had been listening.

"Veracruz," I answered. "Yes. It's closer."

A lot closer, and it wasn't in the heart of a big marijuana-growing region. The straight stretch of coastal route from Veracruz to the Rio Grande could probably be driven in one ten-hour stretch.

"It would have to be safe. Foolproof," I said.

A voice came over Tom's citizens band radio. "Breaker one-nine for anyone with their ears on. Smokey at Gessner I-10 looking west."

Radar detectors were illegal in Texas and many other states, so some drivers, particularly truck drivers, used CB radios to warn each other about Smokey Bear, aka the police. I had listened to Tom's conversations on our trip to Florida.

Tom picked up his microphone.

"Roger that, Yankee Down, ears on. Got your back door."

An idea began to focus; two cars, two CB radios. One in front as point, the other behind with the load. I looked down at

Tom's CB. Would it work? If the person driving point saw a checkpoint or anything suspicious ahead, he could notify the car behind, which would be far enough away to turn around and get out of Dodge.

"I don't have a connection in Veracruz," I said.

"You didn't have one in Oaxaca when you went there the first time."

I pictured where Dan and I bought that first paloma of flower tops near the market. Where would that pot have come from? The mountains west of Veracruz? I told Tom my idea. He was ready to go, of course.

"It may just be an exploratory trip," I said. "It's been a year and half since I've driven those roads. There could be checkpoints now."

We installed a CB radio in my Bug and worked a month.

When we asked the boss if we could take another break, he said, "Sure, but don't count on having a job when you get back."

He wasn't happy about it. I had become his right-hand man, and Tom was the best laborer he had.

Tom and I delayed our departure a few days for the premiere of a science fiction movie. The trailers looked like nothing I'd ever seen, and in case anything went wrong in Mexico, I didn't want to miss it. We waited in line an hour at the Galleria to see *Star Wars* and departed the next day.

As our two-Bug caravan made its way south on Highway 77, most of the Sunday traffic was headed north, back to Houston. When we approached the Kingsville intersection where Deputy Bubba had nabbed our friends and shaved their heads, I picked up the microphone.

"Breaker one-nine for Yankee Down, this here's Beer Belly. Our twenty is the King Ranch. Keep your pedal off the metal and your ears and goggles on. This is redneck territory."

"Ten-four," Tom replied.

I ad-libbed the lingo. Other than Tom's conversations on our trip to Florida, my experience with CB radios amounted to listening to Schneider on the new TV show *One Day at a Time*.

His handle was Super Stud, so I used his friend's less ostentatious handle.

"Breaker one-nine for Beer Belly, this here's Fire Ranger Four, what's your twenty?"

Another compadre. Cool. "Fire Ranger Four, Beer Belly is southbound 77 exit 56. What's your twenty?"

"Roger, Beer Belly. Fire Four is one of them rednecks you was referrin' to. We're 77 north passing Lewiston and we got our goggles on for y'all."

Shit. Several trucks drove by in the northbound lane while Tom and I maintained radio silence. No sign of hostiles materialized. I turned up The Eagles' latest album, *Hotel California*, and Don Henley sang about the warm smell of colitas rising up through the air. With luck, Tom and I would soon be inhaling likewise. Did The Eagles know about smuggling weed?

Forty miles north of Brownsville, buzzards loitered in the opposite lane. Just for Tom, I turned toward them. One buzzard flapped away in slower motion than I anticipated, and the impact of the VW's curved hood ejected the bird skyward. I watched in the rearview mirror to see if it would be a threat to Tom. He swerved to try to nail the vulture on the way down but missed. I was going to have to watch that guy.

We met at Margarita's restaurant in Brownsville, and I laid a map with our highlighted route on the table. I told Tom to keep his visa and car papers all in one place and hand them to the soldiers or officials as soon as they requested them. I explained the importance of being a Man of Papers.

Tom would go through Mexican customs first, and we'd rendezvous beyond the twenty-kilometer checkpoint wherever he thought looked good. After that, we could stick together. Cars often traveled in small caravans in Mexico. I handed him some pesos and a map with our highlighted route.

After exiting the twenty-kilometer checkpoint, I pushed in the tape, and "Already Gone" played through the speakers just like old times. Ten minutes down the road, I spotted Tom's shiny red Bug parked at a tienda on the right. He was sitting on a bench outside, drinking a Dos Equis. Fast learner. I went inside to get my own beer and joined him on the bench.

We continued south and turned onto the road for the beach north of Tuxpan. On our left, moonlight reflected off the Gulf between the palms. No other cars were around, so I extinguished my headlights and drove by moonlight. Tom's lights blinked off, and we drove in stealth formation for a couple of minutes.

After parking at the beach, we set up our tents in the same pine grove where Dan and I had camped two and a half years earlier. Inside the tent, I fell asleep listening to the surf as a comfortable Gulf breeze washed over me.

In the morning, Tom and I swam in the warm, clear water, and I looked above the pine trees to the mountains. Thin plumes of smoke spotted the green landscape where campesinos were preparing breakfast. In the Gulf, just past the breaking waves, pelicans flew by, skimming the swells for lift while grazing the water with a feather tip. In the U.S., I had harbored some anxiety about returning to Mexico. A web of fear and insecurity had spun around me. The only way to keep that web from hardening was to break through and just go for it. Nothing down here had changed.

In Tuxpan, we ate breakfast at an outdoor restaurant adjacent the town zocalo. Afterward, Tom leaned his chair back against the wall, and I began teaching him important Spanish words like beer and bathroom and food. We got in our cars, and he followed me to Veracruz and along the Gulf boulevard south of town. I remembered the Hotel Mocambo from my trip with Dan. Its location just outside the city would make it a good base of operations.

We checked into the Mocambo and drove to town in the evening. I parked near the outdoor market where Dan and I had bought that first paloma.

During the actual run, Tom would be driving the load. We planned to do everything regarding procurement of the weed using my VW. That way, if our new connection set us up, the police would be looking for my car, which would be clean.

We sat on a cement bench near the market and waited. After a while, we walked across the boulevard to the ocean. The Gulf was subdued by a long rock jetty to our left, and a peaceful breeze blew across the water and rattled the palms along the boulevard. We continued walking to the jetty and looked through a chain link fence into a shipyard. Under high yellow lights, workers and cranes loaded cargo onto ships.

Tom went for beers, and I sat on the seawall and watched yellow light from the shipyard reflect off the black Gulf. He returned with two cold cans of Tecate and we sat quietly. After half an hour, I was about to suggest we try the zocalo when Tom nudged me. To our left, people were exiting the shipyard through the main gate. We watched the silhouette of a slim man walk toward us and sit down on the seawall. He faced the Gulf, away from us.

A familiar scent soon made its way through the breeze. With his back still to us, the guy held up a burning joint. We walked over and sat next to him. As the doobie made the rounds, we learned Ramon was a 50-year-old dockworker.

"You are looking to buy mota?" he asked in Spanish.

I told him yes, and he said he could tell us the availability and price the next day.

"Es esta mota buena para ustedes?" he asked. *Is this pot good for you?*

I took another hit and answered, "Yes."

"Nos gustan sinsemilla si posible. Quince kilos," I said. *We would like sinsemilla if possible. Fifteen kilos.*

I wanted to be able to get $350 a pound for whatever we brought back. Tom planned to drive to New York and sell his half for more.

The following evening, Tom stayed in the hotel while I met with Ramon. We passed through the gate into the shipyard and walked past several dockworkers. No one seemed to take notice of me, and we sat down on a wooden crate against the outside wall of a warehouse. I looked around at the amber nocturnal world. No colors showed other than yellow and black.

"This is available," Ramon said in Spanish.

He removed a joint from his pack of cigarettes and lit it. After taking a hit, he handed it to me. Ramon's coworkers were not far, but if Ramon wasn't concerned, neither was I. He removed a flower top wrapped in cellophane from his shirt pocket. Inside was a seedless, dark green bud laced with orange and red threads. I unwrapped it and squeezed. Resin stuck to my fingers. Ramon pulled the flower apart and rolled another joint. We puffed away on our respective doobies. The pot was good—fresh from the mountains.

"There are fifty kilos of red hair," he said.

"Bueno, but I only need fifteen kilos," I told him.

"Six hundred pesos per kilo," he said. "Nine thousand for fifteen kilos."

Forty-eight dollars a kilo was a decent price. Seven hundred and twenty dollars for thirty-three pounds would keep us on budget. Ramon told me to meet him at a bar on the southern outskirts of town at six p.m. the next day. From there, we would drive to his house.

"It has to be good," I said, remembering how our friends in the mountains sometimes needed a little prompting to come up with what we wanted.

"Of course," he said as he smoked his joint.

I had never smoked weed with a guy his age, nor had I toked up in the amber world of a Mexican shipyard.

In my periphery, I sensed a disturbance. People had stopped working and were looking toward the gate. Two uniformed policemen stood just inside the entrance, talking with workers. They began walking toward Ramon and me.

"Tranquilo," Ramon said.

I had already pinched my joint and stuck it in my sock and hoped this old man did something similar. I relaxed on the crate as Ramon stood next to me—just an old Mexican dockworker and a semi-long-haired gringo hanging out at the shipyard on a Saturday night. Ramon's joint had disappeared. Where?

The cops said, "Buenas noches" to Ramon and me, then spoke with Ramon for a minute before walking away. Relief. Ramon smiled, opened his mouth and removed his half joint. When the cops were out of sight, he lit it. I left mine in my sock for Tom.

The night's business was finished. Ramon sat down next to me, and we watched cranes swing wood crates onto the high deck of a ship.

"I have a question about the United States," he said in Spanish. "It is the United States, I know. But what is it the United States of? United States of Nueva York?"

I laughed. "No. Not New York. It is the United States of America."

Ramon nodded and looked up at the ship. I saw how he had gotten that idea. New York was stenciled on the sterns and bows of the two ships in front of us.

"Many ships come from Nueva York," he said, still processing the information.

To kill time before the connection the next day, Tom and I hung around the pool, then walked across the road to the beach. In the late afternoon, we drove his Bug into town for dinner. When we returned to the car, the triangular window vent in front of the right window had been shoved in. Someone had stolen his tape player and CB radio. Fuck.

I doubted we could find another CB radio in Veracruz and certainly not this late. We developed an alternate plan. There had been no checkpoints on the way down except the usual twenty-kilometer stop for southbound traffic. If a checkpoint or roadblock popped up on our run, I would alert Tom with a series of brake light flashes. If I came to a halt, Tom would stop way behind and use discretion on whether he needed to get out of there. I had faith in him. He had displayed prowess on the sands of Daytona Beach. And except for trying to nail a falling vulture, he'd shown good judgment. (My hit had been unintentional.)

When I arrived at the rendezvous bar, Ramon was waiting outside, and we drove to his house in a southeast barrio of

Veracruz. On both sides of the dirt street, wooden shacks blended into each other. Two dogs lay on their sides and eyed me, ready to bark if I spoke one word of English and confirmed I didn't belong. Gray and blue light escaped from front windows, and I heard television voices. A few houses away, four kids play-kicked and punched each other in the street David Carradine style.

Ramon and I went through the front door of his house, and he pointed to a sofa. I sat down as he disappeared into a room in the back. He returned with a burlap bag brimming with flower tops. I pinched a bud and rolled it between my fingers. The pot looked and smelled good. There were seeds, but minimal. It would suffice.

Ramon spoke to someone in the back, and a young woman about my age with long black hair came through the door carrying a fish scale. She handed Ramon the scale and smiled at me before returning to the back room. Ramon removed a hanging plant from the ceiling and attached the scale to a hook. The bag registered a hair over fifteen kilos.

I placed the kilos into a plastic garbage bag, then double-bagged it. The weed went inside a suitcase, which went into the trunk of my Bug. When Ramon and I shook hands goodbye, he told me to come directly to his house the next time. I didn't mention there would be no next time.

It was almost seven o'clock and already dark. I drove to the Mocambo while staying alert for signs of an imminent bust. If Ramon had snitched to someone, the short drive to the hotel could be where they'd try to get me.

Tom and I checked out of the Mocambo and walked to our cars. I removed the suitcase from my trunk and waited for Tom to unlatch the hood of his Bug. He stood there, looking at me.

"Come on, let's go," I said.

I glanced around the parking lot. It was not a good time to be discussing anything. Was he chickening out?

"I was thinking it might be better to keep it inside with me," he said.

"Inside?"

"You'll get stopped first, so I'll have a warning. If anything happens, I'll blast off. If I need to toss the suitcase or hide it somewhere, I can do it a lot quicker if it's inside the car."

That made sense. And he was the one carrying it.

I hoisted the suitcase over his back seat and set it upright with the handle on top. Clothes, towels and pillows went up against it to keep it in place. We didn't need to mask the smell with fish because the double bagging and suitcase would contain the odor for the short ten-hour drive.

It was seven thirty. We were on schedule. I led Tom north along the boulevard and out of Veracruz. Throughout the night, we drank Cokes to stay awake and rendezvoused to refuel and take a break. We passed the infernal gas flames of Tuxpan and the turnoff for the pine tree beach. I listened to old music and new. All my favorite groups had recorded at least one new album since my last trip south. Genesis had definitely lost their edge without Peter Gabriel, but Gabriel's solo album was excellent. Music was surviving disco. Tom and I arrived at the river just before sunrise.

I decided to cross the pot the old-fashioned way—from the U.S. side after clearing customs. Crossing from the Mexican side with Jack last time had made me uneasy. I wasn't sure why. Both techniques had their risks.

We removed the bag from the suitcase and hiked into the dunes. After burying it, we drove down the beach and I tossed the suitcase. We slept a few hours, then I briefed Tom on what customs would ask and how to respond. He left, and I waited half an hour before departing the beach with "On the Border" playing on the cassette deck. Would I show up on a criminal list at customs? It didn't matter. I was clean.

*

After clearing customs, Tom and I met at Denny's for breakfast, then checked into the Motel 6. I woke up before him and slipped out to buy a Styrofoam boogie board, plastic sandwich bags and two penlights. On the way back to the motel,

I stopped at a hardware store for a can of black spray paint. At twenty past midnight, we left for the river in Tom's Bug and pulled off the road to spray-paint the Styrofoam board.

As we cruised south on the beach, a half moon played hide and seek with clouds over the Gulf. After parking at the river, I zipped my penlight into a plastic baggie and waded in with the Styrofoam board. Tom drove away. He would return in twenty minutes and wait for one blink of my flashlight. If everything was cool, he would flash once. If not, twice.

I paddled across the river and carried the board across the hard sand, then dropped it where the dunes began. Upriver, a dog barked. I looked and saw the same distant light on the Mexican side I had seen before. The dog continued barking—certainly not at me. I watched. The lone light erupted into several lights. Voices. A car motor. Two pairs of headlights began racing along the river bank in my direction. I dropped to the sand and watched. They kept coming. I grabbed the Styrofoam board and stayed low as I moved to the dunes.

I planted the board's nose into the sand, shoved it down, and frantically covered it with sand. A few dunes away, I dug a hole with my hands the size of a body or a prisoner or a corpse. I sat in it and covered my legs with sand, then lay back and concealed my torso, my other arm and my face. Afterward I dug my working arm into the sand. Soon I heard talking in Spanish. The voices grew louder, then diminished, then grew louder again. The cycle continued for what seemed like hours until they faded for the last time. Engines started and also faded.

I had no idea of the time and feared dawn would soon arrive. When I finally moved my face out of the sand, it was still dark. The moon had set, but the east horizon was a shade lighter than the sky overhead. I crawled a few yards and looked upriver, then across. Quiet. No activity. I dug up the weed and Styrofoam board and crouched back to the river.

I flashed Tom once. No reply. I flashed again. And again. Nothing. I swam across, pushing the board with the bag of weed duct-taped to the top. When I got to the other side, Tom was missing in action. It would not be cool to be standing next to the Rio Grande at sunrise with thirty-three pounds of sinsemilla. I dragged everything into the dunes.

Forty-five minutes later, I heard a car approach. As I peered over the rim of a dune, the silhouette of Tom's Bug made a right turn from the beach and parked near the river. The sun was still below the horizon, but the sky was on the verge of morning.

"What happened?" he asked.

"Let's get outta here. Pull closer to the dunes," I said.

I fetched the weed and we drove away. My arm rested on the window frame as the salt air blow-dried my hair. I looked over my right shoulder at the top of a big orange emerging from the sea.

"Man, I thought they got you," he said.

"What did you see?" I asked.

"Two cars or trucks. They drove to where you probably got out of the water. I heard people talking in Spanish, and they shined flashlights all along the river and in the dunes. I thought they got you for sure. I didn't know what to do."

I would have cut Tom some slack if he had driven up within ten maybe fifteen minutes after I crossed back. Dan or Jack would not have left me in such a vulnerable position—I don't think.

"What did you do? How come they didn't catch you?" Tom asked.

"I buried myself in the sand."

"Man, I can't believe this shit. I can't believe you made it. And with the kilos."

We returned to the Motel 6 and slept.

Our plan had been to caravan back to Houston and divide the weed so Tom could drive his share to New York.

"Tom, you're still going to New York, right?" I asked in the morning.

"Right."

"Why don't we divide the kilos here and you can head back now if you want."

"Okay, but I've got to go by my apartment anyway."

"That's okay. We can divide it here. There won't be a problem driving to Houston. We always get waved through the Border Patrol check."

In Houston, Todd sold my share.

CHAPTER TWENTY-TWO

Cocaine All Around My Brain

My money from the run with Tom went into the bank, and I returned to my job. But I wanted more freedom, so I searched for a house to contract myself. In the wetlands of Addicks Reservoir west of Highway 6, prefabricated houses were going up in a new subdivision. Stacks of complete eight-foot wall sections sat next to fresh cement slabs. It looked interesting. The superintendent handed me a set of blueprints, and I called a worker I had gotten along with at my old job. We became partners.

Matt was a laid-back 28 year old from St. Louis. The two of us put up a house a week—two days for the framing and three for the siding and cornice. I occasionally took off to surf and fly, and made it up by working late and on weekends. Matt didn't like disco either, and we found clubs in Houston that weren't devoted to it—places like Foxhunter, Fizz and Struts.

We also drove down to Mickey Gilley's honky-tonk in Pasadena where country and western bands played for the line dancers on a vast wood dance floor. Gilley's down-to-earth ambiance made the place more comfortable than the discos in Houston, so long as you didn't mind an occasional beer bottle flying past your head. No one cared that Matt and I weren't real cowboys (or fake ones). A mechanical bucking bull was set up away from the dance floor and allowed real (and inebriated) cowboys and cowgirls to display their rodeo skills before being thrown. Soft padding surrounded the bull.

Matt had gone to Vietnam, and something about it remained with him. Normally, he was the mellowest person I'd ever met. At work, he never got mad. Whenever we had a disagreement, he'd wander away. Later, I would find him sitting quietly in a cubbyhole or entranceway.

But alcohol triggered something and made him rowdy and unpredictable. He once picked up a tip jar at a nightclub and walked out the door with it. I didn't understand why. It certainly wasn't for the money. I chased him and got him to return it, but it was like I had to break through to the person inside.

Matt had been an MP (Military Police) in Vietnam, and he always brushed off my questions about his experiences. He only said he and his buddies used to climb a hill, smoke a Thai stick and watch bullet tracers sail through the night sky. But there had to have been more.

*

Todd loved flying and began taking lessons. When we flew together, I let him use the second set of flight controls at the right seat, and we split the rental cost. Todd's friends, Billy and his wife, Julie, also liked to fly. And what they liked most was to climb to 9,000 feet at night where the air was dry enough to chop up their cocaine in the back seat. When they finished snorting, I pulled the throttle to idle, and we silently spiraled down over the lights of Houston. At 700 feet per minute, the peaceful descent lasted ten minutes.

I didn't indulge in the festivities until we got back on the ground. It was illegal to fly within eight hours of drinking alcohol, and snorting cocaine probably fell within that rule. Billy and Julie chipped in for the plane rental, so, thanks to everyone, I was getting in a lot of inexpensive flying.

One day Todd asked if I'd be interested in flying a friend of his to Lakeway Airport on Lake Travis, north of Austin. I couldn't legally fly for money without a commercial license, but the FAA allowed flight expenses to be shared. Todd said his friend would cover the cost of the plane rental. (The rules didn't specify that the sharing of expenses had to be equal.) Todd told me Joseph needed to fly to Austin to show samples of cocaine to a potential buyer.

The nicest plane I'd gotten checked out in was the Cherokee Archer, a four-place, low-wing Piper with 180 horsepower. Because of its higher cost, I had only flown it a couple of hours. I took a chance Todd's friend wouldn't mind the expense.

Todd and Joseph met me inside Andrau Airpark's small general aviation terminal. Joseph was tall, clean-cut, and dressed in Texas casual business attire; long-sleeve cowboy shirt with snaps instead of buttons, Levi jeans and silver belt buckle.

We walked across the ramp and I stepped up onto the right wing, opened the door and slid over to the left seat. There is only one door on most small Pipers, and Joseph climbed up behind me in his ostrich-skin boots. I held the front seat forward as he maneuvered into the back. Todd sat copilot to my right.

During the flight, Joseph asked me questions about airplanes and flying. I mentioned the ride wasn't always as smooth, and that I could only fly in good weather until I got an instrument rating.

"What does that take?" he asked.

"I need another twenty hours of instruction in instrument conditions or under the hood. A hood is a plastic helmet you wear so you can't see outside while flying—only the instruments."

When we returned to Andrau, instead of dropping off Joseph and Todd at the terminal, Joseph asked me to taxi to where I had rented the plane. Todd got out, and Joseph sat down in the copilot's seat next to me. He opened his briefcase and asked the cost of the plane rental. I read the hour meter. Three and a half hours would be $150. Joseph handed me three hundred dollars.

"Todd said you can't accept money for flying me, so maybe you can use the extra for some instrument training," he said.

He pushed the door open and looked around at the planes on

the ramp.

"Are all these airplanes available to rent?" he asked.

"Most of them," I answered.

I went into the office and paid for the plane, then drove Todd and Joseph to the terminal. Before Joseph got out, he handed me a small, green triangular packet.

"Thanks," I said and put it in my shirt pocket.

The packet was a holster of cocaine fashioned from, most likely, a hundred-dollar bill—a sort of cocaine paloma. Snorting coke through a rolled-up bill less than a hundred was considered crass, and I presumed a similar protocol existed for the cocaine paloma. I had learned all this from Todd.

At his apartment, Todd removed one of the milky-brown chunks of coke from the packet and used a razor blade to chop it up on the glass of a framed picture. He retrieved a short plastic straw from the kitchen, and we each snorted a rail. Then he poured the rest of the coke into a small brown vial and gave it to me. I was impressed with Todd's methodology. He took it all quite seriously. Before handing me the hundred-dollar paloma, he scraped the remaining coke from it with the razor blade and rubbed the residue on his teeth.

*

After our next flight a week later, Joseph asked if anything bigger was available to fly. I pointed to a Piper Cherokee Six.

"That one has six seats," I told him.

We walked over, and Joseph peered through the Plexiglas. In the back, two rows of velour seats faced each other. A door behind the wing on the left side allowed passengers to enter the cabin without having to climb onto a wing.

"Can you fly this?" Joseph asked.

"I'm not checked out in it. Rental places make you get a check-out for each type of plane. I could fly it if I got checked out."

The Cherokee Six had a 300-horsepower engine, which meant I also needed a logbook endorsement for high-performance aircraft.

"How much would it take?"

"A hundred and forty dollars. Maybe less." I figured I could do it in two hours.

"I mean, how many days would it take you to check out in it? Can we fly it next week?"

"Oh. Probably. If it's available."

Joseph handed me enough cash to cover our flight, an additional $300 to get checked out in the Cherokee Six, and another cocaine paloma.

"See if you can schedule it for next Thursday at ten in the morning," he said.

"I'll go over to the flight office now and call Todd this evening," I told him.

I bought a manual for the Cherokee Six and studied. My check-out took an hour and a half. When Joseph arrived for the flight, he had his partner with him. They sat in the back row facing forward with their legs stretched out and their briefcases on the seats in front of them. We flew the Cherokee Six at Andrau Airpark two more times before I deemed it prudent to spread our activity. Flying around with a small amount of coke didn't bother me. Getting nailed by the FAA for flying for money without a commercial license did. I called around and located another Cherokee Six at Weiser Air Park.

*

While working construction, the length of my hair hadn't been a concern, but now I kept it somewhat trim so I wouldn't appear to be a hippie-bum when I rented airplanes.

I turned my new '78 El Camino off Highway 290 and made a sharp right after Carl's Barbecue. Airplanes were tied down along a chain-link fence on the right. To my left, a blue-and-white plastic sign atop a small building advertised Ray's Flying Service as a Piper Flite Center. I stepped up onto the porch and entered. On the right was a small cubbyhole office with a gray-haired man leaning back in a chair. His eyes were closed, and a toothpick hung from his lips. I walked quietly past him and read postings of airplanes for sale on a bulletin board.

When I returned, Ray's eyes were open. He glanced at my logbook and handed me the plane's clipboard and keys. After preflighting the Six, I sat in the pilot's seat and examined the radios and instrument panel. The instruments were the same as the Cherokee Six at Andrau. The radios were different, but a radio was a radio.

During the flight, I learned Ray had been a lieutenant colonel in the Air Force and flew fighter jets in Korea. He asked me to perform two stall recoveries and two steep turns, then we returned to Weiser Airpark for three landings on the grass strip. That was the checkout. Ray wrote one hour in my logbook to satisfy his insurance company but only charged me for the actual seven-tenths of an hour aircraft and instructor time.

Ray had been laid-back in the plane. Nothing seemed urgent. That calm had to be the result of decades of flying experience. I scheduled an instrument flight lesson with him, and as I exited the building, Ray was already settled into his chair with his eyes closed.

*

On my next flight with Joseph, he explained that he and his partner were dealing two types of coke: Peruvian flake, which had a pink tint, and Bolivian crystal, which was brown. He showed me two different crystals the size of thumbnails and said they brought the cocaine in from South America, all of it uncut.

Afterward, the four of us sat in the leather seats of Joseph's green Jaguar as he placed a pink cube on a small mirror and chipped at it with a razor blade. A thin wafer separated from the cube's side, and he chopped it into powder. Joseph repeated the process with the Bolivian coke, then spread out a two-inch line from each mound with the razor blade.

He handed me a rolled-up hundred-dollar bill and said, "We'd like your opinion of the two types of coke."

"Me? That's a laugh. I'm no expert."

"That's why we want your input. The membranes in our noses are burnt out. We can't tell if it's harsh or not. Your nose is undamaged."

My virgin nose took the taste test and decided the Peruvian flake was smoother than the Bolivian crystal.

*

Hanging out with Todd expanded my minimal social life a bit, although I still lacked in the girlfriend department. Some evenings, I accompanied him to Billy and Julie's apartment where Billy laid out fat rails of coke four inches long, and another and another. We enjoyed nonstop games of backgammon and discussed topics ranging from theology of the masses to why malls supplied their bathrooms with toilet paper that didn't absorb, only smeared. We drank Heinekens, smoked pot, and listened to music. Before calling it a night, we often indulged in a Quaalude nightcap to take the edge off.

Matt and I got along well and continued to fine tune our two-worker house-raising system. The only thing he wasn't happy about was my participation in the coke scene. He considered cocaine a ridiculous drug and couldn't understand why anyone did it. Its rush lasted all of twenty minutes, he said, and when you started coming down, you had to do more to keep from feeling like shit, and more, and more. He said that even speed was better than coke because it lasted a long time and made you productive. Matt may have had some experience with speed, but I never saw him do anything other than smoke pot. Matt associated Todd with cocaine, and whenever I invited him to do something with us, he declined. On Saturday nights, Matt's excuse was that *Love Boat* was on, followed by *Fantasy Island.*

*

When Joseph asked me what it would take to get checked out in a plane with two engines, I explained that pilots normally trained first in a single-engine plane with retractable-gear, then transitioned to a twin. He asked again if I could do it, like he just wanted a yes or a no. Yes, of course. He handed me some cash.

I drove to David Wayne Hooks airport in northwest Houston the next afternoon and began training in a twin-engine Piper Seneca. The fuselage and interior were identical to the Cherokee

Six, so I had a head start. The instrument panel and control quadrant also looked the same except there were two of everything. Piper had basically just added a second engine to the Cherokee Six. It didn't seem complicated. The instructor told me transitioning to a twin would take ten hours, give or take.

I continued to fly Joseph in the Cherokee Six while I worked on my multi-engine rating. After I passed the multi checkride, I concentrated on instrument flight training at Ray's Flying Service. Todd earned his private pilot ticket and began serving as my official safety pilot when I practiced instrument procedures wearing the view-limiting hood.

*

After a night of backgammon at Billy and Julie's place, I awoke at three a.m. itching like crazy. Red welts covered my body, and I felt feverish. I drove to an emergency clinic and was told I had hives, probably caused by an allergic reaction to something I had eaten. A nurse asked me to list everything I ate and drank in the last twenty-four hours. I omitted the cocaine. She gave me Benadryl capsules, and two hours later, the welts were gone. I quit doing coke, cold-turkey, and the hives didn't return. Matt may have had a point about cocaine.

My logbook now showed 240 flight hours and an unused multi-engine rating. It had been a month since Todd heard from Joseph. As much as Todd and I wanted to fly the twin-engine Seneca, renting it for $120 an hour was not in either of our budgets, especially without my stipend from the Godfather (Todd's nickname for Joseph).

Todd and I had grown accustomed to flying to new places with Joseph. Just floating over Houston now bored us. I checked out in Ray's 180-horsepower 1968 Piper Arrow with retractable gear, and Todd and I searched the chart for new airports to explore. One of our favorites became Matagorda Island, an hour south of Houston, where we landed at an abandoned air force base and body-surfed in the Gulf.

Eventually, Todd learned that the Godfather had run into trouble. No specifics were given (at least to me). Our cross-country flights were on hiatus. I worked more hours with Matt.

One Saturday, Todd and I took off for Brownsville in the Piper Arrow—our excuse being to rent a car and drive to Padre Island. When the sky got hazy over Corpus Christi, we radioed Air Traffic Control for airplane traffic advisories. The controller gave us a four-number code to set in the plane's transponder, then informed us we were in radar contact. We had most likely been on his radar earlier, but now the signal was amplified by our transponder, and a specific code moved with the target on his radar screen.

As we descended, Houston Center transferred us to Brownsville Approach Control and told us radar contact was lost. I looked at the transponder and saw its blue light still blinking. Somewhere, a radar station had us in contact. We continued our descent into Brownsville, and the transponder light extinguished at about 700 feet. We had probably still been on Houston Center's radar until then. Apparently, Brownsville Approach did not have radar.

Todd rented a car, and we headed for South Padre Island. As we passed the turnoff to Laguna Vista, I wondered if Jack and Beth still lived in the same rental house. I hadn't heard from Jack since about half a year after prison. Beth had been pregnant at the time and they planned to get married. Most likely, they had moved elsewhere in the two years since then.

It was still daylight when Todd and I returned to the airport from the beach, so we flew along the Rio Grande to the Gulf. I leveled at 1,000 feet and kept a little distance from the river. The transponder's blue light blinked steady and strong. I inched down, and the light quit blinking at 700 feet. When I climbed above 720 feet, it blinked back on.

Todd looked at me. "No radar below seven hundred feet," he said.

"Appears not."

We did a couple of three-sixties near the river mouth, and I pointed out where I used to bury the pot on the other side. I aimed the Arrow toward Houston and handed the controls to

Todd.

He leveled at 5,500 feet, and night gradually consumed the world. In an hour, Houston's mass of lights appeared on the horizon.

*

Without the Godfather's blessings, I didn't have extra cash to continue instrument training. I worried that if I didn't practice regularly, I'd lose everything Ray had taught me. There were also the monthly payments on my El Camino. Matt and I worked longer hours together, which made him happy.

One night as I flew a practice instrument approach into Andrau Airpark, Todd said to me out of the blue, "You know, if we could figure how to do a run in a plane, I would finance it and we'd split the profit."

He sat in the right seat, and no doubt had been watching the transponder light blinking in and out of radar coverage at our low altitude.

"Flying low across the border?" I asked.

"Under the radar," he said.

I took the plastic hood off my head and adjusted my eyes to the million lights that spread across southwest Houston.

"Where would we load it? What about fuel? The Arrow doesn't have the range to fly all the way from Veracruz to Houston. I don't know if Ray will even let me take the plane to Mexico."

"We could drive the weed somewhere closer to the border, then fly down and pick it up," he said.

"Something like that might be possible but isn't the whole point to do it by air?"

I couldn't get a plan to focus. There were too many variables. It would take some investigation.

A few days later, I asked Ray if he allowed his rental planes to fly to Mexico.

"Sure. If you buy the additional insurance. And it'll have to be a dry rate," he answered.

A plane rented at a dry rate meant the pilot paid for the fuel separately, and the hourly rental rate was lower. That would work out fine.

But Todd and I didn't know anything about flying in Mexico, and I wasn't about to do a run in an airplane, half-cocked. We would take a flying vacation and see what the options were—play it by ear.

CHAPTER TWENTY-THREE

Volcán Orizaba

We landed at McAllen Airport, and I filed an international flight plan for the hop across the border to Reynosa. After takeoff, Todd and I watched the transponder light start to blink as we climbed through 700 feet. Ahead, a pale green Rio Grande snaked east through plowed fields. After crossing the river, a conglomeration of unpainted cement block houses and wooden shacks passed below us. I looked down on a mosaic of rusty tin roofs decorated with water tanks of various sizes and colors, wooden crates, a few bicycles and a truck camper shell. Litter was spread across vacant lots and curbs.

"Is it time to call Reynosa?" Todd asked.

I looked up and saw the airport ahead.

"You can do it," I said. Todd enjoyed being copilot.

At Reynosa International Airport, we parked on the ramp and walked under a big, flapping Mexican flag and into a building where we cleared customs. In the general aviation office next door, I handed our flight plan from McAllen to an official in a blue uniform. He helped me fill out a flight plan to Tampico, then signed it, stamped it and handed me the bottom two copies. Like the flight plans in the U.S., the Mexican ones listed the departure and destination airports, number of people on board, departure time, route, ETA, time en route and fuel on board.

"Buen viaje, Capitán," the agent told me as Todd and I

walked out to the ramp.

In Mexico, I was a Capitán.

Todd sat in the left seat and flew us to Tampico. He leveled off at 5,500 feet with the Gulf fifty miles to our left. A line of mountains paralleled us on the right and merged with our course in the distance. I had Todd aim for where the mountains met the sea. With full fuel, we could have flown all the way to Veracruz, but this was an exploratory mission. We needed to learn the lay of the land—and the air. With an extra stop, we would gain more information about flight procedures in Mexico.

We passed over two small airstrips: one with asphalt and one with grass. I looked at the highlighted course on the chart and noted the time over each airport in my notebook.

"What's to stop us from landing at one of these airports?" Todd asked.

"Nothing, I guess, except we didn't put them as our destination on the flight plan we filed. And we don't know who or what's down there."

In Tampico's general aviation office, we caught the official unaware. He had not been advised of our arrival. I reached into my flight case and handed him the two copies of the flight plan and our aircraft documents. He smiled and inspected them. Being a Man of Papers was a valuable trait.

Even though Todd and I wore jeans, polo shirts and sneakers, we were treated with respect. Only the elite traveled in private airplanes, and I was a Capitán. I filled out a flight plan to Veracruz in triplicate, and the agent signed and stamped them and handed back two copies.

Through the office window, I watched three soldiers with rifles walk around the Arrow. They peered through the Plexiglas windows but avoided touching the plane. We topped off the tanks again, and Todd flew us south.

After landing in Veracruz and turning in our flight plan, the official pointed through the window to where we could tie down the plane. Todd walked to the terminal to see about our rental car.

"Can I fly to airports that don't have these offices?" I asked the agent in Spanish.

"Yes. Of course," he answered.

He explained that I could fly to an airport without facilities, and just hold on to the original flight plan to turn in at the next manned airport.

"But to which airport do you wish to fly?" he asked. "There is no gasoline at many airports because of the shortage. Sometimes pilots carry fuel in containers."

I removed the chart from my briefcase and pointed to an airport near the beach.

"There is no gasoline there," he told me.

"Gracias."

I taxied the plane to the tie-down area and met Todd at the rental car counter. I told him what the official said about airports and fuel.

We checked into the Hotel Mocambo, and in the evening I drove our VW Rabbit to town and parked near the docks. I sat for a while on the same bench outside the shipyard as a year and a half before, then walked over to the gate and looked inside. Wooden crates swung from cranes under the yellow lights, and dockworkers milled about, but there was no sign of Ramon. I didn't think it would be cool to enter the yard uninvited, so I sat on the bench for another thirty minutes before returning to the Mocambo.

"What are you going to do?" asked Todd.

Everything on the Mexican side of the border was my expertise and my responsibility. Todd trusted me. He only wanted to know our next move.

"Ramon told me to come directly to his house the last time I saw him. It's been so long, I thought I'd try the shipyard first. I'll go to his house tomorrow."

The next afternoon, I drove to Ramon's home in the barrio. Sitting outside in the shade of the front wall was the girl who had brought Ramon the fish scale when he weighed the kilos for me.

She watched me as I got out of the car and walked toward her.

"Buenas tardes," I said.

She sat up straight and smiled. Did she recognize me?

"Está Don Ramon aqui?" I asked.

Her smile disappeared.

"No está," she said.

We continued in Spanish.

"When will he return?"

"Not soon." She paused. "He is in jail."

Ramon in jail? Shit. Maybe he had only gotten drunk and created a Scorpio-like disturbance. He might be out soon.

"For how long?" I asked.

She looked down at the dirt.

"A long time. He is in the penitentiary for molesting a young girl."

And he seemed like such a nice guy.

"Oh. Gracias," I said

I paused, then turned toward the car.

"You want like before?" she asked.

She remembered me.

I turned back. "Si."

She stood up and held out her hand.

"I am Maria. Ramon is my uncle," she said.

"Soy Steve," I said and shook her hand.

"I know where there is marijuana. But we must go to the mountains." She pointed over the roof of her house to the west.

Maria looked to be only a few years older than me and didn't seem the type to have experience in such business. But what did I know? Mexico was the land of mystery and surprise. I explained to her that I had an airplane this time, un avion, and I needed to find a field or road or private airstrip to land and load the weed.

She knew of places, she said, and could go with me to the mountains in three days. I wasn't entirely convinced of her ability, but she sounded confident—and I didn't have a better option. She told me we would get mota at least as good as what her uncle had sold me. We agreed to meet Friday afternoon.

For the next two days, Todd and I lounged around the pool, body-surfed in the warm Gulf, shopped at the outdoor market and hung out in town listening to mariachis and marimbas while sampling cervezas. We also purchased four plastic five-gallon gas containers and stowed them in the baggage compartment of the Arrow (as recommended by our friendly airport official).

While I studied the chart for potential refueling airports, Punta Roca Partida kept poking into view. Todd and I still had another day to kill, so I suggested a day trip. Toro Prieto was only a two-hour drive. It had been five years.

The road to Toro was now graded with crushed rock, and power lines ran alongside it. We parked in front of El Mio's store as chickens and roosters dispersed around the side of the building. An electric wire hung from a wood pole down to the store, and another wire ran to a nearby electric water well. I wondered if the town's residents still used the bushes as their bathroom, and if the pigs still cleaned the corn cobs afterward.

El Mio raised the counter's center section and came out to greet us. Wc shook hands, and I introduced him to Todd.

"Buenas tardes, El Mio," I said.

"Buenas tardes, Esteef," he said. "Mucho tiempo."

"Si. Mucho tiempo."

He and his coal-black hair looked the same.

"Su otro amigo," he said. "No viene?" *Your other friend. He does not come?*

"No. Dan no está conmigo. Solamente Todd," I said.

"Ta," El Mio attempted, and he shook Todd's hand again. "Chaparrito," he added, smiling. Chaparrito was a nickname for a short or small person.

Todd was only five foot four inches or so, but I never thought of him as small, even though he was also thin. And he didn't have the so-called short man complex. Being a black belt in karate may have had something to do with it—that and his intelligence. Todd and I sat down at a table under the roof.

"Refrescos?"

"Si." I turned to Todd. "Cervezas?"

He smiled and nodded.

When El Mio went for the beers, I looked down the sandy path that led to the Gulf and thought about the storm surf Dan and I had tried to ride. It seemed so long ago. El Mio returned with two sweating bottles of Superior and sat down. We talked a bit, and before I could ask about Isidra, two girls walked into view around the outside of the building. They stopped talking when they spotted our car and did a quick glance in our direction before continuing under the roof and walking behind the counter.

El Mio's brown eyes shined. "La negrita," he said and smiled.

The little black one? Which one? Neither looked black to me.

El Mio turned to the girls.

"Isidra," he said.

Isidra? I looked. She stood behind the counter, wiping it with a rag. Her hair was no longer straight or long or sun-tinted. It was cut in what U.S. fashion called a shag, and her face looked rounder. Had she gained weight? Probably just the haircut. She did appear a little dark, but certainly not a negrita. I hadn't noticed that before.

"She is engaged to a maestro," El Mio told me, emphasizing "maestro" like it was prestigious, which it was. It meant teacher.

"Hablas con ella," El Mio nudged me. *Talk with her.*

I walked to the counter. Isidra looked up.

"Isidra," I said and paused. "Me recuerdas?" *Do you remember me?*

"Si," she said. "Esteef."

She looked down at the rag and folded it. I vaguely recalled telling her five years before that I would be back. This probably didn't count. I wondered if she remembered. Or cared.

Isidra and I walked past El Mio and Todd and along the path to the beach. She told me she lived most of the time in San

Andrés Tuxtla but often visited Toro Prieto. I didn't tell her I had driven past the road to Toro many times but couldn't stop because I was racing through the night with a load of weed. I also didn't tell her I had been an inmate in a prison in her own country. There wasn't much I could tell her. I didn't even mention I was now a pilot and had come to Mexico in an airplane. How would a girl in a remote Mexican village process that?

So we talked about improvements to the road, the new electricity, the water well, her fiancé the maestro—Mexico small talk. Five years had passed, yet she still possessed the same natural beauty as when we listened to *Dark Side of the Moon* while sitting in my VW Bug. We had been twenty years old together once, but mucha agua had flowed under the bridge. She touched my hair and dropped her fingers to my shoulder where it extended last time. My hair barely made it to the bottom of my ears now.

"Yo lo corté," I said. "Usted, igualmente." *I cut it. You, too.*

I moved my right hand close to her shoulder but didn't touch her.

Isidra invited me and Todd to go swimming at a nearby public pool with her and her cousin. We said adios to El Mio, and the four of us drove back down the graded road. At the community pool, we lounged in the shade of tall mango trees, had a few beers, and took turns jumping off the high board. When the sun descended to the tree tops, I offered to drive Isidra and her cousin back to Toro, but they insisted on waiting for a bus that would soon pass by. I reached out my hand, and Isidra held it. She asked if I would be returning, and I said I didn't know.

"Es posible," I added.

She told me that in two months she would be living full-time in San Andrés Tuxtla. Did Isidra want me to return? She was engaged.

As Todd drove us to the main road, Jackson Browne's "Running on Empty" played while the countryside drifted by.

Aside from the electricity and Isidra's new hairstyle, everything at Toro looked the same as it had five years earlier. Time passed differently on this side of the border. If I hadn't gotten sick in Costa Rica, would I have made it back to Toro? Would it have changed anything?

On the highway, we saw a sign with a symbol for a pyramid. Todd turned onto the side road, and we ended up at three unrestored pyramids a hundred feet high. After climbing the middle one—the least dilapidated—we sat at the edge of its flat top and gazed west. The sun was below the horizon, and several tall thunderclouds had merged in the distance with their upper halves brightly illuminated from behind. The sky slowly changed from pink to red to dark. Lightning bugs began to flicker around the other two pyramids. The flickering spread to our pyramid and encompassed us. We sat quietly and watched. The tiny blinking lights were nowhere else—just around the three pyramids. Dan would have declared it a good omen.

The next afternoon, I picked up Maria, and we drove west toward Puebla where her cousin would help with procurement of the weed. I was curious to see the judicial black hole that dispensed the fates of narcotraficantes internacionales and fun-seeking tourists. We climbed away from Veracruz's coastal jungle on a long, straight road. As the sun set ahead, a tall cone-shaped volcano with a snowy cap rose above the world.

"Es Pico de Orizaba, un volcan," Maria said. "La montaña más alta de Mexico." *It is Orizaba Peak. A volcano. The highest mountain in Mexico.*

We drove through the shadow of Volcan Orizaba and emerged onto Mexico's central plateau. An hour later, the hazy glow of Puebla shone ahead in the night sky. At the city's outskirts, we left the highway and maneuvered through dimly lit narrow streets. Puebla did not appear mythical. Houses were ramshackle, and trash was scattered along the curbs. But this was just a barrio of Puebla. The Emerald City district most likely lay elsewhere.

Maria's cousin lived in a duplicate of Ramon's abode in

Veracruz. While Maria talked with her cousin in the kitchen, I sat on a wicker sofa rooted into the dirt floor of the living room. In front of me, four children lay sprawled on the dirt, mesmerized by Fred and Wilma Flintstone speaking Spanish on a black-and-white television.

That night, the wicker sofa made for an uncomfortable bed, and in the morning, we retraced our drive halfway back to Veracruz to the city of Cordoba. At a restaurant near the town's impressive zocalo, we joined a friend of Ramon's named Jorge. He told us he would hear from his people in the mountains in the evening. I wondered if I would be purchasing the pot directly from Indians as I had done in Oaxaca, or through a middle man like Ramon.

"Maria said you need to locate somewhere to land un avion," he said.

"Yes."

"There are possibilities. If you like, we can go now to see."

Jorge sat in the passenger seat and directed us through the foothills, pointing out dirt roads and cow pastures, usually at the bottom or sides of narrow valleys. I rejected all of them. Every location Jorge showed me was either too sloped, too rocky, too short or surrounded by too high terrain. He had no idea of the requirements of un avion. Why should he?

After exploring for three hours, I realized I had made an impossible request. No flat land existed. The image of Tony's charred, mummified friends inside their burned Aero Commander remained etched in my mind. I wasn't about to end up like them.

We had better luck with the weed. Jorge's contact informed him they had some good sinsemilla, and it would be available the next day. I put in an order for thirty kilos. Maria and I slept together on Jorge's sofa—her on the seat cushions, and me on the top of the backrest—another restless night.

Jorge didn't accompany us to the rendezvous. He gave Maria directions, and we drove away at eleven p.m. Just past the town of Fortin de las Flores, we turned right onto a dirt road and passed through several sleeping villages. The road curved left, and we gradually ascended through a valley of moonlit silhouettes. We crossed a narrow metal bridge and wound up steeply. After reaching a plateau, we turned left.

"You have been here before?" I asked Maria in Spanish.

Our route seemed complicated.

"I know Coscomatepec. The last town. My aunt lives there. When I was young, we swam at a pool built into the river," she answered.

We drove by a shack and made another left. Leaves brushed the sides of the VW Rabbit, and I drove for less than a minute before Maria told me to stop. Through the windshield, the symmetrical snowcap of Volcan Orizaba shined surreal in the moonlight. Between it and us, a wide black ribbon ran left and right. We were parked at the edge of a deep ravine.

"It is the Jamapa Canyon. The river is below," she said.

Maria told me she had been instructed to make the connection alone—that they expected only her. I was not happy about it, but I handed over the cash Todd had given me—$1,200 in pesos. She disappeared to the right along the edge of the ravine.

I waited and waited. Always the waiting—it was coming back to me. Across the ravine, Orizaba's crown blazed white under the full moon, yet a million stars still pin-pricked a jet black sky. Scraggly trees on my right cast shadows of hunched women in front of the car. As the moon slowly descended toward a dark ridge, the first shadow witch made her way across the road, clutching the dirt with her long crooked fingers.

Maria was taking too long. Was I getting ripped off? Was she getting ripped off? Would the weed be any good? I had never done a deal without seeing and sampling the materiál before handing over the dinero—and it wasn't even my money this time.

I removed a flashlight and a miniature canister of Mace from the glove box, locked the car, and retraced Maria's path. As I hiked alongside the chasm, moonlight reflecting from Orizaba's peak on my left made the flashlight unnecessary. I had no idea where I was going or what I would find, but a thought did enter my head that I might end up at the bottom of the ravine.

In a few minutes, I saw light ahead to the right. I turned away from the canyon and continued. Under a thatched roof set on four posts, Maria and three Indians dressed in white squatted around two burlap bags. An oil lamp on the dirt cast light on their surprised faces. I put the Mace in the front pocket of my jeans and walked under the roof. We shook hands, and they smiled.

The burlap bags contained red-hair sinsemilla flower tops as good as I'd seen except for maybe the rainbow weed. An Indian rolled a joint, and one toke confirmed its quality. I exhaled and handed the joint back. Maria paid them, and we all shook hands goodbye.

She and I hiked back along the ravine, each with a burlap bag over our shoulder as the moon and Orizaba's snowcap illuminated our path.

"Which Indios are they?" I asked Maria in Spanish as we drove home to Veracruz.

"They are Nahual," she answered.

"Nahual," I repeated.

"We prefer to say Indígenas, not Indios," she said. (In-dee-hay-nas).

"Indígenas," I repeated. It took me a few tries. Indigenous. That made sense, and it was a lot shorter than "the people who live in the mountains."

When we arrived back at Maria's house in Veracruz, I gave her a hundred dollars in pesos even though she had told me she got her cut from los Indijenos. She said she would be at the same house when I wanted to buy more. I told her gracias.

At the Mocambo, I flipped on the light switch as I closed the door. Todd had been asleep. He turned to me and squinted. His hand rose to block the light.

"How'd it go?" he asked.

I had been gone three days.

"Good," I said. "But some changes."

Todd pushed off his blanket and sat up. He turned and placed his feet on the floor.

"We have to use a real runway," I said. "All the possible strips Maria showed me were no good. Rocks and slopes. It'd be suicide."

I pulled the flight chart from my back pocket and laid it out on his bed.

"I'm going to file a flight plan from Veracruz to this airport at Los Leones."

I put my finger on a spot 280 miles north of Veracruz.

"It's a grass strip and has no facilities. There won't be anyone to take my flight plan or issue a new one."

I gave Todd time to study the map.

"But what I'll actually do after taking off from Veracruz is head south, not north. I'm going to fly to this airport first."

I pointed to an airport forty miles southwest of Veracruz. The chart showed it had an east-west paved runway 3,300 feet long.

"You're going to drive the kilos here and hand them to me," I said.

I held my finger on the airport.

"Have you been to this airport?" Todd asked.

"No, but the runway is paved and long, and the map shows no facilities." I paused to let it sink in. "After you hand me the kilos, you'll drive back to Veracruz, turn in the rental car and fly commercial to Houston."

Todd pointed to a gray line on the map that connected the highway to the hand-off airport.

"This road?" he asked.

"Yes."

Todd was double checking.

"From there, I'll fly north to the strip at Los Leones." I pointed to the airport north of Tampico again. "I'll refuel with the gas cans in the baggage compartment. If you and I meet at the first airport around three in the afternoon, I can be at the

Leones grass strip before six. I'll wait there until dark, then take off for Houston."

Todd nodded.

I continued, "Afterward, I need to fly back into Mexico so I can close the flight plan and clear Mexican and U.S. customs legally. Otherwise they may start a search for the airplane, and they've got my name and address on file."

Todd and I had already decided that we needed to do everything paper-legal.

"I'll get a few hours of sleep at my apartment, then cross back into Mexico just before dawn and land at the strip at Los Leones again. From there, I'll fly to Reynosa and turn in my flight plan from Veracruz as if I had spent the night at Los Leones."

Todd looked at the chart. "How do you know the grass runway is in good condition?"

We knew from experience together that weather, disuse and time could render a grass runway unsafe. I pointed to two other airports within fifty miles of the Los Leones airstrip.

"I'll have enough fuel and daylight to get to either of these."

"When are we going to do it?" he asked.

"We can sleep late. I could use some rest. You should probably drop me off at the airport around one o'clock."

"Tomorrow?"

He looked at the digital clock on the nightstand. 0325.

"When do we pick up the pot?" he asked.

"It's in the trunk. I'll bring it in now, and we can put it in the suitcases."

Todd appeared only a little surprised.

"Tomorrow, I'll wait on the runway as long as I can. If you have a problem meeting me, I'll fly back to Veracruz and see you here at the Mocambo. You do the same if I don't show up."

I went out to the car and brought in the kilos.

CHAPTER TWENTY-FOUR

Flying Home

"Buenas tardes, Capitán."

"Buenas tardes," I replied.

I sat down at the desk along the right wall of Veracruz's flight office and began filling out a flight plan.

"A dónde vas?" the agent asked from behind the counter.

The collar of his blue shirt was unbuttoned and his tie was loose.

"I am flying to Los Leones north of Tampico to go fishing," I answered. We spoke in Spanish.

"Ah. Very good. And your friend? He is not accompanying you?"

"No. He must return to the United States for work."

The printer behind the counter ran for half a minute.

"Tampico has clear skies," the agent informed me.

I handed him my flight plan from Veracruz to Los Leones. He laid it on the counter and marked it with a pen while I read the printout of Tampico's weather.

"Muy bueno," he said and smiled, proud of me.

"Gracias."

He signed the top copy and detached it, then handed me the two carbons.

"Buen viaje," he bid.

I taxied the plane to the gas pumps where the young fuelers topped off the wing tanks and filled the four plastic gas cans in the baggage compartment. We joked as they polished the windscreen, and I added a nice tip when I paid.

Although the wind blew from the east, planes were taking off toward the west to avoid making noise over Veracruz. The tailwind would increase my take-off distance, but Veracruz's main runway was a mile and a half long, so the slight increase in the take-off run wouldn't be a factor for the small Piper. I radioed ground control and taxied to the end of the runway.

After lifting off, I raised the landing gear and continued straight out farther than normal so the control tower wouldn't notice my turn to the south. I flew the highlighted course on the chart in my lap and watched for the landmarks circled in ink: a road, a power line, a river and another road. Eighteen minutes after takeoff, a narrow rectangle of gray appeared ahead in the green jungle. Even with 260 flight hours under my belt, I still got a feeling of accomplishment when an airport or even a landmark showed up exactly where it should.

I lined up with the runway and landed east, into the wind. On the rollout, I spotted our VW Rabbit parked behind some bushes two-thirds down the runway on the left. I spun around and set the parking brake adjacent to where Todd was dragging the two suitcases through the weeds. With the engine still running, he climbed onto the right wing and hoisted the suitcases behind him one at a time. I reached over and pushed the door open against the wind from the spinning propeller. Todd kept his back to the door as he shoved the luggage onto the rear seats. He started to say something but stopped in mid-sentence as he stared through the windshield.

"Fuck," I read on his lips.

I looked ahead. A truck painted in army green was hauling ass down the runway toward us.

"See you in Houston," I said.

Todd jumped off the back of the wing, and I latched the door.

If there had been enough runway behind me, I would have

spun around and taken off in the proper direction—into the wind and away from the truck. But there wasn't enough runway behind me. I'd go off the end before I could get airborne. My only option was to take off where I had enough runway—toward the truck. I shoved the throttle to the firewall and held constant, adrenaline-driven pressure against it.

Getting into the air before our paths met was not something I could hope for. When it comes to aeronautics, physics beats hope every time. It was down to an old-fashioned game of chicken. I stayed on the centerline of the runway and watched the airspeed needle slowly rise as the truck got bigger. If we hit, then we hit. Stopping and giving up was not an alternative. One stint in a Mexican penitentiary was enough for one lifetime.

Six seconds into the game—six eons—the truck veered off my left and disappeared. My hand maintained its pressure against the throttle, and the Arrow lifted from the ground as the asphalt became dirt. Would the truck driver radio ahead to someone about me? Would he go after Todd?

I finally banked north but flew low over the jungle. Veracruz had no air force that I knew of, although I did see a fleet of Piper Cherokees painted in a military scheme on the ramp. If that was the Veracruz air force, I needn't worry. At 155 miles per hour, the Piper Arrow could outrun any fixed-gear Piper Cherokee.

I stayed west of Veracruz, then turned northeast to intercept the coastline. After passing over a couple of small fishing villages, I climbed to 1,000 feet where I could see farther ahead and had room to relax. An hour later, a triangular green lagoon appeared on the left, and five huge rocks emerged from the Gulf on my right. According to the chart, Tampico was fifty-five miles ahead. Its big airport was too close to the coast for comfort so I detoured inland until past the city, then turned right and intercepted the coastline again. As I continued north, patches of cumulus clouds thickened over the land, but the Gulf and beach remained clear.

My flight case lay on the right seat, and I pulled out the *Pilot's Guide to Mexico.* It listed all Mexican AM radio stations that broadcast a signal strong enough to use for navigation. I tuned the ADF radio to XEGW in Ciudad Victoria and used the needle on the gauge to cross-reference my progress north—the same navigation I used for the instrument approaches at Andrau Airpark.

Clouds obscured the mainland when I reached Los Leones, but an inlet in the barrier island confirmed my position. I descended over the water until I was below the clouds, then followed a road to the grass runway.

Fields surrounded the strip, and there were no houses or other buildings nearby. I made one low pass to check out the runway, then landed. Tall grass slapped the wing's leading edge as I settled to the ground and slowed. After taxiing back to the take-off end, I emptied the gas cans into the wing tanks and tossed the containers over a barbed wire fence—gifts to a worthy campesino. The sun would set in forty-five minutes. I waited in my seat with the key in the ignition, vigilant.

When it got dark enough to barely see the barbed wire fence along the sides of the runway, I applied power and listened to the grass hit the wing as the Arrow picked up speed. The plane lifted from the runway, the noise ceased, and I banked quietly north toward the USA.

Thirty miles south of the Rio Grande, the yellow lights of Matamoros appeared, followed by the white lights of Brownsville just beyond. I aimed for a point just west of where the river spilled into the Gulf and began a descent to my crossing altitude.

For the hundredth time, I looked at the transponder switch to make sure it was in the off position. Turning it on now to verify I wasn't being interrogated by radar was not an option. It would amplify my signal. At 700 feet, I knew I was below radar coverage. But I didn't fly at 700 feet. When the Rio Grande reflected ahead in the moonlight, I was level at 200 feet. I put on the headphones and pressed play on my portable cassette deck. As I flew over the river, "On the Border" played, and The Eagles voiced our disdain for law and order. We only wanted to turn our water to wine.

After crossing into the U.S., I stayed low and close to the beach for the next twenty minutes, then climbed to 1,000 feet, the minimum safe altitude for the next hundred miles. Close to Corpus Christi, small airports populated the chart. I flew near Alice's airport, turned on the transponder and climbed to 5,500 feet. Air Traffic Control's radar would paint me as just another small plane moving across the Texas night sky.

At Andrau Airpark, I taxied to the terminal and had the gas truck top me off. My El Camino was waiting in the parking lot, and I drove to Todd's apartment and put the suitcases in his bedroom closet. I went to my apartment and slept until the alarm woke me at three a.m.

By three forty, I was in the air, heading back to Mexico. Dawn broke when I was thirty minutes south of the border, and it dawned on me I didn't need to fly all the way to Los Leones. No one would know I hadn't taken off from there in the morning. I reversed direction and flew to Reynosa. The Mexican flight office accepted my flight plan from Veracruz without question, and I filed an international plan to McAllen where I cleared U.S. customs. Three hours later, I was in bed again.

When Todd hadn't telephoned by evening, I began to worry. His Aeromexico flight was supposed to have landed in Houston the day before. I called his apartment a few times, then drove over. There was no sign of him, so I returned to my place and stayed by the phone.

Could the federales or army or municipal police have set up a roadblock in time to catch Todd? I doubted it. Would the truck on the runway have gone after him? Of course. Losing our game of chicken on the runway would have been a serious blow to the driver's Latino machismo. I called Aeromexico and was told they couldn't give out passenger information. If Todd didn't arrive or call the following day, he was in trouble.

*

Just before three the next afternoon, the phone rang. I hurried to answer it and wondered if the news would be good or bad. I had once been on the other end of the line.

"Will you accept a collect call from Todd?"

"Yes."

"Steve, this is Todd." His voice was distant.

"Where are you? Are you okay?" I asked.

"Yeah. Fine. I'm taking off from Brownsville in thirty minutes. The plane lands at Intercontinental at five fifteen. Aeromexico Airlines."

"I'll be outside," I told him.

*

At Houston Intercontinental, Todd's suitcase went onto the bed of my El Camino, and we headed for the freeway.

"Any problems?" he asked.

"Everything went as planned. Better than planned. The suitcases are in your closet. What happened to *you*?"

"I looked back at the runway when I went under the barbed wire," he said. "Man, I *knew* you didn't have enough room to take off before the truck got to you."

"You're two days late. What happened?" I asked again.

"The truck stopped on the runway after it dodged you, then the driver spotted me. I jumped in the car and got out of there. He broke through the barbed wire and chased me. I spun the wheel left and right to throw up dirt, and when I hit the main road, I went south instead of north to Veracruz. After a while, I realized I was on the road to Toro."

"You went to Toro Prieto?"

"I didn't know where else to go. I figured going south would be safer. I hung out with El Mio until it got dark, then drove back to the Mocambo."

At Todd's apartment, we opened the suitcases. The weed was more vibrant and fragrant than when I had examined it under the lamplight with Maria and the Nahuals. I gazed at the flower tops and remembered Volcan Orizaba's shining white snowcap under the full moon and the deep ravine I had hiked alongside. It was a shame that partakers of this weed would never know the story of how it got here.

EPILOGUE

A month after my trip to Mexico with Todd, I passed my commercial and instrument checkrides in the same Piper Arrow we used for the run. Six weeks later, I got my flight instructor license. Midnight crossings on (and over) the Rio Grande ceased.

Ray was hesitant to hire another flight instructor for his little flight school, but Ray's Flying Service was where I wanted to work. The day after I passed my instructor checkride, I sat patiently on the sofa in Ray's building until he gave me one new student. It was a test. I was ready. The student soloed in a week, and Ray handed me almost every new student that came through the door. He kept the upscale ones for himself, in case they needed to buy a new airplane and lease it back to him. I flew a hundred hours a month, the FAA maximum limit.

Joseph, aka the Godfather, resurfaced and told Todd he wanted to talk with me. We met at a restaurant off of I-10 near Highway 6, and he said he needed me to fly cocaine from Colombia across northern Venezuela. Their previous pilot had crashed.

"Your plan is to have me fly the same route your other pilot flew when he crashed?"

"Yes. We already have another Cessna 310 ready to go."

"The same type plane?"

"We'll pay you ten thousand dollars."

The money did not motivate me. I was where I wanted to be. How could I bow out without offending the Godfather?

"I don't think it would be safe to repeat exactly what you were doing before," I answered. "Especially after crashing with cocaine on board. If you come up with a different plan, I would consider it."

Todd and I were surfing a month later, and I asked if the Godfather had found another pilot. Todd said he wasn't sure, then told me Joseph and his partner had considered having me eliminated. I was somewhat shocked.

*

Nine years after my stay in the Oaxaca penitentiary, I had flown 5,000 hours and was hired by a major airline. Twenty years later, I retired as a Capitán.

I departed Houston for good when I started flying for the airlines and only returned to visit family and friends. I began as a probationary flight engineer on Boeing 727s and DC-10s, then got checked out in 737s, 757s, 767s and DC-9-80s.

My father finally accepted my not finishing college. He and I bought a Cessna 150 together, and I taught him how to fly. He had logged a hundred flight hours during his initial Navy officer training at Annapolis in 1947, and we used his original logbook to complete the requirements for his private pilot license.

My prison mate Jack and I went our separate ways early on, although we talked on the phone occasionally. After I retired, we reunited in Houston for Roger Waters' futuristic, techno-production of Pink Floyd's *The Wall*. Jack helped greatly in remembering many of the details of our Oaxaca ordeal and the rainbow weed run. Although he has even more stories to tell regarding his life *after* the peni, he is now a happy grandfather who dedicates much of his time guiding the youth of his local Catholic church.

Todd passed away in 1996 without me knowing it for ten

years. I had lost touch with him and Dan and almost everyone from that era when I began flying for a living. Todd and cocaine had apparently remained close, and he passed away from cirrhosis of the liver at forty-four years of age. He had been a good copilot, responsible business partner and reliable friend.

To put the finishing touches on this book, I returned to Mexico in July 2016 and visited many of the places I knew forty years earlier: Puebla, Orizaba, Veracruz and Toro Prieto. At the time, Oaxaca was involved in a militaristic teachers' strike that blocked all roads into the city, so I didn't make it there.

From Veracruz, I hired a taxi and ventured to the still-remote Toro Prieto, where I learned El Mio had passed away. I also found out we had his name wrong. El Mio's real name was Hermillo Camacho. With the H silent and the double L sounding like a Y, the correct pronunciation of his first name would have been "Air-mee-yo."

Isidra's maestro husband had also passed, and she recently returned to the village to build a house near where her father's store used to be. She cooked lunch for me, and we are now social media friends.

I sent Isidra the first chapter of this book, and someone translated it to her and a group of relatives and friends. She messaged me that she was delighted I had written about her village and her father, and said she was looking forward to reading more.

But I wonder how a woman living in a remote Mexican village would process my tale of a young gringo narcotraficante internacional.

THANKS,
Mr. Cole

I am deeply grateful to Jack's father, Mr. Cole, for traveling to Oaxaca and taking on the mission of getting two young narcotraficantes internacionales released from the Oaxaca State Penitentiary. I learned years later that the U.S. firm he worked for had connections in Mexico, which had put things on a special track for Jack and me. Without Mr. Cole, this book would likely have had a different ending.

THE AUTHOR

After several years of flight instructing, Paul Ogier flew as a corporate, charter and commuter pilot before being hired by a major airline.

He is responsible for the aviation tabloid, *Houston Air News*, and has written stories for national and regional publications, including the *General Aviation News,* the *Portsmouth Herald and the Texas Flyer*.

Back Then, 1975

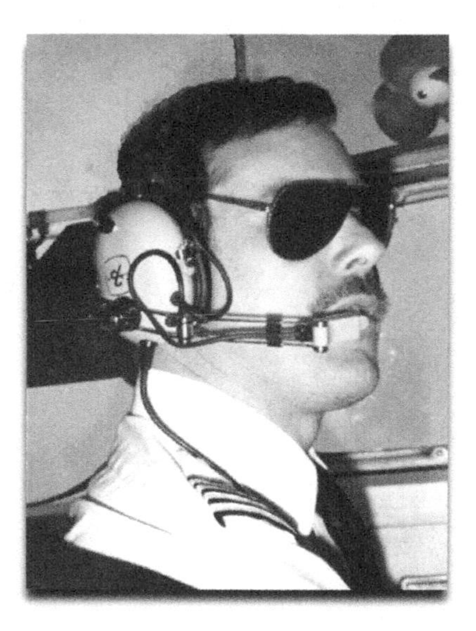

7 Years After this Book Ends

Paul Ogier did 20 years easy time at American Airlines before retiring. He spends summers in New Hampshire and winters in Costa Rica where he still surfs.

Made in the USA
Las Vegas, NV
26 April 2021